Tom Stoppard has always distinguished between his rompy farces designed for amusement and a different kind of play which, however amusing, is not merely amusing: 'All along I thought of myself as writing entertainments like *The Real Inspector Hound* and plays of ideas like *Jumpers*'. Assessing his canon as if such plays are of equal significance, Stoppard says, would be like 'using *Old Possum's Book of Practical Cats* to show that *The Waste Land* is essentially a frivolous work'. Delaney's is the first book to focus on the plays of ideas, the major plays which form the core of Stoppard's achievement.

Delaney shows the seriousness of the whole frothy enterprise without making the comedy appear sombre or the moral implications appear frivolous. He presents Stoppard's work whole, appreciating the wit but showing the serious core of moral concerns which lie at the heart of all his major plays. The book demonstrates that Stoppard's major plays develop from moral affirmation to moral application, from the assertion of moral principles to the enactment of moral practice.

Written in a lively, engaging style, *Tom Stoppard: The Moral Vision of the Major Plays* is accessible to the theater-going public while challenging a number of academic misconceptions of Stoppard's work. The volume makes substantial use of Stoppard's own words about his work and contains the most extensive bibliography and discography of Stoppard interviews (over 200 including print and broadcast sources) ever compiled.

For a note on the author, please see the back flap.

include articles on Stoppard in *Modern Lan-guage Quarterly* and *Critical Quarterly*.

TOM STOPPARD

Tom Stoppard

The Moral Vision of the Major Plays

Paul Delaney
Professor of English
Westmont College
Santa Barbara

St. Martin's Press   New York

First published in the United States of America in 1990

Printed in Hong Kong

ISBN 0–312–03556–X

Library of Congress Cataloging-in-Publication Data
Delaney, Paul, 1948–
Tom Stoppard: the moral vision of the major plays / Paul Delaney.
p. cm.
Bibliography: p.
Includes index.
ISBN 0–312–03556–X
1. Stoppard, Tom—Ethics.   I. Title.
PR6069.T6Z64   1989
822'.914—dc20   89–34360
                                                                        CIP

For Dianne

Contents

Contents

Preface

Insisting that a play is an event rather than a text, Tom Stoppard does not write plays to be discussed or even to be read. He writes plays to be performed and to be seen in performance. Although the present study discusses the texts, I have tried throughout to suggest something of the theatrical zest and energy of the plays. The same intelligent undergraduates who finish a Stoppard script in bewildered perplexity leave a Stoppard performance in unfeigned delight. And yet the most enthusiastic appreciation of Stoppard's stage wizardry sometimes needs to be yoked with greater comprehension of what is at issue amid the theatrical high jinks.

I try to show the seriousness of the whole frothy enterprise without making the comedy appear sombre or the moral implications appear frivolous. Indeed, both the comedy and the morality lead us to eff the ineffable, to glimpse possibilities which lie outside our blinkered vision of the 'real'. I seek to present his work whole, appreciating Stoppard's wit but showing the serious core of moral concerns which lie at the heart of all of Stoppard's major plays. My study traces the paths by which Stoppard's theatre develops from moral affirmation to moral application, from the assertion of moral principles to the enactment of moral practice.

Throughout, I have sought to make each chapter a readable whole. Putting the right words in the right order may not be 'what life's about', but as *The Real Thing* attests, 'it's traditionally considered advantageous for a writer'. To allow each chapter to stand on its own and to meet the needs of students who may have read or seen only one or two of Stoppard's plays, I have sometimes included key quotations in more than one chapter. Throughout, I quote Stoppard from his earliest interviews to his most recent – both to show the nature of his concerns and to demonstrate the continuity of his moral vision.

Santa Barbara, California   PAUL DELANEY

Acknowledgements

Quotations from the published plays of Tom Stoppard are reprinted with the permission of Faber and Faber, London and Boston, and Grove Press, New York. Quotations from unpublished material are reprinted with the kind permission of Tom Stoppard. An earlier version of Chapter 3 appeared in *Modern Language Quarterly* and an earlier version of Chapter 6 appeared in *Critical Quarterly*.

For support and assistance in the completion of this book, I owe debts of gratitude to my family, my students and my colleagues.

My greatest debt is to my wife, Dianne, who has been a perceptive companion at the theatre and a helpful collaborator in the study. Others have read sequential drafts of chapters; she has read sequential drafts of paragraphs. She has always helped to sharpen my ideas or my prose, and sometimes has been the source of those ideas. In particular, her response to *The Real Thing* has shaped my own.

Secondly (to begin at the beginning), there was a time when my pages on *Jumpers* resembled George's own. Though my convictions were intact and my ideas coherent, my writings on *Jumpers* might have remained fragments shored against my ruin had it not been for the encouragement and assistance of Phyllis Potter. She was the first of several students who have left a mark on these pages. Jay Hochstedt deepened my understanding of the significance of Carr in *Travesties*. Jan Faller pointed out a connection between language and morality in *Professional Foul*. Martin Mushik spent several late nights explaining quantum mechanics and talking about *Hapgood*. Vance Smith, Christine Bunten, Bryan Reinhard, Tom Pott, Garett Neudeck and Allyson Cole have read, responded to, and helped to shape various chapters.

My colleague David Downing forced me to rethink the focus of my chapter on *Hapgood*. He has read multiple versions of every chapter and offered comments at once voluminous, specific and incisive. When his comments have been about my writing, I've even appreciated his bluntness. No person other than my wife has offered more sustained help than he. Heather Speirs and Logan Speirs have provided encouragement (gratefully received) along with encouragements toward conciseness (usually adopted). They and Richard Hansen have been particularly influential in helping me come to terms with *Hapgood*. Colleagues and former colleagues Steve Cook, Arthur Lynip, Rebecca Ankeny and Ed Ericson read various chapters and offered helpful responses.

Former Academic Dean Tom Andrews, a gentleman and a scholar (which latter fact in part explains the 'former'), proffered encouragement both pecuniary and personal during his untenured tenure. His vision for a community of scholars continues to be an inspiration. I am happy to acknowledge continuing financial assistance from Westmont College, arranged through the good offices of Dean George Blankenbaker, to bring the manuscript of this book to completion.

I've been writing what turns out to be this book for as long as my children have been alive. The plays of Tom Stoppard have been intriguing, amusing, moving company. Elizabeth and Arthur have provided, and continue to provide, the greater joy.

1
Art as a Moral Matrix

Tom Stoppard has a vision of life which permeates all of his major plays, a vision which has for the most part been misunderstood. Though thoroughly conversant with the currents of thought which prevail in his own day, Stoppard chooses to stand largely opposed to them. He accepts a direct connection between art and morality, between art and life, however distinctly unfashionable such a view may be. Even more importantly, he relegates politics to a secondary status, acknowledging that he is 'more interested in the metaphysical condition of man rather than the social position'.[1] Simply and unequivocally Stoppard continues to declare, 'I'm not a moral relativist; I'm not a political relativist'.[2] Stoppard's vision is of man as a moral being, a being subject to a moral order which is not contingent on intellectual fashion or political expedience or ideological imperatives or national interest. He writes of mankind as existing in a realm in which right and wrong are universal metaphysical absolutes.

Indeed, asserting that human beings are not just organisms, that 'there is more in me than meets the microscope' (as George says in *Jumpers*), Stoppard has from the first pitted himself against the whole gamut of materialist philosophy. Such a concern with the moral is not, Stoppard insists, a form of withdrawing with style from the chaos but of dealing most directly and honestly with reality: 'The truths which are important don't reside in particular events in the physical world. . . . On the contrary, the essential truths are much foggier things which we recognise instinctively rather than analyse and establish by demonstrative proof.'[3] But if such truths may be apprehended by instinct, that does not mean – for Stoppard – that they can be altered either by individual will or by group consensus. 'The difference between moral rules and the rules of tennis', Stoppard declares, 'is that the rules of tennis can be changed.' 'I think it's a dangerous idea', Stoppard adds, 'that what constitutes "good behaviour" depends on social conventions – dangerous and unacceptable.'[4] Indeed, consistency not of ideological doctrine but of moral vision is what Stoppard

1

says he values pre-eminently. As opposed to such dangerous relativism, Stoppard affirms, 'I subscribe . . . to objective truth and to absolute morality'.[5]

Whether such a moral order is of divine origin is a question Stoppard has pondered long and hard. Embracing a moral order derived from Christianity while finding it intellectually or spiritually impossible to embrace Christianity may contribute to Stoppard's much-vaunted uncertainty. But if he is not certain of the source of moral absolutes, his conviction is unshakeable that moral standards are certain. If a measure of indecision remains in his plays, there is a far greater level of certitude than has generally been recognised. Stoppard's plays clearly affirm that art reflects a real and objective world, even if a world more complex than we may have imagined; that social and political realities are subject to and derived from moral realities; that life is profoundly meaningful and ineluctably moral.

Yet the potential ponderousness of such moral perception is always alleviated in Stoppard by the ebullience of his wit. What emerges is less a numbing exposé of the forces of death than an exuberant celebration of the moral value of life. Stoppard writes with an *élan*, a verve, a *joie de vivre* which is as far removed from the turgid political propagandizing of some of Stoppard's fellow dramatists as from the numbingly existential *angst* of others. Indeed, after an extended exposure to the dark negations of much of modern drama, one may, upon discovering the work of Tom Stoppard, be dazzled not just by razzmatazz theatrics but by the light of moral illumination.

Tom Stoppard catapulted to international acclaim overnight with *Rosencrantz and Guildenstern are Dead*. Not only did he become the youngest playwright to have a play staged by the National Theatre, but that 1967 production was hailed as 'the most important event in the British professional theatre of the last nine years',[6] that is, since the production of Harold Pinter's first play in 1958. Within a month of its London opening, productions of *Rosencrantz* were being mounted in Paris, Vienna, Berlin, Munich, Stockholm and The Hague; and young Stoppard's play became the first National Theatre production to cross the Atlantic for a production on Broadway.[7] The hitherto unknown writer whose works had not received professional live production just six months earlier was hailed in New York as one of 'the finest English-speaking writers of our stage'.[8]

Such unalloyed acclaim was to last but six months until Stoppard's next stage play, *The Real Inspector Hound*, began to prompt charges that his plays were detached cerebral exercises in wit which lacked a sense of felt life, that his humour was merely 'a grin without a cat'.[9] The adulation and the disparagement have continued throughout Stoppard's career, with some praising him as the most brilliant playwright on either side of the Atlantic and others dismissing him as merely brilliant, some lauding his vaulting wit and others finding him too clever by half. Early on, the charges began to appear that he avoided social and political realities; that his work was, therefore, a stylish withdrawal from actualities; that his plays remained, essentially, unreal. From other quarters came the response that Stoppard was to be praised precisely for his unreality; for the supposedly absurdist or surrealistic quality of his work.

Attacking Stoppardian theatre for not seeking to alter 'the nature of the society of which it is a part', Philip Roberts disparages the plays as apolitical opportunities 'for wit, parody and metaphysical dalliance'.[10] But if such detractors as Roberts dismiss Stoppard's plays as being merely playful, Thomas Whitaker takes the opposite tack of praising them for being merely playful. The 'single task' of all Stoppard's plays, Whitaker insists, has been that of 'exploring the playfulness to which he early committed himself'.[11] Such a skewed view of Stoppard's dramatic universe leads Whitaker to praise such 'dandified' stylists as Lord Malquist, the Player in *Rosencrantz*, Archie in *Jumpers*, and Tzara in *Travesties*. At the same time Whitaker faults such characters as Mr Moon, Rosencrantz and Guildenstern, George, and Henry Carr because they 'have not known how to divorce themselves from the homely texture of our moral experience'[12] – as if that were a separation devoutly to be wished!

Given his penchant for puns, Stoppard's plays are nothing if not playful. However such observers as Whitaker have toyed with the notion of playfulness in Stoppard until they reach the regrettable conclusion that Stoppard's plays are nothing but playful. Asserting that all Stoppard characters are stylists, Whitaker argues that 'all tacitly assume that style is our main clue to meaning' and that Stoppard himself seems to share that same assumption. Whitaker sees in the 'stylistic virtuosity' of *Lord Malquist and Mr Moon* a 'labyrinthine riddle' because for Stoppard 'fiction had now become a parodic and self-parodic game between writer and reader'.[13] More recently Tim Brassell has given a much more satisfactory account of Stoppard's novel demonstrating that even at the very outset of his career 'the short-comings of . . . verbal cleverness are exposed'. Malquist's 'style', Brassell argues persuasively, is 'a thing of superficial brilliance which glosses over his outright irresponsibility'.[14] Such later commentators as Kenneth Tynan would take Malquist's desire to 'withdraw with style from the chaos' as expressing Stoppard's own stance.[15] Brassell aptly demonstrates that from the first 'such withdrawal is not only impossible but, as Stoppard is progressively concerned to reveal, implies a complete lack of concern with all human and social values'.[16]

In response to the charge of being apolitical, as early as 1974 Stoppard voiced his 'belief that all political acts have a moral basis to them and are meaningless without it'.[17] Acknowledging that such a belief 'goes against Marxist-Leninism in particular, and against all materialistic philosophy', Stoppard continued to declare (to the profound discomfiture of his interviewers from *Theatre Quarterly*) that 'I believe all political acts must be judged in moral terms' and that from such a moral framework the opposing political arguments of Leninism and Fascism may simply be 'restatements of each other':

> The repression which for better or worse turned out to be Leninism in action after 1917 was very much worse than anything which had gone on in Tsarist Russia. . . . But the point is not to compare one ruthless regime against another – it is to set each one up against a moral standard, a consistent idea of what constitutes good and bad in the way human beings treat each other regardless of class, colour or ideology. ('Ambushes', p. 12)

Throughout his career, in other words, Stoppard has affirmed that human experience is inherently moral, and that a Marxist view of human beings as material objects is reprehensibly reductive. On that point he could scarcely have spoken more plainly for those who had ears to hear. In 1974 after acknowledging 'a sort of infinite leap-frog' in his plays – 'you know, an argument, a refutation, then a rebuttal of the refutation, then a counter-rebuttal' – Stoppard proceeded to affirm with adamantine conviction the primacy of the moral, rather than the political, however much such an insistence on timeless criteria might run against the prevailing temper of the times. To eliminate any possibility of ambiguity Stoppard returned to the topic moments later: 'Few statements remain unrebutted. But I'm not going to rebut the things I have been saying just now. One thing I feel sure about is that a materialistic view of history is an insult to the human race' ('Ambushes', pp. 7, 13). Such unambiguous affirmations of the fundamentally moral nature of human experience have, for the most part, fallen on deaf ears.

To be sure, one may acknowledge that there is more to man 'than meets the microscope', may acknowledge a moral dimension to experience, without claiming that absolute, timeless, and immutable standards of right and wrong exist. Even the promulgation of 'a moral standard, a consistent idea of what constitutes good and bad in the way human beings treat each other' leaves open the possibility that such consistency might exist in the mind of the observer rather than being rooted in the essential nature of things.

Not until 1977 did Stoppard publicly affirm his belief in 'a moral order derived from Christian absolutes'.[18] Such a moral order, he makes clear, is not merely contingent on social mores or some subjective sense of desirable behaviour but, in fact, exists outside of and apart from any human creation. In the same context Stoppard applauds 'the defence of objective truth from the attacks of Marxist relativists'. Affirming the existence of 'objectivity and truth in science, in nature and in logic', Stoppard offers a stinging refutation of relativists who would deny the existence of facts, truth and logic:

> These are now the quite familiar teachings of well-educated men and women holding responsible positions in respectable universities, and the thing to say about such teaching is not that it is 'radical' but that it is not true. What it is, is false. To claim the contrary is not 'interesting'. It is silly. Daft. Not very bright. Moreover, it is wicked.[19]

It is, thus, to the pre-eminent existence of the moral realm that Stoppard recurs. What Stoppard publicly acknowledged in 1977 was his belief in a moral standard which is not merely consistent but timeless, immutable, and universal: 'I've always felt that whether or not "God-given" means anything, there has to be an ultimate external reference for our actions. Our view of good behaviour *must* not be relativist.'[20]

Such a deep and abiding conviction of the reality of the moral realm impelled Stoppard, he acknowledged at the same time, to a belief in the reality not only of moral absolutes but of God. Rejection of a relativist view of behaviour, Stoppard confessed to an interviewer, 'led me to the conclusion, not reached all that willingly, that if our behaviour is open to absolute judgement, there must be an absolute judge'.[21] Stoppard says he set out to reflect such a theistic conclusion in his writing for the stage: 'I felt that nobody was saying this and it tended to be assumed that nobody held such a view. So I wanted to write a theist play, to combat the arrogant view that anyone who believes in God is some kind of cripple, using God as a crutch. I wanted to suggest that atheists may be the cripples, lacking the strength to live with the idea of God.'[22]

The significance of Stoppard's writing, however, has been as unrecognised, as misperceived as that of the early T.S. Eliot, or that of another writer Stoppard admires, Aleksandr Solzhenitsyn. In a 1979 interview Stoppard could declare: 'I'm a conservative in politics, literature, education and theatre.'[23] Stoppard's comment to a *New York Times* reporter perhaps lacks the stately cadences of T.S. Eliot's famous self-description as 'a royalist in politics, a classicist in literature, and an Anglo-Catholic in religion'. However, just as the 'absurd' juxtapositions within 'Prufrock' and *The Waste Land* provoked first bafflement and then misplaced praise for Eliot as a spokesman for the avant-garde before the traditional elements of his art were recognised and the spiritual quest embodied in his poetry was grasped, so Stoppard has been both wrongly denounced as an obscurantist and wrongly praised as an existentialist, an absurdist, and a surrealist. Indeed, recognising the inextricable rootedness of the individual talent within the context of tradition, Stoppard both transforms and preserves art and is thereby conservative artistically in the same sense as is Eliot or Joyce. Further, the informing impulse behind his art is profoundly moral and implicitly theistic.

Ironically, just such a concern for the timeless had previously pitted Stoppard against those who saw immediate social change as the sole reason or purpose for art and had, at times, seemed to pit him against any form of 'socially engaged' or 'committed' art. Indeed, the verbal texture and high wit of his plays have caused some who see reality in fundamentally political terms to conclude that Stoppard's art is frivolous, stylish nonsense. Even Kenneth Tynan, who was instrumental in bringing both *Rosencrantz and Guildenstern are Dead* and *Jumpers* into the National Theatre repertoire, charged more in sorrow than in anger that, because Stoppard did not focus primarily on immediate social and political issues, his plays constituted a form of 'withdrawing with style from the chaos'.[24] Less charitably, Philip Roberts accused Stoppard of writing plays which are 'anodyne and anaesthetising', 'beloved by those for whom theatre is an end and not a means, diversionary and not central, a ramification and not a modifier of the *status quo*, a soother of worried minds and not an irritant'.[25] Roberts would deny that Stoppard is a 'serious artist' because of the playwright's alleged 'refusal to believe in the efficacy, in any sense, of theatre to affect anything, including an audience'.[26] Tynan concludes similarly that Stoppard rejects 'any pretensions that art might have to change, challenge, or criticize the world, or to modify, however marginally, our view of it'.[27] The thing to say about such charges is not that they are radical but that they are not true.

Modifying our view of the world is, Stoppard asserts, precisely what art does adeptly: 'Art is very much better at laying down inch-by-inch a matrix for the sensibilities which we ultimately use to make our value-judgements on society, than in making an immediate value-judgement on an immediate situation. Particularly, much better at that than at changing a situation. . . . Art is intensely important for reasons other than writing angrily about this morning's headlines.'[28] Such importance as art has, Stoppard insists, is inherently moral. Here Stoppard does indeed pit himself directly against the prevailing temper of the times by assuming a direct and open connection between art and morality. 'Art . . . is important', Stoppard asserts, 'because it provides the moral matrix, the moral sensibility, from which we make our judgments about the world' ('Ambushes', p. 14).

To illustrate his point Stoppard compares the work of Adam Raphael, a *Guardian* journalist who has written on South Africa, and Athol Fugard, a South African playwright. While journalism may throw light on an immediate situation, art puts the immediate situation within a universal or timeless context. Thus, when Adam Raphael broke a story on wages in South Africa, Stoppard notes, 'within 48 hours the wages went up. Now Athol Fugard can't do that.' However, what the art of Athol Fugard can do is to demonstrate within a South African context that the difference between justice and injustice, between freedom and oppression, between decent treatment and indecent, is absolute and stands as a judgement on any regime which flouts the essential humanness of its citizens. 'The plain truth', Stoppard continues, 'is that if you are angered or disgusted by a particular injustice or immorality, and you want to do something about it, *now, at once*, then you can hardly do worse than write a play about it. That's what art is bad at. But the less plain truth is that *without* that play and plays like it, without artists, the injustice will *never* be eradicated. In other words, because of Athol Fugard, to stretch a point, *The Guardian* understood that the Raphael piece was worth leading the paper with, worth printing' ('Ambushes', p. 14). Thus what art can do most adeptly is to awaken, modify, refine our moral sensibilities. The editors of *The Guardian*, theatre audiences, members of civilised society can have their view of the world changed, challenged, criticised by art as it lays down inch-by-inch a moral matrix which demonstrates how in a new time and place the eternal verities converge.

Thus when Stoppard did begin to write plays which dealt more explicitly with social situations there was not the profound trans-formation, the wrenching metamorphosis in his work which many critics have supposed. 'There was', Stoppard insists, 'no sudden conversion on the road to Damascus',[29] no epiphany in which he discovered that politics were what really mattered, that the body politic was the ultimate frame of reference. Indeed, Stoppard maintains, his concerns have not fundamentally changed. Both *Jumpers* and *Professional Foul*, for example, 'are about the way human beings are supposed to behave towards each other'.[30]

The entire canon of Stoppard's major plays demonstrates just such a consistency, a consistency which has been largely ignored by most observers. Having seen only the glitter and sheen of the early theatrics, some critics were unprepared to recognise the naturalistic form of more recent plays as even 'identifiable as Stoppard's work'.[31] Instead, his plays of the late 1970s prompted much talk of the 'politicization' of Tom Stoppard, talk which either praised Stoppard for finally getting it right by addressing political realities or faulted him for abandoning an exhilarating if vacuous realm of wit. But both praise and blame wrongly insist on a bifurcation in Stoppard's writing career, a Damascene conversion from the parodic to the prosaic, from mindless wit to earnest politics.

Critics who first labelled Stoppard an absurdist, a surrealist, an existentialist, have more recently been announcing a radical transformation, the 'politicization' of a 'cool, apolitical stylist'. At the same time they have essayed some wrenching convolutions of logic to try to cling to the validity of earlier misjudgements. 'We were right', Andrew K. Kennedy insists defensively, 'to stress the vertiginous interplay . . . surrealistic quasi-encounters, and self-breeding verbal games' in the early plays. But Kennedy proceeds to announce a 'remarkable change in Stoppard's comedy from a relativistic and parodic universe of wit'.[32] Seldom have charges of leapfrogging in Stoppard been taken to such a cosmic degree. Indeed, rather than acknowledge the simple truth that Stoppard writes about moral behaviour in the real world and has been doing so for some while now, Kennedy persuades himself that the new Stoppard 'seems to be governed by a non-absurd vision of absurdity',[33] whatever that may mean. However, *pace* Kennedy, reports that Stoppard has changed universes are greatly exaggerated.

That there is development in Stoppard is clear, but the development is from moral affirmation to moral application, from the assertion of moral principles to the enactment of moral practice. Such development from precept to praxis demonstrates organic growth rather than radical, or cosmic, metamorphosis. Failing to recognise the moral affirmation in Stoppard's early work, many critics have been unprepared to recognise the application of those moral affirmations in the more recent plays dealing overtly with socio-political situations. Some observers suppose Stoppard has shifted from uncommitted stylish wit to a committed political stance. They thereby miss the figure which Stoppard from the first has been weaving in his theatrical tapestry. What separates Stoppard from the masses of current British playwrights writing about the masses is not a right-wing political stance as opposed to a left-wing stance, but a metaphysical perspective as opposed to a political perspective, a moral view of individuals and regimes as opposed to a materialistic or ideological view. Indeed, to ignore the affirmation of moral absolutes in the early plays and to ignore the application of moral absolutes in the more recent and more realistic plays is fundamentally to misconstrue Stoppard's entire canon.

Eric Salmon was the first to observe that Stoppard's self-proclaimed '"lack of conviction" is more assumed than real'.[34] Stoppard himself confirmed in 1981 that the earlier proclamations of indecision and leapfrogging were greatly exaggerated. Given a highly politicized climate in which 'theatre seemed to exist for the specific purpose of commenting on our own society directly', Stoppard explains, 'I took on a sort of "travelling pose" which exaggerated my insecurity'.[35] But if he 'over-reacted with a bon mot about having "the courage of my lack of convictions"', his truthful feeling even at that time, he says, was 'not that I had no convictions, but that a lot of my work connected with the same sort of areas of interest as more overtly social plays, but did so in much more generalised terms'.[36] That connection, Stoppard insists, was always a matter of moral vision: 'I was always morally, if not politically, involved.'[37]

Despite Stoppard's assertions that 'a lot' of his work was 'always morally . . . involved', attempts to see the figure in Stoppard's carpet are obscured in part by the amount of time he has devoted to weaving throw rugs. A craftsman as well as an artist, Stoppard has always found time to ply the tools of his trade on a variety of projects besides his major stage plays. In terms of sheer quantity, his scripts for radio and television plays, farces like *The Real Inspector Hound* and *Dirty Linen*, his adaptations and 'translations' for screen and stage together bulk larger than his serious plays (whether comic or not). The range of Stoppard's writing is not only impressive but has generated some confusion in assessments of the nature of his achievement and the continuity of his dramatic career.

Stoppard, however, clearly delineates between writing he has done 'for hire' and works he has written 'from pure choice' just as he further distinguishes between rompy farces designed for amusement and a different kind of play which, however amusing, is not merely amusing. He freely acknowledges how some might confuse the two quite different registers of his writing: 'All along I thought of myself as writing entertainments like *The Real Inspector Hound* and plays of ideas like *Jumpers*. The confusion arises because I treat plays of ideas in just about the same knockabout way as I treat the entertainments.'[38] Yet the difference between the two is profound: '*Jumpers* is a serious play dealt with in the farcical terms which in *Hound* actually *constitute* the play' ('Ambushes', p. 11). Therefore, disregarding the vast bulk of his writing, Stoppard preferred to present himself in 1974 as 'the author of *Jumpers*, *Travesties*, and of my next unwritten unthought-of-play' ('Ambushes', p. 11). More than two years later Stoppard still regarded his dramatic canon in much the same terms: 'I haven't done a large play since *Travesties*. . . . I haven't got anywhere near . . . what would be for me a true successor to *Jumpers* and *Travesties*, i.e. stage plays with all the stops pulled out.'[39] *Night and Day* (1978), although a full-length stage play, is in some ways a less satisfying successor to *Jumpers* and *Travesties* than is *Professional Foul* which Stoppard wrote for broadcast on the BBC in 1977. But if not previously, then assuredly with *The Real Thing* (1982) Stoppard pulled out all the stops to write such a successor. That masterwork was followed six years later by *Hapgood* (1988). If in *Jumpers* Stoppard came to terms with the ideas of Wittgenstein, Bertrand Russell and G.E. Moore, in *Hapgood* Stoppard deals with the ideas of Einstein and Heisenberg in a play which incorporates something of the mysteries of quantum mechanics.

Any attempt to assess the achievement or to recognise the continuity of Stoppard's dramatic career must focus on those major plays. The minor pieces have provided many diverting moments in the theatre and, as importantly, have provided a stage to Stoppard on which he could rehearse his art. But it is as fundamentally misleading to assess his canon as if such plays were of equal significance, Stoppard says, as it would be to 'use "Old Possum's Book of Practical Cats" to show that *The Waste Land* is essentially a frivolous work'.[40] This study seeks to deal with the way of seeing which informs Stoppard's serious plays: with the ideas which are most fundamental to his plays of ideas. To that end, separate chapters are devoted to Stoppard's most-discussed play *Rosencrantz and Guildenstern are Dead*; to his second major play *Jumpers*, the work which Kenneth Tynan, rightly in 1977, termed as Stoppard's masterpiece; and to the erudite *Travesties*. Perhaps more problematic to consider as major plays are *Every Good Boy Deserves Favour* (1977) and *Dogg's Hamlet, Cahoot's Macbeth* (1979). The latter play is no longer than *Dirty Linen* and *New-Found-Land*

(and not wholly unlike that work in being essentially two discrete one-act plays tenuously connected); the script of the former play bulks no larger than a brief one-act. But it is equally clear that these plays are more substantial in their concerns than such entertainments as *Dirty Linen* or even the full-length *On the Razzle* or *Rough Crossing*, which proved to be box office bonanzas for the National Theatre in 1981 and 1984. *Every Good Boy Deserves Favour* and *Dogg's Hamlet, Cahoot's Macbeth* are here grouped with Stoppard's remarkable television drama *Professional Foul* and the full-length *Night and Day* which also deal overtly with social issues. However, *The Real Thing* is the true successor to *Jumpers* and *Travesties*. As a magisterial refinement of many of Stoppard's concerns, *The Real Thing* should force recognition, however belatedly, that throughout his career Stoppard has set his major plays firmly within the realm of the real. Even *Hapgood*, with its focus on what one character calls 'the real world' of particle physics, also dramatises the moral obligations of human relationships in the real world.

Indeed, Stoppard's entire canon dramatises a movement towards incarnation, towards enfleshing the abstract word of moral precept in the corporeal realm of action. 'Words, words. They're all we have to go on', laments one of the title characters in *Rosencrantz and Guildenstern are Dead*. But the import of words in a text forever hidden from them remains unknown to Stoppard's courtiers. Hamlet is a planet out of their sphere; *Hamlet* a cosmos beyond their ken. In *Rosencrantz* the gulf is unbridgeable between the timeless stage world of *Hamlet* with its metaphysical resonances and the all too physical realm of Rosencrantz and Guildenstern who, by the end of things, *are Dead*. Apart from words, the rest is silence. In *Jumpers* Stoppard gives us the flesh and the words, the transcendent realm of moral absolutes and the sublunary sphere of musical comedy, the affirmation of moral precepts and a world of experience which can be quite remarkably without moral practice. We see the bifurcation, the lack of connection, the lack of incarnation: the flesh and the words. In such plays, Stoppard says, he is aiming for the perfect marriage of farce and the comedy of ideas. But thematically he is also concerned with marriages, unions, knowing and being known, becoming one flesh, the urge toward wholeness in union, the fusion of the flesh and the word. In *Travesties* the emphasis is on the way in which the passing world of the flesh can receive some permanence in art, how the mortal can be granted literary (if not literal) immortality, the mundane realities of life transmuted into the artifice of eternity, the flesh made words.

In his 'political' plays of the late 1970s, Stoppard's exploration proceeds in an opposite direction but the concerns are the same. Dealing with dissidents in a Soviet psychiatric prison, moral philosophers subject to a left-wing totalitarian Czech regime, journalists subject to a right-wing totalitarian African regime, artists and actors under Czech oppression, such plays as *Every Good Boy Deserves Favour*, *Professional Foul*, *Night and Day*, and *Dogg's Hamlet*, *Cahoot's Macbeth* question how the precepts of moral philosophy can be practised in the body politic, how timeless moral absolutes can be wed to action in the real world, how such words can be made flesh. From the body politic Stoppard turns his attention to the realm where the two should become one flesh, to the intimate confines of the relationship between one man and one woman. Stoppard continues to deal with the ethics of political action and the aesthetic possibility of achieving immortality in the words of art. But the focus of the moral vision in Stoppard's more recent work is on the ineluctably moral commitment of intimacy, on the responsibilities of personal commitment which turns out to be *The Real Thing*. And in *Hapgood* Stoppard pits the personal against the technical, an intuitive recognition of the worth of a person against an inhuman view of persons as objects to be used, the moral bond of parent and child against the value of a career, in a wrenching choice which remains inherently moral.

2

Through a Glass Darkly: Mortality and the Outer Mystery in *Rosencrantz and Guildenstern are Dead*

Rosencrantz and Guildenstern, spear carriers from the wings of Shakespeare's imagination, are summoned to centre stage by Tom Stoppard. With three acts before them and no acts to perform, Rosencrantz and Guildenstern spin coins, devise word games, parry questions and answers, delve and glean, draw Hamlet on to pleasures, play at playing, take a stab at killing (though the intended victim never gets the point), and, finally, wind up on the receiving end of the point themselves. And yet the whole point of Stoppard's play, in so far as it has one, is – surely – that Rosencrantz and Guildenstern never get the point. Although the courtiers come to see that their quietus will be made for them, the rest is silence. Stoppard's two courtiers remain – and the word gathers weight throughout the playwright's career – mystified. The bafflement of Rosencrantz and Guildenstern has tempted some observers to conclude with Tzara in *Travesties* that 'everything is Chance, including design'.[1] Stoppard's play more nearly forces us to see that even chance appearances mask a reality of design. If Stoppard's courtiers sense the mystery in the clockwork of *Hamlet*, they always do so with the sense that what evades their grasp is unknown to them but not unknowable. That which Rosencrantz and Guildenstern do not comprehend is not necessarily incomprehensible. Offering a helpful analogy between Stoppard's play and T.S. Eliot's poem 'Marina', Tim Brassell suggests that 'Stoppard, like Eliot, calls attention to what is present but cannot be perceived'.[2] But if Stoppard's play conjures up an image of man surrounded by an uncomprehended but comprehensible outer mystery, such resonances were not perceived by the author himself while he was writing the play.

14

Indeed, while acknowledging that his canon divides into stage entertainments and more substantial drama, Stoppard does not group *Rosencrantz and Guildenstern are Dead* among such works as *Jumpers* and *Travesties*, works which he frequently describes as 'serious plays', 'large plays', or 'plays of ideas'.[3] Although in *Jumpers*, *Travesties*, and some of the later plays Stoppard consciously set out – he now readily avers – to deal with certain philosophical issues, he steadfastly rejects the notion that *Rosencrantz* had such a genesis: 'I would absolutely deny that an intellectual or philosophical motive was in my mind when I wrote it.'[4] Any thematic freight that *Rosencrantz* may carry apart from its function as entertainment is, Stoppard claims, unintentional: 'The play had no substance beyond its own terms, beyond its apparent situation. It was about two courtiers in a Danish castle. Two nonentities surrounded by intrigue, given very little information and much of that false. It had nothing to do with the condition of modern man or the decline of metaphysics. One wasn't thinking, "Life is an anteroom in which one has to kill time". Or I wasn't, at any rate.'[5]

What the 28-year-old former journalist was thinking of as he put pen to paper was how 'to entertain a roomful of people' ('Ambushes', p. 6). 'When I was writing *Rosencrantz*', he recalled, 'I was in no sense engaged in any sort of esoteric work. It was like music-hall, if anything, a slightly literate music-hall, perhaps.'[6] Just how lightly Stoppard took his Shakespearean music-hall is indicated by his willingness to dismiss his courtiers before they were ever summoned to the stage. By the time Rosencrantz and Guildenstern were ready to tread the boards for the first time as title characters, Stoppard had already consigned them to the wings of his imagination having decided that his fame would come as a novelist. 'I was very light-hearted about the whole thing', Stoppard says of *Rosencrantz*'s opening on the Edinburgh fringe, 'because I had a novel published in the same week that the play opened, and there was no doubt in my mind whatsoever that the novel would make my reputation, and the play would be of little consequence either way'.[7]

Then came the life-changing review by Ronald Bryden; Kenneth Tynan cabled requesting a script; and in less than a year Rosencrantz and Guildenstern were not the only bit players called to centre stage at the Old Vic. Suddenly the former Bristol journalist, whose novel had meanwhile achieved worldwide sales

of 688 copies, was in the limelight of London. After the National
Theatre Company opening, Stoppard celebrated at a first-night
party, and then spent the early hours 'dashing up and down Fleet
Street from one machine-room to the next' to read the glowing
reviews of morning newspaper critics. The next day, drinking
glucose and water to ease his hangover after 'the most wildly
successful night of his life', he confessed to a reporter for the *Sun*
that 'As I went to bed last night, I had an awful thought that this
was some monstrous hoax the world was perpetrating on me'.[8] The
young writer who had set out to amuse a roomful of people with
a music-hall entertainment found his work hailed as a landmark
in British dramatic history. Even twenty years later it is difficult
to reconcile the wonderment of the awestruck young playwright
– dashing about the early-morning streets of London reading his
notices – with some academic views of his earliest play which
postulate the conscious artistry of an assured master.

At the same time, however, Stoppard acknowledges that
Rosencrantz reveals the extent to which a playwright can be
'the beneficiary of one's subconscious'.[9] 'It would be pointless
to deny', Stoppard explains, 'that in writing the play – in the act
of writing it – I was continually confronted by the opportunity
to say something which was more than a joke, or beyond a joke.
But these opportunities were very welcome as they came along
without actually being premeditated.'[10] If Stoppard's explanation
of the play's genesis should serve as a caveat against imputing
any overly elaborate or sophisticated interpretation to the play as
a conscious intention, it nevertheless invites our consideration of
what serious concerns – more than a joke or beyond a joke – the
play reveals.

Stoppard says that what attracted him to the predicament of
Rosencrantz and Guildenstern was, in part, its 'combination of
specificity and vague generality' ('Ambushes', p. 6). That same
combination of specificity and vague generality seems to have
made the play particularly fallow ground for a remarkable out-
cropping of critical interpretations. Although *Rosencrantz* was first
hailed as an existentialist or absurdist or Pirandellian or Beckettian
work, and, indeed, continues to be regarded in those terms by
some,[11] more thoughtful critics have been coming to recognise
the inaccuracy of such labels.

Beckett scholar Ruby Cohn catalogues an impressive array

of dramatic devices and theatrical techniques which she persuasively argues that *Rosencrantz* derives from *Waiting for Godot*.
Despite such elaborate interconnections between the two plays,
Cohn reaches a conclusion we should regard as judicious: 'with
hindsight, we can see that *Godot* was stylistically rather than
philosophically seminal for Stoppard'.[12] But if the philosophic
implications of *Rosencrantz* are utterly irreconcilable with those
of *Godot*, if 'the chasm is unbridgeable' between the two plays,
what should we recognise as the philosophic implications of the
Stoppard play? Although that is the important question, Cohn
chooses – in an appropriately Beckettian silence – for her answer
not to be.

While Jim Hunter may not, by opposing, end the sea of
troubles attendant on such a question, he does take a stab at
an answer: 'If Ros and Guil's position is to be taken, as some
spectators wish to take it, as in any way allegorical of human life,
then it is allegory not of existentialism, materialism, or chance,
but of a fixed purpose, a logic beyond and outside us which we
cannot visualize.'[13] Sketchy as Hunter's account is, it points us
in the right direction. The gulf between *Godot* and *Rosencrantz* is
more painstakingly mapped by William E. Gruber who rightly
rejects as 'simply incorrect' any attempt to label Stoppard's
play as 'Absurdist drama' or even '"post-Absurdist" drama'.[14]
Stoppard's dramatisation of Rosencrantz and Guildenstern, he
notes, simply 'does not illustrate the baffling absurdity or the
blind fatality that has sometimes been said to arrange their lives'
(Gruber, p. 302). Gruber definitively catalogues the manifold ways
in which *Rosencrantz* bodies forth a vision of life, of language, of the
cosmos, which is utterly incompatible with – indeed antithetical
to – absurdist negations.

However, of the two most cogent commentators on *Rosencrantz*,
Brassell emphasises the courtiers' innocence while Gruber argues
for their culpability. Brassell convincingly demonstrates that
Stoppard excises every patch of dialogue from *Hamlet* which
might point toward the courtiers' complicity. Gruber, with equal
accuracy, argues that Stoppard invented the scene on board ship
in which Rosencrantz and Guildenstern discover Claudius's death
warrant for Hamlet precisely to show that by their inaction they
become willing accomplices. Although Brassell argues that the
playwright's omission of numerous passages from *Hamlet* 'enables
him to leave out a number of exchanges which cut across the

grain of his interpretation' (pp. 43–4), Brassell in his turn fails
to deal with a passage which cuts across the grain of his
interpretation, the scene in Stoppard (but not in Shakespeare) in
which the courtiers discover the contents of Claudius's letter to
England importing the swift death of Hamlet. By contrast, Gruber
emphasises the courtiers' culpability, arguing that when they do
finally learn the contents of Claudius's letter seeking Hamlet's
death, they refrain from taking any action which might avert the
wrongful death of their childhood friend. If Stoppard's intention
were to excise any evidence which might point to the courtiers'
complicity, why invent a scene in which by their silence they
seem far guiltier than they ever do in *Hamlet*? For a playwright who
will come to make much of the morality of one man's dealings
with another man, Stoppard here seems not just ambiguous but
ambivalent on the question of whether we should see Rosencrantz
and Guildenstern as innocent or culpable.

Stoppard seems to be feeling his way in the dark – inherently
attracted to the question of individual culpability but not prepared
to explore the subject in his Shakespearean music-hall. What does
emerge clearly from *Rosencrantz* is the picture of characters who
inhabit a world which is stranger than they had supposed, a world
which they know is not as it seems, but which, finally, is not just
a matter of what seems but what is. Brassell rightly notes that in
Stoppard's play the 'ideas of rôle and fate' 'invoke the inability of all
mankind to understand those forces ultimately in control of their
lives and fates'. 'Yet', Brassell judiciously continues, 'precisely
because Rosencrantz and Guildenstern's fate is determined by
Hamlet, and not by random forces, Stoppard further suggests
that there is some method behind the seeming madness of their
lives' (Brassell, p. 53). In making applications from the world of
Stoppard's play to the realm of real life, however, Brassell seems
to follow in the path of so many observers who see more the madness than any method in 't. 'What tempers our recognition of the
courtiers' amusingly ironic plight is a latent awareness that, like
them, we cannot see the "design" behind our own lives', Brassell
reflects ruefully, 'Our sympathies are thus directed towards these
two men groping in an existential void which, to varying degrees,
may mirror our own'. We see Rosencrantz and Guildenstern 'as
human beings trapped in a world which does not make sense,
which refuses to follow the expected rules' (Brassell, p. 54).
But if the courtiers' world mirrors our own then ours is

not just an existential void. It may be a world which does not *seem* to make sense, which refuses to follow the rules *we* might expect. But to the extent that the world of Rosencrantz and Guildenstern mirrors our own it shows us the inability of all mankind to understand those forces ultimately in control of their lives and fates at the same time that it asserts that such forces beyond human control or understanding do exist. While man may question whether the other country beyond this mortal sphere may be or not be, ultimately Stoppard's play leads us to recognise that whether we can comprehend it or not that there is 'design at work' in life as well as art, that there is order and coherence to the cosmos beyond man's ability to grasp. Although Brassell spends a couple of paragraphs flirting with the 'existential void', he is much nearer to achieving an understanding of what lies beyond our understanding in his telling evocation of Eliotic mystery: 'what is present but cannot be perceived' (p. 55).

A comparison with 'Albert's Bridge', a radio drama Stoppard wrote at about the same time proves instructive. In that play, all seems chaotic, bizarre, and baffling from ground level though from the altitude of the bridge Albert is able to see order and pattern in the events on the street. In *Rosencrantz*, Stoppard is working with something of the same contrast in perspectives that we see in 'Albert's Bridge'. The mistake some observers have made is in supposing that the groundlings' view which the two courtiers obtain at street level in Elsinore is the only perspective offered in the play. In fact, just as 'Albert's Bridge' hinges on our simultaneous awareness of two points of view so *Rosencrantz* keeps constantly before us the disjunction between the way events appear at ground level as contrasted to the loftier vantage point of *Hamlet*.

But if Stoppard is echoing the technique of 'Albert's Bridge', he is also anticipating some of the concerns of his next major play, *Jumpers*. Just as George can assert that 'there is more in me than meets the microscope', so Rosencrantz and Guildenstern are sensing that there is more to life than is explainable in purely naturalistic terms. However positive Rosencrantz and Guildenstern may have been that their world was logical and natural, whatever their natural expectation that they could count on heads coming up more or less as often as tails in this life, they're having to reckon with life being somewhat more, or less, than they had counted on. Their dawning awareness at the outset of the play that the laws of probability no longer obtain ushers them into a realm which must be 'un-, sub- or supernatural'. That tentative invocation of a supernatural realm anticipates the discussion in *Jumpers* of a realm which is 'super, both natural and stitious'. Although George may have difficulty finding the right words in which to clothe his ideas, Rosencrantz and Guildenstern are even less articulate. However, what they are sensing, however dimly, is the existence of a realm beyond natural explanation, a realm which cannot be accounted for by microscopes or probability.

Brassell's caveat against allegorising Stoppard's play seems judicious. 'Although the pattern of *Rosencrantz* is susceptible to allegorisation in quasi-religious terms – that God or Destiny's design does exist, however comfortless and obscure its manifestations – this is not its *raison d'être*', Brassell argues. 'Stoppard's viewpoint here, and throughout his subsequent work, is essentially humanist, bound up with the consequences of a *given* determinism, not with an inquiry into the universe's determined or non-determined nature' (Brassell, p. 266). Indeed, it is possible to invest Rosencrantz and Guildenstern's games and banter with more weight than they can bear. However, Stoppard's next major play, *Jumpers*, is devoted specifically to just such an exploration of the nature of the cosmos. In that work Stoppard set out, he says, 'to write a theist play'.[15] If we are to see the sort of continuity in Stoppard's theatrical career which Brassell is, rightly, so concerned to demonstrate, we would do well to ask how it comes to be that among Stoppard's major works *Rosencrantz* serves as the immediate predecessor for a theist play.

Countering Gruber's claims that Rosencrantz and Guildenstern are tragic figures, Tim Brassell cites Stoppard's description of his two courtiers as 'a couple of bewildered innocents'.[16] Although Brassell may be quite right in arguing that *Rosencrantz* 'is not . . . an attempt to produce *Hamlet* with a new pair of tragic heroes', it does not follow that Stoppard is 'primarily . . . interested in Rosencrantz and Guildenstern as victims'[17] as Brassell maintains.

Stoppard does not depict Rosencrantz and Guildenstern primarily as victims (exploring the injustice that is done to them) or as tragic figures (exploring the justice of their deaths). Jim Hunter rightly argues that 'as well as sympathy for Ros and Guil in their innocence surrounded by seediness, we may also feel a degree of moral respect'.[18] However, the innocence of Stoppard's courtiers is not primarily a lack of evil but a lack of knowledge; they are *naïfs*. In Stoppard's description of them as 'bewildered innocents', the focus is on their bewilderment. Stoppard's emphasis is on their awed recognition of a frame of meaning which they can never grasp. Rosencrantz and Guildenstern exist within a realm which is greater than they can recognise but not beyond their apprehension; their intuitive reach exceeds their cognitive grasp. If something is rotten in the body politic of Denmark, there is also in Shakespeare's created world of Elsinore that which is glorious; there is – in Hamlet himself – a quintessence of more than dust. As Gruber rightly notes, we feel the wonder, the power, the splendour of that world even though it passes with its immense gravitational field just outside our view. On our own little globe – even if a great stage of fools – we may be able to sense the splendour and power of that celestial body without quite being able, with the naked eye, to discern just what it is. But whatever else may be true it is apparent that something is out there. Rosencrantz and Guildenstern are never led to feel that theirs is an isolation amid a cosmic void.

At the outset of the play Rosencrantz remains oblivious to any oddity in their coin-tossing, describing the improbable run of 85 heads as merely a new record. But Guildenstern, as the opening stage directions indicate, is 'well alive to the oddity of it', not concerned about his loss of money but 'worried by the implications'.[19] 'Is that *it*, then?' Guildenstern asks Rosencrantz only five minutes into the play, 'Is that all? . . . A new record? Is that as far as you are prepared to go?' (p. 9). To ask just what is encompassed when Guildenstern refers to '*it*' is to ask a question which runs throughout the whole play. 'But it's this, is it?' (p. 20), Guildenstern asks when it appears that 'getting caught up in the action' would consist of nothing more than becoming a participant in one of the players' pornographic pageants. Guildenstern insists that '*it*' could have been something more – 'It could have been – a bird out of season, dropping bright-feathered on my shoulder . . . . It could have been a tongueless dwarf standing by the road to point the way. . . . I was *prepared*. But it's this, is it?' (p. 20). The destiny which awaits Rosencrantz and Guildenstern consists of nothing for which they are prepared. Instead they are to be 'kept intrigued without ever quite being enlightened' (p. 31). 'Where's it going to end?' Rosencrantz asks and Guildenstern echoes 'That's the question' (p. 33). How much is encompassed by Rosencrantz's word 'it'? What is 'it' that is happening? 'That', indeed, is the question.

While Guildenstern may be 'aware but not going to panic about it' (p. 7), it is clear that panic for him would involve questions of 'faith': 'A weaker man might be moved to re-examine his faith, if in nothing else at least in the law of probability' (p. 8). Clearly for Guildenstern the law of probability is not as far as he is prepared to go in his reassessment. Just how much Guildenstern is prepared to reassess seems itself somewhat vague. Jonathan Bennett offers the helpful analysis that Rosencrantz and Guildenstern are confronting 'a small cluster of intimately connected concepts . . . *identity, memory, activity* and *death*'.[20] In this complex of epistemic questions, what is up for grabs for Guildenstern is reality itself. But if Guildenstern is questioning the nature of reality, it is also clear that from the outset he has ruled out certain possibilities. 'It must be indicative of something', Guildenstern insists, 'besides the redistribution of wealth' (pp. 10–11). Years later Stoppard would declare in his own voice and with utterly unequivocal firmness, 'One thing I feel sure about is that a materialistic view of history is an insult to the human race' ('Ambushes', p. 13). In retrospect it is possible to see from Guildenstern's remark at the outset of *Rosencrantz* just how early in his career Stoppard was prepared to discount Marxist materialist explanations of reality.

At the same time Guildenstern also insists that 'the scientific approach to the examination of phenomena is a defence against the pure emotion of fear' (p. 12). Throughout Stoppard's career, acknowledgement of such intimations of immortality seems more a fearful prospect than a source of comfort or reassurance. Guildenstern accuses Rosencrantz of being ignorant in his complacency: 'Is *that* what you imagine? Is that it? No *fear*? . . . *Fear!* The crack that might flood your brain with light!' (p. 10). Guildenstern describes the equanimity of their past existence in terms of complacency. The 'mathematically calculable chance, which ensures that [a tosser of coins] will not upset himself by losing too much nor upset his opponent by winning too often', Guildenstern says, 'made for a kind of harmony and a kind of confidence':

It related the fortuitous and the ordained into a reassuring union which we recognized as nature. The sun came up about as often as it went down, in the long run, and a coin showed heads about as often as it showed tails. Then a messenger arrived. We had been sent for. (p. 13)

The anxiety of Rosencrantz and Guildenstern is less like that of Gogo or Didi endlessly *Waiting for Godot* than like that of the Chorus of Canterbury Women who have already intuited a *Murder in the Cathedral*. The mystery in *Godot* is unplumbable. The realm beyond, in *Godot*, is not only unknown but unknowable, mysterious not only to Gogo and Didi but to us. Will Godot come or will he not? The audience is able to provide no more of an answer than can Gogo or Didi. By comparison, the realm beyond in *Rosencrantz* is the world of *Hamlet*. But Rosencrantz and Guildenstern do not wait – hopefully or fearfully – for something to alter an endless mundane existence. Rather, their fear is that their mundane but ordinary existence, their conventional lives in a known and knowable world, has already been disrupted by some force beyond their understanding. Just as the Chorus of Canterbury Women may have preferred living – living and partly living – amid such known pains as crop failures and taxes, so Guildenstern senses 'fear' that something is happening outside of anything accounted for by materialistic, scientific, or naturalistic law. The Chorus of Canterbury Women are filled with anxiety that something extraordinary has already been set in motion; the return of Thomas, Archbishop, raises their inchoate fears of the supernatural, of the eternal breaking into their lives in ways they are unprepared for. Just so, in *Rosencrantz* the extraordinary has already broken into the realm of the ordinary, wheels within wheels have already been set in motion.

Just what this new fear that has come upon them may consist of is not precisely defined in either work – but Guildenstern is ready to allow the possibility that what they may have become subject to are 'un-, sub- or supernatural forces'. Although Guildenstern says it would be a great relief to him personally if 'un-, sub- or supernatural forces' are not at work, it is again to the possibility of the supernatural that he recurs in comparing their experience to that of two men seeing a unicorn. However frustrating it may have been for Guildenstern to be alone in his perception of the oddity of their situation, it is even more alarming when Rosencrantz too hears the mystical music which has heretofore been the private perception of Guildenstern. It is the fact of Rosencrantz hearing

the music too which prompts Guildenstern's meditation on unicorns:

> A man breaking his journey between one place and another at
> a third place of no name, character, population or significance,
> sees a unicorn cross his path and disappear. That in itself is
> startling, but there are precedents for mystical encounters of
> various kinds, or to be less extreme, a choice of persuasions to
> put it down to fancy; until – 'My God,' says a second man, 'I
> must be dreaming, I thought I saw a unicorn.' At which point,
> a dimension is added that makes the experience as alarming as
> it will ever be. (p. 15)

Guildenstern is wrestling with the 'alarming' possibility that
something they had assumed 'couldn't have been real' is in fact
affirmed by another witness. Not only the materialistic redistribution of wealth and the scientific examination of phenomena
but also that which is 'reasonable' proves to be 'as thin as reality,
the name we give to the common experience'. What truly alarms
Guildenstern is the possibility that they might be apprehending a
'dimension' outside 'the common experience' which is, nonethe-
less, real.

Rosencrantz and Guildenstern's perceptions of such a reality may
be fleeting and fragmentary without being fantastical, irrational, or
hallucinatory. Stoppard demonstrates the difference between the
two with his 'peacock story', which he has repeated on numerous
occasions to illustrate his whole approach to playwriting:

> A couple of years ago I went to see a man who had peacocks
> in his garden and he was telling me that when peacocks are
> new they tend to run away, and he was shaving one morning
> and looked out of the window and he saw . . . his pet peacock
> leap over the garden hedge and make off down the road. Pea-
> cocks being rare birds, he dropped his razor and, barefoot and
> lathered, he pursued it. . . . It crossed the main road but on the
> other side of the road he caught it. He picked it up and then
> cars started going by and he couldn't get back and he stood
> there for a little while watching these people in cars.

What fascinates Stoppard about the peacock story is not any confusion between appearance and reality. The peacock is real, the man shaving is real, and the way they appear is not misleading. Stoppard is bemused by the way a coherent chain of events can result in a scene which at first glance resembles an irrational fantasy but is, emphatically, real. Although the peacock owner may clearly comprehend the whole situation, Stoppard continues,

> I don't write about him, I don't write about the peacock, what I write about is two people who drive by in a car . . . . And they see this fellow in pyjamas with shaving cream on his face, barefoot, carrying a peacock, walking down the road. And they see this fellow for about 5/8ths of a second – never again, and they are never quite sure exactly what they saw.[21]

'I mean, *Rosencrantz and Guildenstern are Dead* is a bit like that you know', Stoppard confided to a bemused but bewildered San Francisco audience, adding gamely if – for this crowd – unpersuasively, 'It makes perfect sense to me'.[22] His play, Stoppard explains, simply presents *Hamlet* as viewed by 'two people driving past Elsinore'.[23]

The events which Rosencrantz and Guildenstern see for perhaps 5/8ths of a second as they are driving past Elsinore may be as alarming as a sudden glimpse of a unicorn. Struggling to understand what is happening to them Rosencrantz suddenly, impossibly, thinks he hears music. But as soon as Guildenstern thinks he hears it also, Rosencrantz relaxes 'It couldn't have been real'. That the seemingly irrational would happen simultaneously to two persons is as impossible, Guildenstern says, as discovering that a second person shares your delusion of having seen a unicorn. The fact that Rosencrantz and Guildenstern share the same impossible glimpse into the Elsinore of *Hamlet* adds the even more alarming dimension that what they have experienced is not individual hallucination but the discovery of the reality of what heretofore they would have regarded as fantastical. Having a second person say 'My God . . . I thought I saw a unicorn' adds a dimension 'that makes the experience as alarming as it will ever be'. The alarming aspect of a second person hearing the knock on the shutters, the knock from the outer darkness, is that beyond the empirical realm in which verification is possible there may exist another realm in which wheels turn within wheels. Rodney

Simard rightly recognises that Stoppard's unicorn resonates with metaphysical, even theological, implications even if he scoffs at the notion that the play might actually take such intimations of divinity seriously.[24]

To be sure, the realm beyond their ken remains mystifying to Rosencrantz and Guildenstern. They remain unable to delve into Hamlet or to glean what afflicts him. But the fact that Rosencrantz and Guildenstern have not the skill to play the frets and stops which are offered to them demonstrates their limitations rather than the instrument's. Indeed, the two courtiers never abandon the belief that within the perplexing character of Hamlet there is something to be gleaned if only they could delve deeply enough. But Hamlet remains opaquely impervious to their delving and they recognise it. 'He murdered us', Rosencrantz says simply after they've tried their wits against Hamlet's, 'Twenty-seven questions he got out in ten minutes, and answered three' (p. 41). Rosencrantz and Guildenstern are left not with the conviction that Hamlet is inexplicable, that what Hamlet says is mindlessly incoherent but rather that they themselves do not have the power to grasp what sits on brood within Hamlet's teeming brain: 'Twenty-seven–three, and you think he might have had the edge?! He *murdered* us' (p. 41).

If the character of Hamlet eludes their grasp, so also do the events of *Hamlet*. Indeed, just how little Rosencrantz and Guildenstern grasp of events around them is reflected in their complete ignorance as to why the king, who had encouraged them to draw Hamlet on to such pleasures as a play, then interrupts the production in mid-performance. That play, which Hamlet stages to snare the conscience of the king, is 'abandoned in some confusion', Rosencrantz confesses in Stoppard's play, 'owing to certain nuances outside our appreciation' (p. 84). Such missed nuances characterise Rosencrantz and Guildenstern's limited perceptions of the whole of the events which they witness from the periphery. They are perplexed as much by Claudius's actions as by Hamlet's introspection. Why Claudius should have chosen them, what Claudius wants them to glean from Hamlet, why Claudius thinks Hamlet's transformation has causes apart from what is already 'well known, common property', remains beyond their sphere. But if they understand neither character nor events, they disarmingly insist that it is their own impercipience rather than the irrationality of events which accounts for the mystery: 'I don't pretend to have understood', Rosencrantz declares, 'Frankly, I'm not very interested. If they won't tell us, that's their affair' (p. 70). Whereas Rosencrantz and Guildenstern humbly recognise their own inability to grasp the nuances which would explain Hamlet's character, *Hamlet*'s events, or their own fate, they never reach the philosophically despairing conclusion that there are no nuances to be grasped, no reasons or explanation or rationale for what has transpired.

The denial that truth exists, that there are no certainties to be grasped, is confined in this play to the voice of the Player. The music which first Guildenstern and then Rosencrantz heard turns out to be that of the band of tragedians who, within *Hamlet*, will play 'The Murder of Gonzago' before the court of Elsinore. But while the music is not what it first seemed to betoken (prompting Guildenstern's 'wistful' remark 'I'm sorry it wasn't a unicorn. It would have been nice to have unicorns') neither are the tragedians what they seem. The players are not just a troupe of mortal thespians but the mediators between the two courtiers and the world of *Hamlet*. 'We're *actors* – we're the opposite of people', the Player explains. As such the Players seems to confront the befuddled mortal Rosencrantz and Guildenstern with the voice of knowledge and experience. From the first the Player adopts the role of the sophisticate, attempting to draw Guildenstern on to such pleasures as the chance to 'get caught up in the action' of a pornographic revue. Hunter perceptively argues that in taking offence at the Player's attempt to arouse him to indecency

> what Guil displays . . . is what we might least expect in routine travesty or routine Absurdism: a sense of values. There is an echo, of course, of the arrival of Pozzo and Lucky . . . in the first Act of *Waiting for Godot*; and in Guil's gentleness to Alfred a little later an echo of Vladimir to the Boy; but the indignation and concern of Stoppard's character are much more deeply felt.[25]

Besides having an intimate knowledge of a certain rottenness in the state of Denmark, the players also seem knowledgeable in being able to predict, foreshadow, even act out Rosencrantz and Guildenstern's fate. They know the score – or the plot – as the case may be. But the plot, artifice, playing, is all they know. The Player speaks with the disembodied voice of art. Thus he can 'know' that 'truth is only that which is taken to be true'. What we should recognise is that in such 'sophisticated' insights – much as in the players' penchant for pornography – the Player does not so much speak with the voice of wisdom as of the worldly wise. Brassell rightly points out that the difference of attitude between the players and the two hapless courtiers 'recalls the central contrast in Stoppard's novel between Moon and Malquist' (Brassell, p. 52). The players, Brassell asserts, follow in the footsteps of Lord Malquist, that prototype for a series of characters who are 'breezily and superficially clever, often very funny, but selfish and ruthless' (Brassell, p. 22). The players may be the opposite of people, but the extent to which that stage world reverses the world of people is not immediately apparent. If they recognise – as Rosencrantz and Guildenstern do not – that they have roles to play, they go to the opposite extreme in supposing that life consists of nothing more than roles.

Rosencrantz and Guildenstern may be obtuse in a number of ways, may never catch on to where they stand in the scheme of things, may never discover 'how to *act*' (p. 49). In contrast the Player offers assurances which are as cheerfully nihilistic as is the slick cynicism of Archie throughout *Jumpers*. The Player contends that any experience can be treated as a role to be played with aplomb and panache. However, like the debonair badinage about adultery in the opening scene of *The Real Thing*, such ironic detachment from the actualities of life is shown to be an imaginative 'House of Cards' which only exists on stage. When confronted by the fact of death, all the world is distinctly not a stage. Rosencrantz and Guildenstern recognise, as the Player does not, the limits of their mortality and the absolute finality of the fact of death. Indeed, of all the concerns expressed in *Rosencrantz*, nothing calls attention to the gulf between reality and the realm of imaginative reality so sharply as the fact of death.

'Do you ever think of yourself', Rosencrantz asks, 'as actually *dead*, lying in a box with a lid on it?' (p. 52). Rosencrantz's plaintive question voices a concern over the fact of human mortality and an anguished need to know something beyond that mortality, a concern which is to run throughout Stoppard's plays. George's discovery in *Jumpers* of the death of a colleague prompts his poignant reflections on whether the human spirit continues to exist after the demise of the human body. 'It's not the dying with me – one knows about pain', George says, 'It's *death* that I'm afraid of'.[26] *Travesties* and *The Real Thing* will offer the reflection that both character and writer can achieve immortality of a sort in the lines of a poem or in the pages of fiction. Still, the artifice of eternity scarcely answers the nagging fear of dissolution that Rosencrantz and Guildenstern and George express. Stoppard has quoted, approvingly if ruefully, Woody Allen's wry quip – 'I don't want to achieve immortality through my work, I want to achieve it through not dying'.[27] While the other plays, and even *Rosencrantz* itself, offer the possibility of enshrinement in words as a sort of consolation, the confrontation of the individual with his own mortality is dealt with more rawly in *Rosencrantz* than in any of Stoppard's subsequent plays. 'Whatever became of the moment when one first knew about death?' Rosencrantz asks, 'There must have been one, a moment, in childhood when it first occurred to you that you don't go on for ever. It must have been shattering – stamped into one's memory. And yet I can't remember it. It never occurred to me at all. What does one make of that? We must be born with an intuition of mortality' (p. 53).

If in growing up, most men lose not only their intimations of immortality but their intuition of mortality, if most men become inured to, oblivious to the idea of their own death, perhaps art – this play speculates – can reawaken such a perception. But such an awareness will not be evoked, Guildenstern asserts, through tawdry theatrics: 'The mechanics of cheap melodrama! That isn't *death*! You scream and choke and sink to your knees, but it doesn't bring death home to anyone – it doesn't catch them unawares and start the whisper in their skulls that says – "One day you are going to die"' (p. 63).

What Guildenstern denounces as 'cheap melodrama' is the players' dumbshow which begins as the mime from 'The Murder of Gonzago' but expands into a mime of the events of *Hamlet*. Although Guildenstern would 'prefer art to mirror life', the mime he is witnessing – though he only vaguely catches the reflection – precisely mirrors his own. Indeed, what prompts his outburst are the impending stage deaths of 'two smiling accomplices – friends – courtiers – ... two spies' dressed in coats identical to those worn by Rosencrantz and Guildenstern themselves. If there is some ambiguity in the Player's introduction of the two figures as 'accomplices' or 'friends', his questions regarding their demise leave matters even more up in the air: 'Traitors hoist by their own petard? – or victims of the gods? – we shall never know!'

(p. 62). The Player's questions apply as much to Rosencrantz and Guildenstern as they do to the 'spies' of the dumbshow.

Brassell may call Rosencrantz and Guildenstern 'victims', Gruber may judge them to be culpable traitors, but the emphasis of Stoppard's play is neither to exonerate nor to convict the courtiers but to dramatise their bewilderment before forces which they do not understand. The plight of Rosencrantz and Guildenstern is to be 'kept intrigued without ever quite being enlightened' (p. 31). Having been summoned to Elsinore, having met the players, having delved and gleaned, having delivered Hamlet to Claudius, Guildenstern is left in perplexity: 'And yet it doesn't seem enough; to have breathed such significance. Can that be all?' (p. 70).

Like Guildenstern, Rosencrantz is left in baffled incomprehension in which he does not 'pretend to have understood'. But, unlike Guildenstern, Rosencrantz supposes 'it' is over (p. 70). Guildenstern, however, not only recognises that events have not yet reached their aesthetic, moral and logical conclusion ('I knew it wasn't the end') but his desire to see things through to their conclusion represents a conscious, deliberate act of the will. Near the end of the second act the courtiers take a remark by Hamlet as permission for them to leave. 'He *said* we can go', Rosencrantz insists, 'Cross my heart'. Although Rosencrantz is ready to depart, Guildenstern demurs. Guildenstern's reluctance to leave Elsinore neither manifests complicity nor innocence but bafflement and the urgency of his desire for enlightenment. 'I like to know where I am', Guildenstern explains, 'Even if I don't know where I am, I like to know *that*. If we go there's no knowing' (p. 72). In admonishing Rosencrantz earlier that he would not find the answer to 'where we stand' by looking 'in the bowl of a compass' (p. 43), Guildenstern had been expressing the need for something other than a geographical location. Just so, Guildenstern's desire to know 'where I am' expresses the need more for a metaphysical than a merely physical grounding. Even leaving Elsinore may not enable the courtiers to escape from 'it' as Rosencrantz sanguinely predicts: 'We'll be well out of it'.[28] Guildenstern is not so optimistic: 'I don't know. It's the same sky' (p. 72). If *Rosencrantz* is the story of two courtiers driving past Elsinore, Guildenstern's fear is that once they have left Elsinore they will never know what they glimpsed while there, what 'significance' they have 'breathed'. Guildenstern's earlier fear of being subject to 'un-, sub- or supernatural forces', the fear of not knowing what might happen to them, seems to have given way to the fear that the experience might be over without their having understood what those forces are.

When the courtiers do leave Elsinore and are on board boat in the third act they still have to 'act on scraps of information' (p. 77). It is, however, a source of some comfort to them that in escorting Hamlet to England they have 'got a letter which explains everything' (p. 79). Thus, in discovering the warrant for Hamlet's death the courtiers' response is not so much one of murderous complicity as a desperate desire at last to know the whys and wherefores of this murder mystery in which they – like characters who will follow them in *Jumpers* and in *The Real Inspector Hound* – have been so fatally caught up.

Just so, their discovery of a warrant for their own deaths evokes a response which is scarcely different in kind from their response to the warrant for Hamlet's death. We cannot very well fault them for murderous complicity unless we are equally prepared – as Gruber seems not to be – to fault them for being wilfully suicidal. If they are prepared with fatalistic abandon to pursue things to their artistic, logical and aesthetic conclusion, they do so in the desperate hope that from their end they might know their beginning.

The realisation that they are about to die does not confront the courtiers with logic nor with justice but simply deepens their sense of mystery. What looms in Guildenstern's mind is, still, the lack of explanation. 'Was it all for this? Who are we that so much should converge on our little deaths?', Guildenstern asks the Player in anguish, 'Who are *we*?' (p. 93). The Player's response 'You are Rosencrantz and Guildenstern. That's enough' is of scant comfort. 'No – it is not enough', Guildenstern protests, 'To be told so little – to such an end – and still, finally, to be denied an explanation . . . . ' (p. 93). Even to the very end Guildenstern does not deny that an explanation exists, does not deny the existence of order and causality, that there are wheels within wheels that have been set in motion. What he protests is that he has not been 'told' the explanation. It is amid just such frustration that he lashes out at the Player: 'If we have a destiny, then so had he – and if this is ours, then that was his – and if there are no explanations for us, then let there be none for him— ' (p. 93).

In performance Guildenstern's rash and bloody deed as he plunges the dagger into the Player frequently evokes an audible

gasp from the audience. Guildenstern has murdered the Player,
he thinks, and we in the audience think so too. 'You see, it *is*
the kind they do believe in', the Player says of his stage-death
as he shows Guildenstern that it had been a stage-dagger. The
Player survives. He will live to tread other boards, to play other
roles. In his acting the murdered Gonzago will live again on other
stages.[29]

But if art survives, the individual does not. Even while the
Player maintains that death can be acted, Guildenstern insists
otherwise: 'No . . . no . . . not for *us*, not like that' (p. 95). In
performance, Guildenstern's line became even more emphatic:
'No, no, no . . . It's not like that'.[30] The Player's death scene,
which turns out to be a play within a play (in *Rosencrantz* which
is itself a play within the play of *Hamlet*) functions in much the
same way as will the opening scene of *The Real Thing* years later in
Stoppard's career. While it is happening we in the audience have
no idea that what we are seeing is artifice. It *looks* real. But the jolt
of recognition when we come to see that we have been taken in
does not serve to convince us of the unreality of life but to throw
into even starker relief the distinction between feigning and real
life, between the conventions of the stage and the conditions of
actual experience, between that which we know to be and that
which we know not to be. Ultimately for the players, as Brassell
asserts, 'nothing, not even death, is "real"' (Brassell, p. 58). 'In
their experience' everything usually ends in death – but their
experience is all the experience of the stage, of artifice, of feigning.

Of all the actions that a man might play, death is a final
reality which passeth show; the Player's stage-death offers but
the trappings and the suits of woe. In reality, as opposed to the
theatre, death is not a stage-death. In the world, as opposed to
the world of the play, 'Death is not romantic . . . death is
not anything . . . Death is . . . not. The absence of presence,
nothing more . . . the endless time of never coming back'.[31] As
the play ends with the disappearance of Rosencrantz unnoticed
by Guildenstern and then with Guildenstern's disappearance
unnoticed at the time by any of the other characters, this play
may, amid its jokiness, catch its audience unawares and start the
whisper in their skulls that says – 'One day you are going to die'.
One senses in the quiet exits of Rosencrantz and Guildenstern an
utter finality. If such exits are entrances somewhere else, they are
entrances to an undiscovered country which gives pause to the

nonentities Rosencrantz and Guildenstern much as to the sublime
Hamlet. Their little fear matters, the play insists. Their little deaths
matter.

But if we can see the significance in the lives of such unimposing
figures as Rosencrantz and Guildenstern, what are we to make of
the realm they confront? Arguing from the form of the work, Peter
J. Rabinowitz demonstrates that Stoppard simultaneously evokes
our sympathy for the hapless Rosencrantz and Guildenstern while
eliciting our respect for the larger pattern, the greater order of
Shakespeare's stage.[32] Even if Gruber goes too far in asserting
that 'Stoppard's play . . . affirms unconditionally the morality of
Shakespeare's' (Gruber p. 307), Rabinowitz conclusively demonstrates that Stoppard does not just parody Shakespeare or present
'a reduction to absurdity of everything noble and weighty in
Hamlet'[33] as Jill Levenson had tried to maintain. Rather, Rabinowitz
concludes, Stoppard wants 'to make us share his characters'
anguish while we transcend their intellectual limitations'.[34]

While it may be, as Hersh Zeifman claims, that *Rosencrantz*
metaphorically dramatises a world in which 'we have no idea of
the plot, our place in the action' or even 'the *purpose* of it all',[35]
it certainly does not follow that life is therefore purposeless; if
there is a 'confusing multiplicity of possible meaning', it does not
follow that 'the whole concept of meaning ultimately becomes
meaningless'.[36] That Rosencrantz and Guildenstern do not grasp
how their world is ordered scarcely demonstrates that there is no
order or that life is, as Zeifman would have it, 'terrible'.[37]

What Rosencrantz and Guildenstern see may appear bizarre.
But it is not inexplicable, irrational, or chaotic, as Michael
Billington implies in his assertion that 'philosophically, Stoppard's
play belongs to the tradition of Theatre of the Absurd as defined
by Ionesco'.[38] In fact, as Stoppard was to explain of *Jumpers*,
Rosencrantz 'suggests that real life can rise to surprising and bizarre
effects. I don't mean absurd – not with a capital A, like Ionesco'.[39]
Nor does the failure of Rosencrantz and Guildenstern to understand their circumstances demonstrate the meaninglessness of
life, the powerlessness of human beings, or the inscrutability of
a cosmic void, as a subsequent interviewer tried to maintain.
Rosencrantz and Guildenstern may not grasp what they have

seen, 'but', Stoppard insists, 'they make continuous attempts to master the situation and comprehend it with the assumption there is something to comprehend, which would be nearer the position that I would take'. Thus while admitting the difficulty of coming to grips with the meaning of existence, Stoppard agreed with his somewhat surprised interlocutor that 'yes' he was asserting that it is possible 'to comprehend . . . purpose in life'.[40]

Just as George can assert that 'there is more in me than meets the microscope', so Rosencrantz and Guildenstern are sensing that there is more to life than is explainable in purely naturalistic terms. Although George may have difficulty finding the right words in which to clothe his ideas, Rosencrantz and Guildenstern are even less articulate. However, what they are sensing, however dimly, is the existence of a realm beyond natural explanation, a realm which cannot be accounted for by microscopes or probability.

But what the play finally leaves us with is not an ironic smirk at Rosencrantz and Guildenstern for their naïveté in believing in a world beyond their ken. If *Jumpers* is 'a theist play',[41] a play which demonstrates that atheists may be the ones without the courage to believe in the reality of God, the groundwork for such metaphysical affirmations was already laid in *Rosencrantz*. Stoppard's play reverberates with a sense of man surrounded by an outer mystery; there may exist more than Rosencrantz and Guildenstern have dreamt of in their philosophy. That outer mystery ineluctably resonates with metaphoric implications of a realm of meaning beyond the materialistic 'redistribution of wealth', a realm of reality beyond what can be empirically verified through the scientific 'examination of phenomena'. In *Rosencrantz* we can already see the seed of Stoppard's future concerns, concerns which he would subsequently express in his acknowledgement that 'yes, it is true that I *am* more interested in the metaphysical condition of man than the social position'.[42]

And that world beyond, that order beyond our ken which is inherently metaphysical, is from the first in Stoppard associated with art, imaged, figured, made known by art. In *Rosencrantz and Guildenstern are Dead*, the courtiers' attempt to understand their fate is greeted by the Player's pronouncement: 'It is written'. Such biblical language has the effect of associating, within the created world of Stoppard's play, the Shakespearean text with the Scriptural. A realm in which a coin can come up heads

92 times in a row must have some significance beyond the materialistic. But that realm is not random, disordered, chaotic. It is the realm of which Shakespeare is the author and finisher. If it is difficult or even, finally, impossible to pluck out the heart of *Hamlet*'s mystery, the play's actions are not full of sound and fury signifying nothing.

Even in Stoppard's first major stage play, we see that his impulses are to celebrate the value and worth of the individual within the context of a complex but coherent cosmos, a cosmos which resonates with metaphysical and moral mystery but never with the meaninglessness of the amoral or the – merely – materialistic. What *Rosencrantz* gives us is less a tragic vision than a moral vision. We are confronted by the significance of the human even in its most insignificant manifestation rather than by the glory and exaaltation of the noblest and most sublimely human. We are confronted by the fact of mortality which will come to all men. But, inexorably, we are confronted by a world of outer mystery which lies beyond the grasp but not beyond the reach of every – not just the exceptional – man. Having had a glimpse of *Hamlet* while 'driving past Elsinore', Rosencrantz and Guildenstern may never be able to make sense of what they have seen as through a glass darkly. And yet they sense more than they can make sense of. The world of *Hamlet* hovering in its tragic power, majesty, and splendour just beyond Rosencrantz and Guildenstern's comprehension figures the transcendent realm which lies beyond the ability of mortal flesh to verify empirically, though not beyond his power to intuit as a verity.

3

The Flesh and the Word
in *Jumpers*

Jumpers explodes on the stage with a burst of flashing lights, puzzling pyramids of gymnasts, an unsynchronised medley of moon songs, and the striptease of a secretary who is, literally, a quite daring young woman on a flying trapeze. Suddenly a gunshot tears one of the jumpers out of the gymnasts' pyramid; the party is over; and we are plunged into a play which is, among other things, a murder mystery. Tom Stoppard's 1972 play has proven so popular that in 1976 it began a remarkable second run at the National Theatre – a 'revival' of a work not five years old. Drawing on the magnificent theatrical facilities available at the National, the production employed a revolving stage, projected televised images on a gargantuan screen, and belted out a concluding musical number which might bring down the house in Las Vegas. Making a most welcome reappearance on the West End stage in 1985, the play counterpointed the ravishing strains of Vivaldi's 'Gloria in Excelsis Deo' with the soundtrack of 'Star Wars', added a jet-propelled space suit for the eye-popping re-entry of Captain Scott to the Coda, and a grapevine for the swinging entry – clad in tuxedo top and loincloth – of Lord Greystoke, a.k.a. Tarzan.[1]

Jumpers, in short, is a good show. Whether or not it is more than a facile revue-sketch, its overt theatricality assures it of a successful place on the modern stage. Although detractors first faulted the play as a 'shallow display of stage pyrotechnics' and admirers praised it for 'a dazzling display of virtuosity', more thoughtful observers have come to recognise that the play possesses the 'weight, authority, stature' of the 'profound'.[2] Surveying Stoppard's canon from *Rosencrantz and Guildenstern are Dead* through *Every Good Boy Deserves Favour*, Kenneth Tynan quite rightly declared *Jumpers* to be Stoppard's 'masterpiece'.[3] Given his desire to contrive 'the perfect marriage between the

play of ideas and farce',[4] Stoppard achieves in *Jumpers* a con-
summation devoutly to be wished. Tynan aptly describes *Jumpers*
as 'something unique in theatre: a farce whose main purpose is to
affirm the existence of God'.[5] Within the play such affirmations
are entrusted to Stoppard's professorial protagonist, George.

However, the deftness with which Stoppard juggles pratfalls
and paradoxes has left many observers up in the air. 'The confusion arises', Stoppard says, 'because I treat plays of ideas in just
about the same knockabout way as I treat the entertainments'.[6]
Even among critics who recognise what is at issue in *Jumpers*, the
most frequent error is the oversimplified notion that either George
is the hero of the play's ideas or he is the comic butt of the play's
farce. Critics either praise George for being acute or dismiss him
as obtuse and neither angle encompasses his role in the play.
Brassell argues that 'George is the play's hero and Stoppard's
own mouthpiece'[7] but omits any sense of George's culpability.
Crump rightly recognises that George 'fails as a husband and as
a detective' but supposes that such 'ineffectuality in the realm
of action' undercuts any affirmation of his moral philosophy.[8]
In fact, the play leads us to a complex vision which precludes
a simple yes or no answer to the question of whether Stoppard
comes down on George's side. In the realm of the word, George's
beliefs possess weight, authority, stature; however haltingly, he
utters profundity and speaks not only for himself but for Stoppard.
In the realm of the flesh, not George but Dotty confronts – both in
her own closet and in the cosmos – the existential fact of human
mortality and human immorality; however uncomprehendingly,
her experience bodies forth not only her own anguish but that
of Stoppard.

I began by describing the overt theatricality of Stoppard's
play. However, we should not conclude that Stoppard's theatrical
devices are a glossy screen behind which are hidden his serious
concerns. More than any other recent playwright, perhaps more
than any playwright since Shakespeare, Stoppard thinks in consciously theatrical terms. The ideas of the play revolve around
issues in moral philosophy which Professor George Moore will be
debating in a departmental symposium. More theatrically, the play
is about a professor dictating a lecture while in the next room his
wife, a former star of musical comedy, is trying to hide the corpse
of the gymnast killed during the party. The situation itself raises
more moral issues than are dreamt of in George's philosophy. It

is not sufficient to pay attention only to what the characters say and to regard the stage action as a kind of illustration.

Indeed, Stoppard says that the 'initial impetus for the play' and one of the threads which provides continuity for the entire production is an 'entirely visual image' in that frenetic opening scene. 'The first thing I had', Stoppard says of the genesis of his play, was 'the image of a pyramid of gymnasts occupying the stage, followed by a gunshot, followed by the image of one gymnast being shot out of the pyramid and the others imploding on the hole'.[9] Stoppard has repeated these observations about his 1972 play in several different contexts – in separate interviews with Ronald Hayman and the *New York Times*[10] in 1974, in programme notes for the National Theatre's 1976 production of *Jumpers*, in a guest lecture at a California university in 1977. Two points seem to me significant in his remarks. First, Stoppard does not just refer generally to the acrobatics the gymnasts perform. The germinal image of the play and the one that lingers in Stoppard's mind years later is, specifically, the human pyramid the jumpers form. Further, although his phrasing naturally varies, Stoppard always uses the word *imploding* to describe the break-up of the pyramid. In this, he is repeating the words of his original stage direction.[11] The pyramid, that is, does not merely collapse; it does not explode; quite pointedly Stoppard insists that the pyramid is drawn into the hole, sucked into the vacuum left by the departed jumper. It implodes.

To ask what we are to make of all this is also to ask what Stoppard made of it because he works inductively – constructing contexts, significances, associations as he goes along. Given a metaphoric association of gymnastics with mental acrobatics, Stoppard quickly identifies his jumpers as a cross section of Radical Liberal academics who have been willing to leap to a bewildering variety of intellectually fashionable positions. Literally, George explains, the acrobatic troupe contains 'a mixture of the more philosophical members of the university gymnastics team and the more gymnastic members of the Philosophy School' (p. 41). But we perceive, more tellingly, the kind of leaps these jumpers are capable of when George catalogues them as 'Logical positivists, mainly, with a linguistic analyst or two, a couple of Benthamite Utilitarians . . . lapsed Kantians and empiricists generally . . . and of course the usual Behaviourists' (p. 41). Indeed, following their party's victory at the polls, the jumpers make the archbishopric of Canterbury a political appointment and fill the post with Sam Clegthorpe – the Radical Liberal spokesman for Agriculture and an agnostic. By equating such mental gymnastics with physical acrobatics, Stoppard has his fun simply by literalising a metaphor.

The jumpers are led by Archie, a jack-of-all-disciplines who holds the office of Vice-Chancellor and is as well 'a doctor of medicine, philosophy, literature and law, with diplomas in psychological medicine and PT including gym' (p. 52). Archie's versatility in leaping from one discipline to another is paralleled by his versatility as to what constitutes truth, his epistemological relativism. Archie is a man of no convictions whose actions spring wholly from an elastic pragmatism. Believing goodness and truth to be equally unknowable, he condones whatever is expedient. Despite Archie's supple leadership, the intellectual 'guardian and figurehead' (p. 54) of the jumpers is Professor Duncan McFee, whom George is preparing to debate. McFee is the jumper most closely identified with ethical, as opposed to epistemological, relativism; he propounds that 'good and bad aren't actually *good* and *bad* in any absolute or metaphysical sense' (p. 38). From there it is a short jump to justifying murder as antisocial and undesirable but not, *philosophically*, inherently wrong. In fact, it is a short jump from McFee's moral relativism to any number of philosophic, psychological, and political positions which – however reprehensible in a moral sphere – are nevertheless tenable in a world where good and bad do not exist. We need to recognise, then, just how basic McFee's premise is to the mental acrobatics of all the jumpers. Standing alone against McFee and the jumpers, George ruefully considers a name for the sort of philosophy which condones murder: 'Mainstream, I'd call it. Orthodox mainstream' (p. 39).

After the intellectual dependence of the jumpers on McFee's moral relativism has been conclusively established, after George has laboured over riposte after riposte to McFee's premise, after an Inspector Bones has arrived on the scene investigating the murder of an acrobatic professor, after we have returned from intermission and are well into the second act, Stoppard finally chooses to disclose that the jumper shot out of the pyramid in the opening scene was – Duncan McFee. But not until the last moments of the second act do we learn that McFee had decided to defect from the ranks of the jumpers; that he had come to recognise the possibility of altruism, and – hence – the existence of good and evil; that he saw amorality as 'giving philosophical respectability to a new pragmatism in public life' which he found 'disturbing' (p. 70); and, in a crowning touch, that he was leaving the university, breaking off an affair with George's secretary, and entering a monastery!

I think we can now see why that image of the pyramid, which Stoppard terms the 'initial impetus for the play', proves so seminal. The moral relativism which McFee represents is the cornerstone for the positions of all the other jumpers. Their leaping to positions (philosophical or gymnastic) that can be held for the required length of time (about a minute for a gymnastic pyramid – maybe twenty minutes for a scholarly paper) is a form of academic gamesmanship founded on the moral relativism which McFee represents. There is a certain amount of fun in calling the philosophers jumpers and saying they will leap to any position. But the satire becomes keener when Stoppard reveals that any position the jumpers leap to will come crashing down as soon as one removes the premise that moral absolutes do not exist. If McFee defects, if the central premise that all value-judgements are relative is removed, the entire intellectual house of cards of the faddish philosophers comes tumbling down. It does not explode. Rather, it disintegrates because of lack of internal consistency; it collapses because of its own hollowness, the moral vacuousness which it has relied on instead of a core of values. The pyramid of gymnasts, Stoppard's stage directions tell us, 'has been defying gravity for these few seconds. Now it slowly collapses into the dark, imploding on the missing part, and rolling and separating, out of sight, leaving only the white spot' (p. 12).

If, then, we are to understand the play at all, we must first recognise that *Jumpers* affirms that moral absolutes do exist and, further, that the position of the jumpers who would deny such absolutes is – both literally and figuratively – undercut. To be sure, Stoppard does enjoy what he calls 'intellectual leap-frog': 'You know, an argument, a refutation, then a rebuttal of the refutation, then a counter-rebuttal, so that there is never any point in this intellectual leap-frog at which I feel *that* is the speech to stop it on, *that* is the last word' ('Ambushes', p. 7). But Stoppard can also make pronouncements with adamantine conviction. When pressed to explain why his plays do not address themselves to political issues, he insists with some verve that all political questions hinge on more basic questions of morality. What is needed, he argues, 'is not to compare one ruthless regime against another – it is to set each one up against a moral standard, a consistent idea of what constitutes good and bad in the way human beings treat each other regardless of class, colour or ideology, and at least my poor professor in *Jumpers* got *that* right' ('Ambushes', p. 12). Well, if George got that right, Archie – who holds a materialistic view of life – must surely have gotten everything wrong. Indeed, a bit later in the interview Stoppard declares adamantly and unequivocally: 'Few statements remain unrebutted. But I'm not going to rebut the things I have been saying just now. One thing I feel sure about is that a materialistic view of history is an insult to the human race' ('Ambushes', p. 13).

More recently Stoppard has issued a ringing denunciation of 'the attacks of Marxist relativists' on 'objective truth'. Stoppard defends 'the idea of objectivity and truth in science, in nature and in logic' from charges that 'all facts are theory-laden',[12] charges which recall Archie's words at the end of the second act: 'The truth to us philosophers . . . is always an interim judgement' (p. 72). Such attempts to deny the existence of objective truth, Stoppard continues,

are now the quite familiar teachings of well-educated men and women holding responsible positions in respectable universities, and the thing to say about such teaching is not that it is 'radical' but that it is not true. What it is, is false. To claim the contrary is not 'interesting'. It is silly. Daft. Not very bright. Moreover, it is wicked.'[13]

Although Stoppard is attacking epistemological relativism, that last word serves as a stinging refutation of ethical relativism as well. More specifically Stoppard is attacking those 'Radical Liberal' political philosophers who have denied the spiritual nature of mankind and who would see humanity wholly in materialistic terms.

Stoppard then, is sure that Archie is wrong, that his 'materialistic argument' – Archie's own words (p. 60) – is invalid. Archie is the great high priest of the nihilistic jumpers, the archbishop of the Rad-Lib revolutionaries, the ever-guileful, ever-alluring archfiend. Of course Archie seems to be in control. The star of the Rad-Libs is in the ascendant. Even McFee at the point of his conversion acknowledges, 'I have seen the future, Henry, . . . and it's yellow' (p. 71). That is, the future belongs to the extending influence of the yellow-clad jumpers who deny all moral absolutes. To see Archie as a spokesman for Stoppard's own beliefs is to misread the play utterly.[14]

More forceful is Crump's challenging thesis that the playwright may be sympathetic to George's position but that the play is not: 'Whatever may be Stoppard's personal views about God, *Jumpers* does not endorse George's position at the expense of those of Bones and Archie'. Crump supposes that George's bumbling detective work points to the weakness of his intuitive philosophy. She sees in George's failure to discover the identity of McFee's murderer a metaphoric inability to obtain 'knowledge of life's ultimate mysteries'.[15] Crump's assumption that the play leaves all philosophic options equally open simply ignores the crucial force of McFee's recantation of logical positivism, revealed in the final scene in a speech Michael Billington rightly terms 'the keynote of the play'.[16] Throughout the evening George has been preparing to debate the guardian and figurehead of philosophical orthodoxy among the logical positivists. Then at the penultimate moment we learn that even McFee had been filled with moral revulsion by the cold-blooded murder on the moon, had recognised the existence of absolute standards of morality, overthrown his part in a system which gave philosophical respectability to murder, and in converting from logical positivism had sought not just the moral but the theological sanctuary of a monastery. Whatever may be Stoppard's personal views of God, the playwright of *Jumpers* describes that work as 'a theist play'.[17] Failing even to mention McFee's pivotal recantation which brings down the house of cards of the logical positivists, Crump's assertion that *Jumpers* does not endorse George's philosophic position flies in the face both of authorial pronouncement and the play's own internal evidence.

Further, her argument that the play precludes any endorsement of George at the expense of Archie will not, upon examination, hold up even within the arena of the murder mystery. To be sure, we may not know who killed McFee. But we *do* know that he did not crawl into a plastic bag in the park and commit suicide, as Archie claims. We may not know the whole truth, but we do know that Archie is a liar. It is instructive in this context to consider Stoppard's explanation of the esteem accorded such a 'highly provocative, fascinating, intelligent, brilliant, wrongheaded oaf' as B.F. Skinner: 'if people write well and epigrammatically and clearly, their ideas gain in authority'. Explicitly terming Archie 'the villain, a pragmatist', Stoppard implicitly refers both to him and to the other jumpers (the 'usual Behaviourists') when he says that 'as much as anything this is an anti-Skinner play'.[18] If one wishes to draw a parallel between the murder mystery and the 'mystery in the clockwork' (p. 63) of the universe, Archie's explanation of phenomena must be dismissed as fraudulent.

And even if we do not know who murdered McFee, we *do* know who orders the murder of Clegthorpe in the Coda. On a signal from Archie, the jumpers move menacingly against Clegthorpe and manoeuvre him into a gymnastic pyramid where, like McFee, he is shot (p. 76). Clegthorpe's only offence is that of deserting the party line, of sensing that there may, after all, be value in having values. Furthermore, Archie stoutly defends Scott's cold-blooded murder of Astronaut Oates as 'natural'.[19]

After we acknowledge a level of certainty in the play – the certainty that the nihilistic, pragmatic materialism of Archie and the jumpers is invalid – it remains to be shown just what George, Stoppard's 'poor professor', got right and what he got wrong. There is a central debate, a sort of 'infinite leap-frog', in *Jumpers*; but the issue is not to be found between George on the one hand and the jumpers on the other. That is, what is at issue in the play should not be confused with what is at issue in the philosophy department's annual symposium on 'Man – good, bad or indifferent?' Rather, the point at stake shifts from the symposium's level of debate over whether moral absolutes exist, to the question of whether the moral absolutes – which do in fact exist – spring from a divine source or human experience: whether God is the progenitor of goodness or goodness is a pre-existent absolute which precedes even God. This central tension of the work is also given intensely theatrical realisation. The entire stage is split between George in his study struggling to 'invent God' and Dotty in her bedroom on the verge of a nervous breakdown. In the National Theatre production the entire set was on a revolve which could quickly spin George's study out of view and bring Dotty's bedroom on stage. In any event, Stoppard specifies it as 'an essential requirement of the play that the bedroom can be blacked out *completely* while the action continues elsewhere'

(p. 7). That is, we can be in either one realm or the other – either George's study or Dotty's bedroom, either the world of moral philosophy or musical comedy. Back and forth we go between the theoretic implications of moral absolutes, on the one hand, and the experience of right and wrong on the other. The central tension in the work, then, is between the perspectives represented by George and Dotty.

In his study, George's bumbling attempts to compose a lecture appear, on first sight, ridiculous. Having just seen the antics of the party in the opening scene, the audience initially pegs George as just one more crazy along with the girl swinging from the chandelier, the ex-musical comedy star who cannot remember the words of moon songs, and the jumpers who laboriously perform gymnastic feats with mediocre skill. George shuffles the pages of his paper, strikes a suitable stance to begin a lecture, and announces: 'Secondly!' (p. 15). Such buffoonery prepares the way for more giggles when George retrieves the missing page and sonorously intones, 'To begin at the beginning: Is God?' (p. 15). Surely, the audience tells itself, such a question is itself absurd in a play with a trapeze striptease, bounding gymnasts, and show biz gunshots. Ah! What rare mirth! This Stoppard fellow is *très amusant!*

The snickers do not last. There is a note of rueful recognition in the laughter when George's philosophising on 'the overwhelming question' of God's existence is interrupted from off stage by Dotty's plaintive, lonely cry: '*Is anybody there?*' (p. 17). Here, as elsewhere, we see that the overwhelming question really is the same on both sides of this split stage. Whereas the jumpers show a dazzling intellectual agility, George plods. There is a slow unfolding of George's argument from his demonstration of the 'irreducible fact of goodness' to his theistic conclusions. But what we begin to recognise as George fumblingly attempts to use a whole armful of audio-visual aids – a rabbit named Thumper and a tortoise named Pat, a target with a bow and arrows, tape recordings of an elephant's trumpet and a bugle falling down steps – is that George is right.

Even when, at the end of the second act, George is reduced to tears by his realisation that he has accidentally killed Thumper with a stray arrow and inadvertently stepped on Pat, we see the ironic demonstration of George's own tenets. George had intended to demonstrate how reality belies such philosophic sophistries as those the jumpers promulgate. Despite Zeno's paradox, 'which showed in every way but experience that an arrow could never reach its target' (p. 21), George's arrow does reach Thumper. When his attempted philosophical illustration with bow and arrow actually kills his beloved rabbit, George's argument from experience is given all too pointed proof.

Despite the sophistries of the relativists, George argues, experience confronts us again and again with actions that are good and bad – 'not more useful, or more convenient, or more popular, but simply pointlessly *better*' (p. 45). As a moral absolutist, George would be happy to stop with a demonstration of the 'irreducible fact of goodness' (p. 46). The first act concludes on precisely that note. Stoppard seems to prefer just such a stopping point for his own beliefs. In a 1977 pronouncement he identified himself as predisposed toward 'Western liberal democracy favouring an intellectual elite and a progressive middle class and based on a moral order derived from Christian absolutes'.[20]

There is an air of the penultimate to that phrase 'derived from'. But if George follows his convictions to ultimate conclusions he arrives, rather embarrassingly, at God. By midway in the second act, George's philosophical investigations have acquired new resonances, and the audience is properly hushed as he confesses his knowledge not just of the existence of moral absolutes but of a realm of the spirit which transcends both a Darwinian view of man as animal and a Marxist view of man as material:

> And yet I tell you that, now and again, not necessarily in the contemplation of rainbows or newborn babes, nor in extremities of pain or joy, but more probably ambushed by some quite trivial moment – say the exchange of signals between two long-distance lorry-drivers in the black sleet of a god-awful night on the old A1 – then, in that dip-flash, dip-flash of headlights in the rain that seems to affirm some common ground that is not animal and not long-distance lorry-driving – then I tell you I *know* – I sound like a joke vicar, new paragraph. (p. 62)

Starting with the intuitive affirmation that human life is inherently moral, that human beings share 'some common ground that is not animal', George is impelled toward the irresistible conclusion that temporal moral values must imply the existence of a transcendent standard of moral perfection, that God – in a word – 'is'. Taking a fresh start at conveying what he 'knows', George refers to the mathematical concept of 'a limiting curve, that is the curve defined as the limit of a polygon with an infinite number of sides' (p. 62). So, for example, if George takes an old threepenny-bit or a 50-pence piece and infinitely doubles the number of sides, he finds that a circle can be logically implied by the existence of polygons. With this new metaphor in mind George pushes beyond a perception of human spiritual communion to a sense of spiritual perfection:

> And now and again, not necessarily in the contemplation of polygons or newborn babes, nor in extremities of pain or joy, but more probably in some quite trivial moment, it seems to me that life itself is the mundane figure which argues perfection at its limiting curve. And if I doubt it, the ability to doubt, to question, to *think*, seems to be the curve itself. *Cogito ergo deus est.* (pp. 62–3)

Such an understanding of the limiting curve is, as John A. Bailey correctly points out, 'George's finest statement'.[21] George's argument neither dismisses humanity as valueless nor offers a humanistic view that mankind is the measure of all values. Rather, George sees human imperfection. In effect he acknowledges that we live in a fallen world. But he still sees in that which is humanly possible a flawed figure which bodies forth the reflection of God. In the flashes of human communion with one's fellow man he senses an image of spiritual communion with God. And yet the evidence for this truth which he apprehends spiritually is so tenuous as to resist logical proof.

I think we hear the rueful note of Stoppard here.[22] Believing in moral absolutes, he is relentlessly impelled toward a belief in God which he finds embarrassing and immediately dissembles. 'When I push *my* convictions to absurdity', confesses the moral absolutist George,

> *I* arrive at God – which is at least as embarrassing nowadays. All I know is that I think that I know that I know that nothing can be created out of nothing, that my moral conscience is different from the rules of my tribe, and that there is more in

me than meets the microscope – and because of *that* I'm saddled
with this incredible, indescribable and definitely shifty *God*, the
trump card of atheism. (p. 58)

Discussing his own religious views and their pertinence for
Jumpers, Stoppard echoes both George's affirmation and discomfiture in his explanation:

> I wanted a device enabling me to set out arguments about
> whether social morality is simply a conditioned response to
> history and environment or whether moral sanctions obey an
> absolute intuitive God-given law. I've always felt that whether
> or not 'God-given' means anything, there has to be an ultimate
> external reference for our actions. Our view of good behaviour
> *must* not be relativist. The difference between moral rules and
> the rules of tennis is that the rules of tennis can be changed.
> I think it's a dangerous idea that what constitutes 'good
> behaviour' depends on social conventions – dangerous and
> unacceptable. That led me to the conclusion, not reached
> all that willingly, that if our behaviour is open to absolute
> judgement, there must be an absolute judge.[23]

Belief in the existence of an absolute judge provided, Stoppard
explains, the thematic impetus to *Jumpers*:

> I felt that nobody was saying this and it tended to be assumed
> that nobody held such a view. So I wanted to write a theist play,
> to combat the arrogant view that anyone who believes in God
> is some kind of cripple, using God as a crutch. I wanted to
> suggest that atheists may be the cripples, lacking the strength
> to live with the idea of God.[24]

Believing in the ineluctably moral nature of human experience,
Stoppard – as well as George – is discomfited to find himself
impelled toward belief in the existence of a transcendent divine
progenitor of absolute moral values. Such a belief in God is
'embarrassing nowadays'. But to draw back from such intuitive
affirmations of the transcendent is to play it safe, to stick to the
verifiable, to avoid putting oneself 'at risk'. 'McFee never made
that mistake', George says of his empiricist colleague, 'never put
himself at risk by finding mystery in the clockwork' (p. 63).

Corballis uses George's rueful remark as a springboard to an interpretation of the entire Stoppard canon.[25] Unfortunately, the way Corballis skews the terms 'mystery' and 'clockwork' makes Stoppard appear to reject some of the very values he is most concerned to affirm. When Corballis associates 'clockwork' with any abstract or artificial view of the world[26] he starts down a slippery slope which leads ultimately to his conclusion that nothing is affirmed in Stoppard plays save instinct. In fact, when George says that McFee never found mystery in the clockwork, he is alluding to McFee's logical positivism which denied the existence of any moral, spiritual or metaphysical dimension to the cosmos or to humankind. The 'clockwork' in which McFee fails to find mystery is the material universe, the cosmos conceived of as a giant machine devoid of any transcendent Creator or transcendent progenitor of moral values – a world in which God are not. Clockwork for Stoppard is repeatedly associated with the mechanistic, the materialistic, the perception of the cosmos as a machine, the perception of the human as mere organism. And 'mystery' for Stoppard suggests a world beyond the material, a sense of the moral and metaphysical depth of human experience, ultimately the unfathomable significance of a universe presided over by a transcendent deity.

As a theist play, *Jumpers* gives dramatic realisation to metaphysical assumptions which Stoppard was voicing – however wryly – when the play first came out. Two months after *Jumpers* opened, Stoppard assured Mel Gussow that the existence of Shakespeare's sonnets impelled him toward theistic affirmations: 'Now a straight line of evolution from amino acid in volcanic rock all the way through to Shakespeare's sonnets – that strikes me as possible, but a very long shot. Why back such an outsider? However preposterous the idea of God is, it seems to have an edge in plausibility.'[27] Shakespeare creates. And in the complex polygon of human art Stoppard sees mankind's approach to the ineffable, an approach that argues perfection at its limiting curve. In Shakespeare's sonnets, Joyce's fiction, even his own plays, Stoppard sees a flawed figure of immortality which bodies forth the very existence of God. Shakespeare thinks: therefore God is. '*Cogito ergo deus est.*' Speaking specifically of *Jumpers*, Stoppard says, 'I identify emotionally with the more sympathetic character in the play who believes that one's mode of behavior has to be judged by absolute moral standards'. When Stoppard turns the tables a moment later, he tacitly accepts George's position as his own: 'intellectually I can shoot *my* argument full of holes'.[28] Like both George Moores, Stoppard himself ultimately bases his judgement on intuition. And like both philosophers, Stoppard is discomfited to find that his intuition leads him to a conclusion that is beyond the logician's proof or disproof.

Sensing the authority of the author's voice in George's words, we must affirm the celebration of spirit within the play, affirm the celebration of a moral instinct and a moral order, affirm the celebration of a metaphysical realm which just comes within the furthest reaches of George's ken. But let us have a little more than ken, or risk being less than kind to Dotty, that nymph in whose orisons be all George's sins remembered. Indeed, in the flow of ideas back and forth between the moral absolutists and the ethical and epistemological relativists, it seems as easy for us, as for George, to ignore Dotty. With such weighty matters to be resolved, it is possible to dismiss the ex-musical comedy star as a daft, amusingly incongruous wife for a professor of moral philosophy. But it is perhaps with her that we find Stoppard's most basic sympathies.

Given Stoppard's immersion in the world of *Hamlet*, the suggestion that the aptly named Dotty recalls the mad Ophelia is not wholly gratuitous. While her Prufrockian husband – 'and "How his hair is growing thin"' (p. 25) – struggles to roll the universe into a ball and push it toward 'the overwhelming question' (p. 17), Dotty is left alone, shut out by her philosophic lover, and has to deal with the reality of a corpse though her husband remains supremely indifferent while she must lug the guts into the neighbour room. Dotty is the first character to appear on stage and has the last words in the play. In her initial appearance we see how close she is to breaking up mentally as she reels off disjointed lyrics from moon songs. But we should not see her plight as simply illustrating – in a general way – the sadness and emptiness of much of modern society. If the jumpers are reprehensible and George's well-meaning conclusion ultimately embarrassing, Dotty is coming to a visceral understanding of the moral issues which the jumpers deny and which George, while affirming, does not experience. It is important, then, to consider why she is so thoroughly shattered.

Dotty is not just a musical comedy performer; she has

placed her belief in a musical comedy view of things. She
has accepted its saccharine romanticism with a mindless optimism. Her belief centres, symbolically, on 'that old-fashioned,
silvery harvest moon, occasionally blue, jumped over by cows
and coupleted by Junes, invariably shining on the one I love;
well-known in Carolina, much loved in Allegheny, familiar in
Vermont' (p. 32). People are not good or bad; they are eternally
hopeful, full of limitless possibilities, occasionally naughty but
usually kind, and – through it all – perky. And if the impossibly
lovely people will only hope upon that Juney old moon, they will
be united with each other in the last reprise, and the antiquated
anachronisms of romantic musicals will be reaffirmed.[29]

Her present crisis is that of a believer who has been forced
to realise – or, more accurately, to feel with visceral intensity –
the ultimate shallowness of all she had put her faith in. On the
immediate level, Dotty has just witnessed – or, perhaps, participated in – a murder. She is wearing, Stoppard tells us with a sense
of the incongruous, a 'blood-stained party frock' (p. 13). But more
than Dotty's frock has been stained. Her musical comedy ideal
has been marred by the landing of the first two Englishmen on
the moon. While Dotty watches television, Stoppard projects on
a screen the size of the stage a huge televised image of the moon
as a 'pitted circle' (p. 13). Viewed from a distance, the moon had
been an image of luminous perfection, 'the fair paradise of nature's
light' (p. 32); seen in relentless close-up, it is shown to be pocked
by craters, a land of ugliness and desolation. Technological man
has defiled Dotty's romantic ideal, and her metaphysical world is
left in fragments: 'When they first landed, it was as though I'd seen
a unicorn on the television news . . . Very interesting, of course.
But it certainly spoils unicorns' (p. 29).

The contrast which Stoppard establishes here is recapitulated
in a number of ways throughout the play. Just so, the jumpers
viewed from a distance seem youthful and athletic, but upon close
examination prove to be paunchy, dogged, and inexpert. Just so,
Dotty herself upon first view appears 'fabulous, stunning' (p. 10),
but at the end of the play her skin becomes the pitted subject
matter for a technological 'dermatograph'. The pits and craters
of her skin fill the screen 'in very big close-up' (1972 text, p. 82)
in an exact analogue to our earlier views of the moon. Both kinds
of 'heavenly bodies' are shown to be flawed.

More profoundly, Stoppard uses the setting of the moon for

a look in very big close-up at mankind. By postulating damage to the space capsule's rockets, he creates a situation in which there is only enough thrust to return one man to earth. Given the certain death of at least one of the two, Captain Scott resolves the situation by simply knocking Astronaut Oates to the ground and announcing, 'I am going up now. I may be gone for some time' (p. 14). Astronaut Oates is last seen by millions of viewers as 'a tiny receding figure waving forlornly from the featureless wastes of the lunar landscape' (p. 14). Stoppard thus creates a situation in which murder is seen in isolation. Sociological, economic, psychoanalytic, and cultural contexts are removed, and we see the cold-blooded decision of one man to kill a fellow human being in order to save his own neck.

The names of Stoppard's imaginary astronauts contrast the astronaut's decision with that of the historic Captain Oates, who sacrificed his life during an Antarctic expedition in order to give his companions a chance of survival. But the action itself may well recall a much older episode in human history. Dotty has seen a re-enactment of the deed which, in the words of Hamlet's uncle, 'hath the primal eldest curse'. Stoppard isolates his Cain and Abel in a new unpeopled world and forces us to witness, in this modern context, the first murder in the world.

It is this glaring close-up not of the moon or of human flesh but of mankind which is ultimately so shattering for Dotty. The realisation she is coming to should not be confused with an existentialist despair that life is meaningless. Indeed, her conclusion is almost diametrically opposed to the existentialist position. Dotty's optimistic platitudes of musical comedy, her belief in a romantic ideal, have been shattered by the fact of human evil. She is discovering that her mindless optimism is inadequate to account for a world in which human evil is real and the concepts of right and wrong are terrifyingly meaningful. She thinks now of the 'Poor moon man, falling home like Lucifer' (p. 29).

Stoppard thus painstakingly constructs an archetypal scene of human evil which must be judged not antisocial or inconvenient or undesirable but simply, irredeemably, wrong. Gabrielle Robinson is certainly incorrect when she says that 'George Moore in *Jumpers* tries to cling to his belief that absolute values do exist. . . . But the parody of Scott on the moon . . . denies this'.[30] That murder exists and that we can know it for murder does not refute but rather reveals the existence of moral absolutes. Indeed, Stoppard's technique here recalls George's own tactic of showing that the rabbit will overtake the tortoise, the arrow will reach the target even though a coherent line of philosophical speculation would seem to prove the contrary. Just so, the direct experience of the reality of evil exposes as inadequate any attempt to account for human actions in morally neutral categories. It is as a direct consequence of the events on the moon that McFee refutes the moral relativism he has been espousing, acknowledging instead that altruism – and moral absolutes – do exist. Comparing the murder of Astronaut Oates with the sacrificial action of his namesake, McFee realises, 'If altruism is a possibility . . . my argument is up a gum-tree' (p. 71). Brassell rightly refers to McFee's recantation as 'the linchpin of Stoppard's "play of ideas"'.[31] In the cold light of reality, the academic philosopher's theorising proves to have no more substance than the pipedreams of musical comedy. If the reality of evil destroys Dotty's mindless optimism, it simultaneously destroys the cheerful nihilism of the intellectually fashionable philosophers who argue that all moral values are relative.

Both Dotty and McFee have been wrong in everything they have believed. However, it is a measure of their sensitivity and character that they are willing to acknowledge their error. Stoppard presents them sympathetically as he shows the painful honesty with which they strip away their former illusions. Their growing awareness of the reality of human evil constitutes an illumination which is a needful, if painful, apprehending of truth. Archie, on the other hand, is not only wrong but persists in error. By refusing to recognise what Dotty and McFee do come to realise, by attempting to pass off McFee's murder as suicide, by attempting to justify Scott's murder of Oates (p. 74), Archie emerges as the most thoroughly discredited figure in the play.

If Archie is discredited, and Dotty intuitively but inarticulately apprehends the fact that good and evil exist, it remains for us to deal with the question raised by Stoppard's assertion that 'at least my poor professor in *Jumpers* got *that* right'. Just how much does Stoppard's '*that*' include, how much does George get right? At the risk of sounding facile, my answer is that in terms of what he believes George gets everything right. I emphasise the word *believes* because *Jumpers* here presents us with a central challenge 'derived from Christian absolutes' – not just to have knowledge of love but to have knowledge incarnated in love, not just to know that good exists but to enflesh goodness.

George knows. He knows that some acts are, objectively, good, and that others are just as objectively bad. He knows that human actions must be judged in terms of moral absolutes, not merely condoned in terms of political expediency. He knows that there is more to life than dust, more than just behaviour. He knows that despite having a spiritual nature, mankind is flawed, fallen, imperfect. He knows that God exists. He knows that God is the divine source of good and evil. He knows that God is the divine perfection which can be glimpsed dimly in the moral imperfection of man created in His image. George knows much. It seems to me that Stoppard concurs – with varying degrees of eagerness and embarrassment – with everything George believes. Where George is adamant that the moral categories of good and evil exist as philosophic absolutes, Stoppard is equally adamant. Where George is reluctant to admit that such a premise forces him to the embarrassing conclusion that a transcendent God exists, Stoppard shares his embarrassment. Not just in his judgements of political regimes but in all his beliefs one could say – at least the poor professor got that right. Yes, George knows much. But he is not transformed by his knowledge.

George knows but he needs to act on his knowledge. While George in his study is proving that man is good or bad but not indifferent, he remains inhumanely indifferent to the pain of his wife in the next room. With his mind on matters of universal philosophic import, George never responds to another human being.[32] The ideal 'other' for George is his secretary, who sits mutely receiving the words of his lecture, never in the course of the entire play uttering a single word.

Stoppard, who acknowledges that 'a lot of the time I've ended up trying to work out the ultimate implications of what I have written' ('Ambushes', p. 13), is wrestling here with a dilemma which finds its resolution in a central mystery of Christianity – the word made flesh. But on the Stoppard stage the categories remain discrete. In Dotty's bedroom of longings, stage right, there are only the lusts and the pain of the flesh, sensation but never knowledge. In George's study of abstract contemplation, stage left, there is absolute doctrinal purity but absolute lack of enfleshment of those doctrines. We see the flesh. We hear the words. The flesh and the words. But never the word made flesh. Stoppard, then, presents us with characters in search of Incarnation. More than that, Stoppard presents us with a playwright in search of Incarnation. But he never sees such a possibility. He sees only the correctness of the belief and the need for something more than correct belief.

In the concluding speech of the second act, Archie tells us: 'We will never even know for certain who did shoot McFee. Unlike mystery novels, life does not guarantee a denouement; and if it came, how would one know whether to believe it?' (p. 72). Although Archie is simply trying to assert the relativity of all things once again, Stoppard has actually done much more than just leave a mystery unsolved. By leaving the finger of guilt pointing ambiguously, Stoppard indicates the murderous capacity within us all. We see in Dotty's mental imbalance, in Archie's professional jealousy, even in the silent Secretary who had been jilted by McFee after three years of secret betrothal, the same potential for murder that we have seen in the astronaut Scott. Archie's words, above, are almost the conclusion to the second act. But after those words have been uttered, we still need to pay astute attention to Stoppard's use of visual theatre.

As the Secretary puts on her coat to leave, we suddenly discover a 'bright splash of blood on its back' (p. 72). Seeking the source of the blood, George discovers that his own misfired arrow had killed Thumper; and then before our eyes George accidentally steps, fatally, on Pat. George too is stained. Even his sobs, which demonstrate his inability to respond to any crisis except the death of his pet animals, pronounce judgement on the limits of his humanity. In George's refusal to get involved, his rigid adherence to philosophic truths to the exclusion of overt action, there is surely culpability. Despite the absolute correctness of his words, we see in him the same murderous capacity we saw in the others. This inefficacy of correct belief I take to be the significance of the Coda which follows the second act without interruption.

The Coda serves as a reprise, a recapitulation, of the themes of the play proper. We see, in bizarre dream form, the departmental symposium, the testimony of Captain Scott,[33] the murder of the archbishop; but all is made explicable by what has gone before. The Coda carries out McFee's prediction: 'I have seen the future . . . and it's yellow' (p. 71). We have earlier seen the jumpers bouncing about in the opening scene or doing a syncopated shuffle while removing McFee's body. But here we see them in control. The symposium itself shows the breakdown of academic discourse into garbled meaninglessness. Billington rightly recognises that *Jumpers* demonstrates 'that a world that denies the metaphysical absolutes of good and evil, that sunders any tolerance of the irrational, that subverts moral sanctions . . . will fall into chaos'.[34] With the appearance of Scott we move from the academic groves which have served as the springboard for the jumpers in the past to see the impact of their pragmatic moral relativism on the political process. McFee's prediction that the murderous astronaut 'was only twenty years ahead of his time' (p. 71) is borne out. We are in the future and see gratuitous murder shrugged off as a 'natural response to a pure situation' (p. 74; cf. 1972 text, p. 84). Finally, with the murder of the archbishop we move simultaneously into the past and future to see the impact of political pragmatism on ecclesiastical structures.

The murder of the archbishop should not be dismissed merely as 'yet another murder' included for 'no dramatic reason'.[35] Its similarity to the murder of McFee enlarges our understanding of the initial crime. Clegthorpe, like McFee, is a jumper who has defected from the nihilistic orthodoxy of the jumpers far enough to recognise the existence of moral absolutes. Indeed, having been moved to compassion by the needs of his new spiritual flock, Clegthorpe now pleads, 'Surely belief in man could find room for man's beliefs' (p. 76). As a result of his transformation, Clegthorpe now objects to the Rad-Lib policies and, in fact, would administer the sacrament to his believers, who are shouting, 'Give us the blood of the lamb. Give us the bread of the body of Christ' (p. 76). Thus Clegthorpe, like McFee, has determined to abandon the academic gymnasium with its stained-glass window and instead enter the ecclesiastical orthodoxy of the Church. But here the threat to the newly converted believer is clearly executed by the jumpers themselves. Archie pronounces the fatal words '*Will no one rid me of this turbulent priest!*' (1973 text, p. 85)[36], and his henchmen, the jumpers, immediately move menacingly against Clegthorpe. The echo of Henry II's words, which led to the martyrdom of Thomas à Becket, is not gratuitous. With sudden jolting clarity we see that the appointment of a socialist spokesman for Agriculture as Archbishop of Canterbury serves as a modern analogue for the earlier political gift of that office to 'Old Tom, gay Tom, Becket of London'. Clegthorpe – with his yellow jumpsuit beneath his coronation robes – reminds us that in both his case and Becket's we see the inexplicable transformation of the secular political operative into the religious believer. Certainly Stoppard's Coda adds to our understanding of the play by putting McFee's transformation into a much broader context.

Finally, the death of Clegthorpe exposes the nature of George's error with a compression not to be found in the rest of the play. Clegthorpe's final words appeal to George both on the philosophic level of moral absolutes and on the personal level: 'Professor – it's not right. George – help' (1973 text, p. 85). Stoppard is choosing his words here with extraordinary succinctness. If the professor does believe in absolute values, he ought to respond to a situation that is not right; but in any event George ought to respond on the human level to a plea for help. However, in a reprise of his failure to respond to Dotty, George does absolutely nothing. 'Well, this seems to be a political quarrel', George stammers. 'Surely only a proper respect for absolute values . . . universal truths – *philosophy*— ' (1973 text, p. 85).[37] While George is stammering his unenacted truths, a gunshot rings out: Clegthorpe is knocked out of the pyramid, and – as in the opening scene – the pyramid disintegrates. We see, with greater clarity than ever before, just how empty George's words ring when they are not made manifest in action.

In his incisive review 'Count Zero Splits the Infinite', Clive James argues that Stoppard's use of multiple perspectives – like Einstein's abandonment of fixed viewpoints – springs 'from the impulse to clarify'. Such a 'plurality of contexts' is not intended to negate, to undercut, or to confuse but is employed 'in order to be precise over a greater range of events'; ambiguities 'are just places where contexts join'.[38] In *Jumpers* Stoppard strives for precision both in the words of George's moral philosophy and in Dotty's experience within the world of the flesh. George's words – as words – ring true. Within the realm of philosophy, *Jumpers* affirms the existence of transcendent moral values and leads us – however reluctantly – to sense the approach of these moral absolutes down awesome corridors from an infinite divine source. Simultaneously, as the great revolve of the National Theatre stage relentlessly wheels Dotty's bedroom into view, *Jumpers* affirms the reality of her plight and the pain of experience within the world of the flesh. But within this plurality of contexts we do not find the still point of the turning wheel, we do not find the point at which the infinite eternal moral truth becomes enfleshed in immediate tangible moral action. The ambiguities of *Jumpers*, the places where the contexts join, are the interstices between the flesh and the word, between the perspectives of George and Dotty, between the existence of divinely established moral absolutes and the irrelevance of such absolutes if not bodied forth in human compassion.

4

Mortal Flesh
in a Moral Matrix of Words:
The Temporal and the Timeless
in *Travesties*

Like *Jumpers*, *Travesties* bursts onto the stage with a dizzying array of fragments which seems unreal, chaotic, devoid of coherence and impervious to sense. Both plays begin, Stoppard says, with a 'pig's breakfast'[1] of seemingly random juxtapositions. But if *Jumpers* opens with a visual montage, *Travesties* opens with a verbal mélange. *Travesties* begins with three pairs of interlocutors exchanging such esoteric declamations as 'Eel ate enormous appletzara', 'Hoopsa, boyaboy, hoopsa!' and 'Bronski prishol'.[2] Not only do the three verbal exchanges have nothing to do with each other, each of the pronouncements is baffling in its own right. In *Jumpers* we may not know what paunchy gymnasts, a trapeze striptease, a bumbling professor and a stumbling waiter have in common – but there is nothing particularly arcane about each one individually. Whereas *Jumpers* presents us with the pieces of a visual puzzle which do not interlock to form any coherent picture, the verbal snippets of *Travesties* not only fail to cohere with each other but each piece of the puzzle seems to defy any attempt to reduce it to rational sense. The untranslated words and seemingly untranslatable syllables first sounded in *Travesties* confront the audience with what sounds like a towering Babel of confusion.

Yet however strange it may sound, the play echoes history. The genesis of *Travesties* was a glimpse of the highly unlikely conjunction, the utterly improbable though historically accurate fact, that in 1916 three of the century's revolutionaries – the Russian ideologue Lenin, the Rumanian artist Tristan Tzara, and the Irish novelist James Joyce – were simultaneously resident in the Swiss city of Zurich. A friend's remark that 'within a stone's throw of each other and using the same cafe were the Dadaist Tristan

58

Tzara, and Lenin, and I think Freud, maybe. Look into it' sparked Stoppard's consideration of the dramatic possibilities. Stoppard first conceived of 'a two-act thing, with one act a Dadaist play on Communist ideology and the other an ideological functional drama about Dadaists'.[3] The play he was contemplating grew out of the essentially negative proposition 'that committed art is really a kind of bogus enterprise'.[4] But when Stoppard looked into his friend's suggestion and the third luminary turned out to be not Freud but James Joyce, he began to give his play a more positive lilt – or, perhaps, brogue. 'It's such a good idea', Stoppard exulted while still revising his script, 'you can never live up to it'.[5]

The situation, said Stoppard, raised 'a question worth asking, can the artist and the revolutionary be the same person or [are] their activities mutually exclusive? How would you justify *Ulysses* to Lenin or Lenin to Joyce?'[6] While untangling that conundrum, however, Stoppard stumbled onto the fact that while in Zurich Joyce had directed a production of Oscar Wilde's *The Importance of Being Earnest*, that a minor British consular official named Henry Carr had appeared in *Earnest* and had attempted to recover the cost of trousers worn in the play by suing Joyce, who was roused to revenge first by countersuing Carr and then by creating a foul-mouthed bully of a British Army private named Henry Carr as a cameo character within the pages of *Ulysses*. The glimpses of the historical Henry Carr are of a litigious bureaucrat with a bourgeois taste for sartorial effect and just enough artistic presumption to fancy himself an actor in amateur theatricals. But Stoppard's cornucopia of serendipity was running over. Stoppard decided to set his play as much within the script of *The Importance of Being Earnest* as *Rosencrantz* had been set within *Hamlet*. And as the cornerstone for his vaultingly clever attempt to span three towering historical figures, Stoppard improbably chose this same Henry Carr, as slight a footnote in the illustrious career of James Joyce as Rosencrantz and Guildenstern were to the sublime progress of Hamlet.

With the addition to Stoppard's play of the *Earnest* framework, Wilde's roster of dramatis personae, the historical nonentity Henry Carr, the eminent James Joyce and the refracted reflections of Joyce as he may have been seen by Henry Carr, the number of perspectives on art and politics increased exponentially. Even within the heightened complexities of *Travesties*, however, Stoppard's original premise that committed art is a bogus enterprise is clearly sounded. On the question of whether art must be an ideological attack on class structure as Lenin propounds, or part of an equally polemical attack on cultural heritage as Tzara petulantly screams, there is no question but that Joyce's celebration of art which is not committed to a cause is also Stoppard's celebration and the play's celebration. Among the historical heavyweights in the play, Joyce wins the debate.

However, as we may surmise from *Jumpers*, winning a debate – whether artistic or ideological or philosophical – is not enough. One may have all the right ideas and, like George, be culpable. Conversely, like Dotty, a character may recite a string of second-hand opinions and still enlist our sympathy. Outside of a realm in which what matters is getting the right words in the right order there is, also, life. And any victory in a battle of words may prove pyrrhic if it somehow omits the actual experience of ordinary people who are not part of the cognoscenti or literati. Part of the literati Henry Carr, to put it circumspectly, is not. Stoppard consistently invests Carr with a bourgeois weakness for clothes, middle-class affirmations of patriotism, and middle-brow taste in art. Carr, in short, is ordinary, typical, average, and undistinguished. But to suppose that Carr is therefore discredited is to risk showing the same indifference to the ordinary and average and common as does George.

Carr may initially appear as insignificant – compared to Lenin, Joyce, and Tzara – as are Rosencrantz and Guildenstern against the backdrop of such mighty opposites as Hamlet and Claudius. However, in Stoppard's Elsinore, Rosencrantz and Guildenstern remain wholly in the dark, oblivious to the motivations and machinations of their betters. By contrast, Carr is granted some of the most piercing insights of any of the international visitors to Zurich. He emerges less as an anonymous nonentity than as a stalwart embodiment of English middle-class common sense. Being able to smile at fastidiousness in fashion (and Stoppard's own penchant for sartorial splendour is legendary) is part of the play's comic structure. That there's something to be said for such popular artists as Gilbert and Sullivan as well as for the vanguards of the literary avant is, perhaps, not merely comic. However, Carr's middle-class affirmations that freedom is worth fighting for, that patriotism is not to be derided, and that high-sounding cultural ideals can only be preserved through the defence of political freedom – these affirmations by no means receive comic dismissal within Stoppard's work. Lenin, Joyce and Tzara may score points off each other throughout the course of the evening. But the debate among such historical antagonists is not the topic which continues to be unresolved within the mind of the playwright.

Joyce may take the stance that an artist need not 'justify himself in political terms *at all*'. But what Stoppard asks himself, he says, is not whether Joyce's position is defensible artistically or feasible politically but whether it is sound morally. 'If Joyce were alive today', Stoppard continues, 'he would say, juntas may come and juntas may go but Homer goes on for ever. And when he was alive he *did* say that the history of Ireland, troubles and all, was justified because it produced *him* and *he* produced *Ulysses* . . . . So clearly one now has to posit a political prisoner taking comfort from the thought that at least he is in the country of Joyce, or of Homer.' What Stoppard then asks himself, he says, is 'whether Joyce, in moral terms, was myopic or had better vision than lesser men'.[7] On that question, Carr serves, within *Travesties*, as the spokesman and embodiment for all of the world's lesser men. But it is precisely at this juncture, on the issue of whether the vision of the artist or of the ordinary citizen is more moral, that Stoppard locates his own indecision: 'my answer to that question is liable to depend', he told his interviewers, 'on the moment at which you run out of tape' ('Ambushes', p. 16). Just as the unresolved tension in *Jumpers* is between the perspectives of George and Dotty, so in *Travesties* the crux of the play is found between the perspectives of the towering figure of James Joyce and the thoroughly ordinary Henry Carr.

Although Stoppard may be undecided on that issue, the commonest misinterpretations of *Travesties*, as of other plays in his canon, continue to spring from the relativist notion that if Stoppard is undecided on some matters it follows that he is equally undecided on all matters. Hersh Zeifman quite rightly sees metaphysical implications even in Stoppard's puns. But if Stoppard's art and even his puns demand our faith that something is more than it appears to be, what we are left with is not, as Zeifman would have it, mere 'metaphysical confusion'.[8] While some tensions remain unresolved in Stoppard's drama, it does not follow that his plays constitute 'an exuberant advertisement for philosophical and linguistic relativity', that they are 'chaotic' reflections of 'a relativistic and parodic universe' demonstrating 'his basic sense of disorder'.[9] Rather, Stoppard's drama exudes an

exuberant 'asseveration of faith in life' and of 'the metaphysical
reality which art celebrates' as Eric Salmon faithfully affirms.[10]
Stoppard's drama celebrates a realm beyond the material, a universe which however complex is not in the least random but
rather, as David Camroux claims, is pervaded by order. Camroux
may overstate his case in claiming that Stoppard's 'view of an
ordered world is mediaeval and catholic, while . . . the value he
places on the individual is Protestant, even humanist'.[11] But in
seeing a celebration of individual worth within the context of
a complex but ordered cosmos, Salmon and Camroux surely
come closer to comprehending Stoppard than a cacophonous
chorus of critics who claim that Stoppard 'likes chaos', sees
'nothing left but parody', writes 'theater of exhaustion' which
reflects 'the relativity of everything', that his plays are themselves
'pan-parodic' or 'chaotic' evidently put together more by Dadaist
chance than by conscious craftsmanship.[12] To see the disjunctions of *Travesties* as a chaotic mélange which pays homage to
Tzarra's willingness to cut up sonnets into – just – words, words,
words, is as wrongheaded as seeing the play as a forum for Lenin
who would reduce art to – just – the promulgation of politically
acceptable ideas.

Whereas Lenin's position self-destructs and Tzara proves a
mere cut-up, Stoppard has made clear on numerous occasions
that he infinitely prefers, he 'absolutely', 'categorically' agrees
with Joyce. 'Lenin', Stoppard says, 'keeps convicting himself out
of his own mouth. It's absurd . . . . It's sheer nonsense.' However,
the playwright adds elsewhere, 'Lenin had no use for the kind of
art represented by Dada, which is one of the few things Lenin
and I agree on': 'Writing a poem by taking words out of a hat
may be amusing fun, but let's not call the result poetry.' 'What it
isn't', Stoppard continues, 'is art'. 'I have no interest in anarchic
or unstructured art', Stoppard declares, 'I have no sympathy at all
with Tristan Tzara'. By contrast, 'Joyce is an artist I can respect'
and admire as 'the finest practitioner of a style of literature with
which I temperamentally agree'. 'It just happens that I'm on his
side', Stoppard asserts, prompting his interlocutor's question as
to what side that may be: 'The side of logic and rationality. And
craftsmanship.'[13]

Coppélia Kahn argues that whatever side Stoppard may be on,
Travesties itself does not take sides: 'Though Stoppard insistently
poses the question of the social role of art, he refuses to answer it.

He mocks Joyce's Homeric high priest of art and Tzara's barbaric yawper and Lenin's "cog in the Social Democratic mechanism" with equal gusto and wit.'[14] Similarly, Allan Rodway claims that 'no principle of decision is made available'[15] in *Travesties* for valuing Joyce more than Lenin. However, Stoppard does not merely say that he personally agrees with one side of a debate which is presented with disinterested objectivity within the play. 'I happen to be on his side', Stoppard reiterates, 'which is why I've given Joyce the last word'. 'Consciously or not', Stoppard continues, 'I loaded the play for him'.[16] As we should see, an affirmation of Joycean craftsmanship rather than Dadaist anti-art or Marxist-Leninist functional art is not merely dependent on authorial pronouncements outside the play but on internal evidence which permeates *Travesties*.

Thus, the first words of the play are plucked out of a hat by Tzara as an exercise in randomness, an attack on coherence and sense and conscious creation. However these same words actually make coherent sense – unbeknownst to Tzara and even, as Stoppard would have it, unbeknownst to the actor playing Tzara[17] – in French. Tzara extracts from his hat such fractured English nonsense as

> Ill raced alas whispers kill later nut east,
> noon avuncular ill day Clara! (p. 18)

which a Francophone may recognise as the phonetic equivalent of the sensible

> *Il reste à la Suisse parce qu'il est un artiste.*
> *'Nous n'avons que l'art,' il déclara.*

which upon being anglicised once more makes coherent sense as

> He lives in Switzerland because he is an artist.
> 'We have only art,' he declared.[18]

The words which Tzara pulls out of his hat clearly were not discovered by Stoppard through a similarly mindless 'creative' process. Rather, the elaborate bi-lingual punning which opens *Travesties* reflects a conscious craftsmanship, a verbal virtuosity, which is joyfully Joycean in its complexity. Similarly, Tzara subjects Shakespeare's eighteenth sonnet to unspeakable violence with quite inadvertently sensible, if libidinously sensual, results, thanks again to Stoppard's prodigal craftsmanship.

Those who dismiss such virtuosity as mere clever nonsense and those who while agreeing that it is nonsense praise it for at least being clever nonsense both miss the point. The point is that the speech makes sense. Stoppard's verbal wizardry may be clever but it's not nonsense and Tzara's attempted attack on sense is, quite sensibly, undercut. Although Tzara claims that 'everything is Chance, including design' (p. 37), *Travesties* more nearly leads us to the conclusion that everything is design, including chance. Indeed, unknown to Tzara, the words which he utters as merest chance not only make sense but possess artistic design: the words form, in French, a limerick.[19] From the very first words of this exceedingly intricate and at times perplexing play, none of *Travesties'* intricacy bodies forth a vision of the cosmos as random, incoherent, chaotic. Tzara's dour attack on conscious creation is quite consciously rebuffed by Stoppard's linguistic *joie de vivre*, his polyglot rejoyceing of language. Indeed, Tzara's position, his attempt to create art by destroying art, his deconstructive, reductive, reputedly revolutionary art self-destructs as the logical consequence of its own illogic.

Tzara denounces causality and proceeds to enumerate the causes for the current degradation, as he sees it, of art. Tzara dismisses logic and proceeds to explain the reasons why one should practice artistic anarchy. Tzara derides the concept of duty and proceeds to announce that 'it is the duty of the artist to jeer and howl and belch' (p. 93) at the notion of causality. The argument is as hollow as it is circular. Tzara is willing to leap to the most contradictory positions and does so, finally, not out of disinterested principle but out of an unprincipled and personally-interested pragmatism.

Thus, Kahn's perplexity as to 'whether dada stands for the supremacy of art or the negation of art or, paradoxically, for both'[20] is understandable. But Tzara's pronouncements are not, finally, centred either on the supremacy of art or its negation but on the supremacy of the artist. 'An artist', Tzara declaims, 'is someone who makes art mean the things he does. A man may be an artist by exhibiting his hindquarters. He may be a poet by drawing words out of a hat' (p. 38). Tzara, that is, voices a position diametrically opposed to that of the playwright

Henry in *The Real Thing* who, proceeding 'with humility', avers 'I don't think writers are sacred, but words are'.[21] Tzara, filled with self-adulation, deifies the writer and desecrates words.

Such verbal vandalism is unleashed in Tzara's scissoring of Shakespeare's sonnets but not more so than in the violence he does to words in his apologia for anti-art. Tzara abuses language itself, physically by cutting up words, intellectually by trying to wrench the meaning of words by main force. Whereas Brodie in *The Real Thing* 'knocks corners off' words 'without knowing he's doing it' (p. 54), Tzara perversely sets out to smash the very building blocks of the artist's craft and then stands amid the piles of rubble, claiming greater glory as an architect because of his supposed superiority to his materials.

Just as Tzara's contradictory and unreal notions about the world begin in his own self-absorption in his identity as an artist, the confusions which Lenin and Lenin's ideological disciple Cecily express about the nature of art and society arise from their failure to apprehend reality in its complex wholeness. Cecily's knowledge is literally (and here again Stoppard has literalised metaphor) encyclopaedic: 'her knowledge of the poets, *as indeed of everything else*, is eccentric, being based on alphabetical precedence' (p. 42, emphasis mine). It begins in the encyclopaedia, with strict definitions. Whereas Tzara defies any definition, and uses words for whatever purposes he pleases, Cecily mistakes words for absolute, concrete realities.[22]

In this she follows Lenin, who, like Cecily, based his knowledge of life, his approach to life, on a bookish intellectualism invalidated by experience. A university student reading Marx as devoutly as he had prepared for his high school final examinations (p. 68), Lenin uncritically accepted Marx's false premise that 'people were a sensational kind of material object' (pp. 76–7) and Marx's false assumption that the classes would inexorably move further apart, a result demonstrable in every way but experience by the 'inexorable working-out of Marx's theory of capital' (p. 76). Lenin's revolutionism is not based on the needs of the masses, but on his own abstract systematic theory divorced from life. Cecily tells Henry that Lenin refused to help organise famine relief because 'he understood that the famine was a force for the revolution' (p. 77). That is, because of an intellectual system conceived privately, he refused to respond to real need. His theoretical perception drove out the reality of the suffering of those whom he intended to save.

Just so, Lenin's ideological dictum, reiterated by Cecily, that 'the sole duty and justification for art is social criticism' (p. 74) drives out the reality of his own visceral response to art. Tzara informs Henry that Lenin flew into a rage against the Dadaists when someone began to play a sonata by Beethoven, the very archetype of romantic individualism. Although his ideology would deny the value or even ability of art to elevate or transport the human soul, which his theory would also deny, upon hearing the 'Appassionata' Lenin can be transported to consideration of the 'superhuman', 'the miracles that human beings can perform', the creation of 'beauty' (p. 89).

Lenin's ideology must postulate a collective ethic divorced from its effect on individual lives. Correspondingly, he promulgates a freedom apart from anything that can be experienced by an individual. Thus he affirms a 'free press' but one which will be *'free from bourgeois anarchist individualism!'* (p. 85). In effect, Lenin, with all the totalitarian zeal if not the humour of President Mageeba in *Night and Day*, affirms a 'relatively free press', a press which will have about as much freedom as one edited by Mageeba's relatives. Hence Lenin involves himself in impossible convolutions of logic, mistaking the terms of his intellectual system for concrete realities. The world of experience is subjected to textbook definitions. Words become arbitrary, dictatorial – just as they do in Tzara's verbal anarchy.

By their words we know them. And in *Travesties* both Lenin and Tzara are convicted by their language. If one of the serious themes in *Jumpers*, as Ronald Hayman correctly notes, is the 'connection between immorality and imprecision in the use of language',[23] *Travesties* leads us to see Lenin and Tzara not only as imprecise in their twisting of words but immoral. Their unscrupulous abuse of language reflects their pervasive lack of scruple. *Travesties*, then, unequivocally answers the question it raises as to whether an artist and a revolutionary can be one and the same person. Lenin may be a revolutionary; but his own visceral response to art demonstrates that his aesthetic theories self-destruct. Tzara, who aspires to be both revolutionary artist and artistic revolutionary, evinces instead political paralysis and artistic aridity. *Travesties* demonstrates conclusively that the revolutionary cannot hope to change the world by pulling random words out of a hat nor can the artist hope to dance within the strait-jacket of ideology.

After we acknowledge a level of certainty within the play – the certainty that the self-serving egocentrism of Tzara and the self-deluding functionalism of Lenin are invalid, the certainty that the randomly destructive aesthetic of the revolutionary artist and the wilfully destructive repression of the political revolutionary self-destruct – it remains to be shown whether an artist 'has to justify himself in political terms *at all'* ('Ambushes', p. 16). It remains to be shown what we are to make of the 'more extreme form' of the question *Travesties* asks of art and politics.

Having begun with the idea of contrasting Tzara and Lenin, Stoppard says he had 'already started to work before I thought, "I'd better see if there's anything in this James Joyce angle." And so a few weeks in, it turned out to be a play about Joyce as well.'[24] Craig Werner maintains that 'the implications of this report should be sobering to at least the most enthusiastic of the pro-Joyce interpreters'. 'If Joyce wasn't even in the original plan, then *Travesties* could hardly have been intended as a forum for the propagation of his esthetic message,' Werner argues, 'A play designed to praise Joyce would not have been likely to develop out of the Joyceless Ur-Travesty'.[25] However, Stoppard has explained that it was precisely the attractiveness of Joyce's aesthetic which led to the Irish novelist's dramatic immigration. 'I brought him in', Stoppard says of Joyce, 'mainly because I didn't want Tzara and the Dadaists to carry the artistic banner in the play, and Joyce was an artist with whom I sympathize a great deal.'[26] As contrasted to the radical aesthetic of Tzara, Stoppard affirms that he 'absolutely', 'categorically' agrees with Joyce.[27]

The entry of Joyce into *Travesties'* artistic design prompted a much more elaborate stylistic complexity than Stoppard's first conception of 'a two-act thing' contrasting Dadaist and Marxist-Leninist styles.[28] Eventually, Stoppard says, what he was trying to do was to write an 'anthology of styles-of-play, styles-of-language'.[29] At the same time, however, Stoppard took care that the play was realistically placed in the mind of Henry Carr. 'My own plays are traditional plays', Stoppard insists, 'They have a fragmented look, but *Travesties* is a logical play. Everything which seems to be illogical and irrational is a projection of a man's faulty memory.' Indeed, without the faulty memory of Henry Carr to provide a realistic framework for the play's disjunctions, *Travesties* 'would be a surrealist play, and I would hate it', Stoppard declares. To say that a work is traditional is not, of course, to say that it will be reassuringly familiar in form. For example, says Stoppard, '*Ulysses* is a book which seemed very bizarre when it was published, but at the same time it's part of a continuing tradition which goes back to Henry Fielding'.[30] But to overthrow consistency, logic, reason, craftsmanship is to risk 'drifting over the edge into a kind of artistic anarchy . . . . and the result is an absolute boring mess'.[31]

Thus, the mélange of memory-play reminiscence, the epigraphic opening in foreign fragments, the epigrammatic wit, the limericks, catechising, occasional light bits of song and dance together with heavy monologues, and Gallagher and Shean vaudeville routines all form a stylistic mosaic unlike anything previously mounted on the stage. But such a bravura polyglot performance is not without its precedents. The entire work in its linguistic complexity, its concatenation of styles, even its appropriation of the fabric of an earlier literary work for its own overarchingly clever architecture succeeds, as Howard D. Pearce rightly argues, in working 'improbability, seemingly chance, into baroque form'. The very structure of the work, seemingly random but undergirded by logic, rationality, craftsmanship, vaultingly 'demonstrates Joyce's aesthetic'.[32] The whole play, that is, is Joycean in its very form.

Unfortunately, some reports of Stoppard's structure mistake high art for anti-art. However, to confuse Stoppard's baroque palace with Dadaist rubble, calling *Travesties* 'chaotic' or 'nothing but a series of "scraps"' for which 'Tzara's pastiche is a metaphor'[33] is to fall into the very folly that even Carr denounces. 'It is a librarian's duty', Carr admonishes Cecily, 'to distinguish between poetry and a sort of belle-litter' (pp. 42–3). The claim by one critic that *Travesties* itself is a sort of 'belle-litter'[34] perhaps suggests that Carr's admonition is needed as much by those who profess, as by those who catalogue, literature.

That *Travesties* shares a Joycean aesthetic is finally revealed not only in the work's architectural form but in its celebratory function. Joyce, the member of the dramatis personae, celebrates both the immortality of art and the immortality which art grants to men. An artist, he says, is 'the magician put among men to gratify – capriciously – their urge for immortality' by creating 'what survives as art, yes even in the celebration of tyrants, yes even in the celebration of nonentities'. And Joyce, the historic author, created in *Ulysses* one of the enduring literary temples to the ordinary life of man within the form of one of mankind's most extraordinary works of art, the *Odyssey*. 'And yet I with my Dublin Odyssey', Joyce says in *Travesties*, 'will double that immortality' (p. 62).

'The celebration of nonentities': the phrase could serve as a paradigm of Stoppard's art. From such cast-off courtiers as Rosencrantz and Guildenstern who do not even survive some directors' cuts of *Hamlet* but live in Stoppard's art, their immortality redoubled; to the haplessly outdated, outmoded, ploddingly pedestrian George; to such obscure figures as a Czech cleaner, his unlettered wife and son in *Professional Foul*, the celebration of nonentities forms a leit-motif in Stoppard's canon. In *Travesties*, as Pearce rightly proclaims, Stoppard 'redoubles the immortalities of *Earnest*, *Ulysses*, . . . Joyce, Tzara, Lenin, the great wars of Troy and the world'.[35] And holding the whole frame together is that mere footnote to history, the ordinary mundane laughably parochial but thoroughly real Henry Carr.

Just as Stoppard can write clever dialogue for Archie and anticipate witty ripostes from McFee without feeling seriously inclined to espouse a materialistic view of mankind or an amoral pragmatic view of politics, so he can create arguments for Tzara and copy declamations from Lenin without ever being seriously inclined toward the functional art of the ideologue or the anarchist anti-art of the Dadaist. And just as in *Jumpers* he is torn between the perspectives of George who wins a pyrrhic victory in the intellectual debate but whose moral affirmations pale beside the mortal anguish of his supposedly peripheral wife, so in *Travesties* Stoppard is torn between the perspectives of the extraordinary sensibility of the artist and the ordinary common sense of the average man. What is finally of interest to Stoppard is not the tension between art and strait-jacketed ideology nor the tension between art and unbridled surrealistic indulgence but the tension between the ordinary human being and the extraordinary artist, between the individual dancer and the enduring pattern of the dance, between the perspectives of the temporal and the timeless. The conflict between the perspectives of Carr and Joyce, then, ultimately figures the tension – as we shall see again in *The Real Thing* – between life and art.

Just as Tzara first enters as 'a Rumanian nonsense' (though with the assurance that 'there will be another one') and Joyce first enters as 'an Irish nonsense', so Carr first appears as a bourgeois British nonsense. In his failure at times to grasp that a social revolution might consist of something more drastic than ladies unattended at operas, he cuts a rather farcical figure. However, Stoppard's self-description, in the year *Travesties* appeared, as 'an English middle-class bourgeois'[36] might suggest a certain sympathy for Carr's values even if we must smile at the taste that an English middle-class bourgeois can manifest in fashion or music. Indeed, three years after *Travesties* appeared, Stoppard would offer a ringing affirmation in his own voice of the propositions that 'Truth is objective. Civilization is the pursuit of truth in freedom. Freedom is the necessary condition of that pursuit. Political freedom and economic freedom are dependent on each other. Material and cultural progress (growth) is dependent on both together. The loss of freedom leads to civilization's decline.' But most of the propositions which Stoppard defends in his 1977 review, which asserts in its title that 'but for the middle classes' civilisation would succumb to the enemies of society,[37] are adumbrated in the positions espoused by Henry Carr, another English middle-class bourgeois, in *Travesties*. It is Carr who defends the objective meaning of language against Tzara's attempts to twist words to mean whatever he wishes them to mean. 'If there is any point in using language at all', Carr insists, 'it is that a word is taken to stand for a particular fact or idea and not for other facts or ideas' (p. 38). In this, Carr is also a forerunner of another Henry who in *The Real Thing* will demolish another 'radical' attempt to redefine language. 'Words don't deserve that kind of malarkey', asserts Henry (not Carr, the other one), 'they're innocent, neutral, precise, standing for this, describing that, meaning the other' (p. 54).

The playwright-protagonist of *The Real Thing* may, unlike Carr, be the chief exemplar of the artist in that later play. But both Henrys insist that the artist is less important than his art, the writer less significant than the words with which he works. Whereas Tzara may exalt the personal power and prestige of the artist, declaiming that 'an artist is someone who makes art mean the things he does' (p. 38), Carr's objection is rooted in the objective meaning of language itself: 'Then you are not actually *an artist* at all?' Just as 'an intelligent child could push . . . over' Brodie's jerry-built verbal structures in *The Real Thing*, so simple common sense could expose the malarkey Tzara inflicts on words, and Henry Carr does just that in a magisterial defence of language. Tzara's attempt to appropriate the word 'artist' for his exhibitionism 'does not', Carr counters, 'make you an artist':

> An artist is someone who is gifted in some way that enables him to do something more or less well which can only be done badly or not at all by someone who is not thus gifted. . . . I might claim to be able to fly . . . Lo, I say, I am flying. But you are not propelling yourself about while suspended in the air, someone may point out. Ah no, I reply, that is no longer considered the proper concern of people who can fly. In fact, it is frowned upon. Nowadays, a flyer never leaves the ground and wouldn't know how. I see, says my somewhat baffled interlocutor, so when you say you can *fly* you are using the word in a purely private sense. I see I have made myself clear, I say. Then, says this chap in some relief, you cannot actually *fly* after all? On the contrary, I say, I have just told you I can.[38] (pp. 38–9)

Carr's refutation of Tzara's anarchic abuse of language, as Richard Ellmann recognised in his review of the original production, 'is definitive'.[39]

And even if Carr's assertion that the words *flying* or *art* signify particular things and not other things is merely common sense, what is so mere about that? 'One of the things which complicates argument at the moment for me', Stoppard has said more recently, 'is that people are so clever that, paradoxically, they can be persuaded of almost anything'.[40] And one form of nonsense which has received wide acceptance among the clever people is that the connection between sign and signified, between language and meaning is wholly arbitrary and subject to capricious reinterpretation. Despite such cleverness, Carr's defence of the integrity of language, his insistence that art is what is meant by the word *art*, that flying is what is meant by the word *flying*, is – quite simply – true. Such simple truth is ignored by those who purport to see in *Travesties* nothing but 'universal parody', 'uncertainty and confusion', a 'chaotic' reflection of a chaotic cosmos.[41] But if such characterisations of *Travesties* 'are now the quite familiar

teachings of well-educated men and women holding responsible
positions in respectable universities',[42] the thing to say about such
teaching is not that it is 'interesting' but that it is not true.

Carr is also invested with the defence of patriotism, duty,
love, and freedom – both the words and the qualities which
those words represent. Like Stoppard himself, Carr draws a clear
connection between political freedom and 'civilised ideals', and
firmly places both within an explicitly moral framework. 'Wars
are fought to make the world safe for artists', Carr asserts
(p. 39). His telescoping of ideas has something of the self-
mocking overstatement of George's *'Cogito ergo deus est'*. But
if George's theistic affirmations carry authorial sanction (and
they do) despite George's 'aptitude for reducing a complex and
logical thesis to a mysticism of staggering banality' (p. 63) so too
do Carr's affirmations of patriotism, duty, love, and freedom.
Indeed, Carr's insistence on a connection between political freedom and 'civilised ideals' anticipates Stoppard's own affirmation
three years later that political freedom is a 'necessary condition'
for civilisation and that 'the loss of freedom leads to civilization's
decline'.[43]

But Carr does not conceive of either the political or the
aesthetic as the ultimate frame of reference. He places both
politics and art within a context which is explicitly moral: 'The
easiest way of knowing whether good has triumphed over evil is
to examine the freedom of the artist' (p. 39). In the more overtly
political plays which follow *Travesties*, Stoppard embarks on just
such an examination. Implicit in Carr's assertion is the belief not
only that moral values exist, but that good and evil are absolutes
which can be used in judging a regime rather than negotiable
commodities which are culturally determined. If art and politics
are connected, as Carr asserts they are, it is not that either is
subservient to the other but that both are subject to a third
realm. The ultimate frame of reference as Carr presents it is
neither political nor aesthetic but moral. The plays after *Travesties*
may explore a variety of regimes examining the freedom of the
press in *Night and Day*, the freedom of philosophic inquiry in
Professional Foul, the freedom of dramatic performance in *Dogg's
Hamlet, Cahoot's Macbeth*, the freedom of political dissent in *Every
Good Boy Deserves Favour*. But in each play the examination of the
political regime focuses on freedom of expression. And in each
play 'the point' (to apply words from a Stoppard interview which

distinctly echo Carr) is to set each regime up against 'a moral standard, a consistent idea of what constitutes good and bad in the way human beings treat each other' ('Ambushes', p. 12). Although they examine freedom of expression, these later plays in fact address the very question regarding the political structure of a society which Carr poses, that of 'whether good has triumphed over evil'.

Indeed, Carr's refutation of Marxism in his second-act confrontation with Cecily is as astute an analysis as Stoppard himself can muster. Parrying the political inquisition of *Theatre Quarterly* interviewers, Stoppard insisted that

> The great irony about Marx was that his impulses were deeply moral while his intellect insisted on a materialistic view of the world. His theory of capital, his theory of value, and his theory of revolution, have all been refuted by modern economics and by history. In short, he got it wrong. ('Ambushes', p. 13)

That was in May 1974. Less than a month later on 10 June 1974 the RSC production of *Travesties* opened at the Aldwych with John Wood, as Henry Carr, declaiming some of the same words, 'No, no, no, no, my dear girl – Marx got it wrong' (p. 76). Arguing that Marx was 'the victim of an historical accident' who encountered the capitalist system after the industrial revolution had crowded people into slums but before it had 'begun to bring them the benefits of an industrialised society', Carr serves rather transparently as the spokesman for Stoppard's own views. To Cicely's leftist dogma that under capitalism 'the gap between rich and poor gets wider', Carr responds with the blunt assertion 'but it doesn't' (p. 76). Carr's insistence that Cecily's ideology ignores the statistical facts echoes Stoppard's own blunt willingness to correct fellow playwright David Hare on the same point ('Ambushes', pp. 14–15). Similarly, Stoppard's ringing affirmation 'One thing I feel sure about is that a materialistic view of history is an insult to the human race' ('Ambushes', p. 13) becomes transmuted, in the art of *Travesties*, to Carr's pithy observation that Marx's 'materialism made a monkey out of him' (p. 76). Carr's witty observation on the origin of the specious evolves into his straightforward declaration that Marx's whole theory was built on the 'false premise . . . that people were a sensational kind of material object and would behave predictably in a material

world' (pp. 76–7). Both in substance and in tone Carr's words
are the clearest possible expression of a position which Stoppard
declares is 'one thing I feel sure about', a position which 'I'm not
going to rebut' ('Ambushes', p. 13).

Despite the fact that Carr associates art with civilised values
and defends war as necessary in order to preserve both political
freedom and civilisation, he later discounts the importance of
art. Carr's notion that art is absurdly overrated (p. 46) may seem
inconsistent with his claims that art 'gratifies a hunger that is
common to princes and peasants' (p. 74). However, in the former
he is rejecting Tzara's insistence on the supernal value of art, in
the latter he is rejecting Cecily's Marxist-Leninist dogma that art
must be ideological. Both Carr's affirmation that art satisfies a
longing wholly apart from its relevance to social change and
his qualification that art is not of supreme importance speak for
Stoppard.

Even Carr's assertion that art is absurdly overrated is echoed
in Stoppard's confession that he is embarrassed by claims that art
is important: 'When Auden said his poetry didn't save one Jew
from the gas chamber, he'd said it all . . . . I've never felt this –
that art is important. That's been my secret guilt. I think it's the
secret guilt of most artists.'[44] Still, this is where we see Stoppard
on the horns of a dilemma. He sees art as timeless, celebratory, and
universal in the way that Joyce does and recognises its capacity
to immortalise whom it will. But at the same time he balances
Joyce's flights of imagination against the less exalted view of a
Carr (or, perhaps, an Auden) which emphasises the present,
the here and now, and the importance of such concerns as
political freedom. However, when Stoppard comes to debate
the contrast between the aesthetic vision of the artist and the
plebeian perception of political realities by the common man, the
questions such a contrast between life and art raises are inherently
moral. Although art may not be important in effecting specific
change in the short term, Stoppard insists that in the long term
'art is important because it provides the moral matrix, the moral
sensibility, from which we make our judgments about the world'
('Ambushes', p. 14).

Eric Salmon rightly calls *Travesties* a 'gage thrown down at
the feet of the materialistic world'.[45] Just as in *Jumpers* there is
more to George than meets the microscope, so *Travesties* asserts
a 'hunger that is common to princes and peasants' that cannot be

satisfied by physical bread alone, an 'urge for immortality' which inexorably reveals not only the moral nature of experience but the spiritual nature of humankind. Thus, the 'meetings' which take place in Zurich are not just those of Tzara and Lenin, Joyce and Tzara, Lenin and Joyce. The 'mystical swissticality' of Zurich, 'the still centre of the wheel of war' (p. 26), becomes an emblem of the timeless locus of art amid the mutabilities of time. And it is against those mutabilities that Joyce celebrates an art which immortalises yes even tyrants, yes even nonentities. Such claims for art echo those offered by innumerable poets whose lyrics still live. Stoppard even manages to include in its entirety Shakespeare's eighteenth sonnet which concludes with a memorable celebration of the immortality which art can grant to mortals:

> Nor shall Death brag thou wander'st in his shade,
> When in eternal lines to time thou growest:
> So long as men can breathe or eyes can see,
> So long lives this and this gives life to thee.

That Shakespeare's lyric celebration of love should be faulted for not having done more to effect social change in Elizabethan England is a view taken by only the most blinkered of Marxist-Leninist materialists. But it is precisely the transcendence of the material state, it is precisely of a spirit above the dust that Joyce sings in his paean to art which 'will dance for some time yet and *leave the world precisely as it finds it*' (p. 63).

However, it does not from that follow that Stoppard is divorcing himself from the world of reality, that he is withdrawing with style from the chaos, as Tynan insists. To conclude, as Tynan does, that 'Stoppard's idol . . . is, unequivocally, Joyce' is as much a half-truth as saying that in *Jumpers* George 'is Stoppard's hero' (which Tynan also says).[46] George may be right in theory but he is culpable in practice. In his rarefied philosophic world praising the importance of experience and real life, George ignores the real-life experience of his wife. Just so, in his rarefied artistic world immortalising the experience of the ordinary average Leopold Bloom, Joyce ignores, slights, the thoroughly ordinary Henry Carr. *Travesties* springs in large part from Stoppard's compassionate perception that the feelings and sensibilities of the all too fallible and mortal Henry Wilfred Carr, 1894–1962, should have mattered more to the author of the immortal *Ulysses*. But Tynan, his sights set on a 'prodigious, polymorphous', and pre-eminently political 'flowering' of 'a Socialist society'[47] slights the significance of anything so unimposing as a mere individual. Like Joyce, Tynan finds it easy to slight Henry Carr.

Whereas Joyce celebrates an art which is changeless, Carr is inextricably associated with the world of time and change. Literally we are reminded of the ravages of time in the transformation before our eyes of young Carr into Old Carr, but not more so than in the ravages of time on Carr's memory. The line 'I have put the newspapers and telegrams on the sideboard, sir', announces Carr's 'time-slips' in both the first and second acts. And in the varied versions of what those headlines might have been we see, as opposed to Joyce's creation of timeless unchanging art, how Carr might have changed the course of history. If art is intensely important for reasons other than writing angrily about this morning's headlines, the political realities reported by those morning headlines, as it turns out, have their own intense importance however separate from the realm of art. Carr speculates that he could have prevented Lenin's departure to the Finland Station. But with 'the lives of millions of people hanging on which way I'd move', Carr was distracted by 'a stroke of luck with a certain little lady' (p. 81).

'What was the right thing?' Carr asks, and only indirectly answers his question by adding, 'and then there were my feelings for Cecily' (p. 81). Moments later he reiterates, 'I should like to make it clear that my feelings for Cecily are genuine' (p. 82) are, in another word, real. At least in hindsight we can see that the love between two insignificant individuals just might be more real than ideology. But how could we tell in such a fleeting moment that Carr's love for Cecily might be translated within the Stoppard canon, into 'The Real Thing'. Don't forget, the playwright Henry Carr wasn't Henry then (not Carr, the other one). Like a Shakespearean comedy, *Travesties* achieves a 'rapid but formal climax' and ends in a dance. Boy gets girl; Cecily says yes; and Carr's affirmations of his genuine love for Cecily prepare the way for the Joycean affirmation of Cecily's 'yes, I said yes when you asked me' (p. 98).

The perspectives of Carr and Joyce are not so much contradictory as complementary. Therefore, instead of a confrontation of their views, the play gives us an endless oscillation between their perspectives. Stoppard's choice of settings reveals where, for him, the conflict is centred. Despite Stoppard's original ground plan, *Jumpers* does not revolve between the Moores' flat and the university but between the moral philosophy of George's study and the musical comedy of Dotty's bedroom, and as we have seen, the central tension of the work comes between the perspectives of George and Dotty. Similarly, if Stoppard had stuck to his original plan to present Tzara and Lenin as mirrored opposites, he might have found settings more apposite than the drawing room of Henry Carr's apartment and the Zurich Public Library. Tzara might have been more in his *métier* at the Meierei Bar and Lenin more in his element behind a rostrum, where we eventually see him in the second act. But it is Joyce the celebrant of mankind's massive literary heritage who is most at home in the Library. And it is on the contrast of Joyce and Carr, reflected in the pervasive contrast of 'The Room' and 'The Library' that *Travesties* ultimately turns.

Carr and Joyce are natural allies. Carr objects to the abuse of language and Joyce is the conserver and renewer of language.[48] Joyce is embarked, in *Ulysses*, on a monumental exaltation of the common life of humanity and Carr is a common human. Carr has sympathy with the underdog and Joyce, an impoverished writer afflicted with numerous eye ailments, private penury and public rejection, is downtrodden. Both also know that civilisation and the arts are connected. 'Wars are fought to make the world safe for artists. It is never quite put in those terms but it is a useful way of grasping what civilised ideals are all about' (p. 39), Carr tells Tzara. 'The temples are built and brought down around him, continuously and contiguously, from Troy to the fields of Flanders. If there is any meaning in any of it, it is in what survives as art . . . . What now of the Trojan War if it had been passed over by the artist's touch? Dust . . . ' declaims Joyce (p. 62). The views supplement each other. Wars are fought for freedom of artistic expression; the artist transfigures and preserves society imaginatively because it cannot be preserved physically. But a pervasive irony of the work is that although Carr and Joyce are natural allies, they never recognise each other as such. Joyce requires the material assistance and the political freedom which Carr can help provide; Carr needs the qualities of imagination and intellect with which Joyce is gifted.

Carr fails to recognise the full importance of artistic freedom even if he acknowledges that civilised ideals are protected by the political freedom for which he is willing to fight. He does not realise that society cannot be physically preserved. His consciousness of the war overlaps at many points his consciousness of clothes. He is obsessed with preserving the outward forms and fashions of society, its cut, and the artist is, to him, a tailor who dresses and adorns the times. 'It is the duty of the artist to beautify existence' (p. 37) is his reply to Tzara. It is appropriate that his entire conflict concerning Joyce be connected with trousers. His disconcertment by Joyce's appearance is also a figure of his disconcertment by Joyce's art: 'And is it a chapter, inordinate in length and erratic in style, remotely connected with midwifery?' (p. 97). Both reflect his belief in the forms of society as against the substance. Nor does Carr recognise that *Ulysses*, even if its author attacked him in its pages and in the courts, is a brief defending him, is Joyce's great exaltation of the common life of humanity.

Conversely, Joyce, for all his exaltation of ordinary humanity in his art, fails to recognise his own dependence on ordinary humans in real life. Joyce may celebrate nonentities but he sees himself as above the political convictions of trench soldiers. The recurrent attention Stoppard gives to Joyce's historical defects of physical vision leads us to question again and again throughout the play his moral vision. 'Surely belief in man could find room for man's beliefs', Clegthorpe says among his last words in *Jumpers* (p. 76). In that context the line applies to the amoral political pragmatist and atheistic materialist philosopher Archie who would deny the validity of any human belief in religion. In *Travesties*, which Stoppard insists is 'so near the knuckle of life', 'closer to the bone'[49] than his earlier plays, Stoppard more directly turns the line on himself as artist. Joyce may be an artist who transmutes the experience of ordinary human beings into art but in doing so he discounts such ordinary human beliefs as patriotism, love of country, love of freedom, and a willingness to defend country and freedom. Carr's artistic tastes may be middle-brow, his penchant for clothing may be middle-class bourgeois, but he believes in freedom, he believes in patriotism – which another Henry will affirm in *The Real Thing* – however laughable his sartorial tastes he has been willing to fight to preserve freedom and Stoppard is by no means as sure as Joyce – much less as sure as Tzara – that in such matters they also serve who only sit and write.

Not only does art capriciously grant immortality to tyrants and nonentities, it emblematically reveals the immortality which all men share, the metaphysical state as opposed to the physical, the eternal spiritual reality as opposed to the social. But both spiritual and social realms are real. Stoppard does not choose between Carr and Joyce because to do so would be to choose between time and the timeless, the metaphysical state of man and the physical state of man. Life within the realm of time and the timeless realm of art which celebrates life are interdependent, symbiotic, part and parcel of one whole. To choose between flesh and spirit is to deny both, is to deny the integrated complex, mystical oneness of the human. Art or politics. Politics or art. The preservation of freedom or the freedom to preserve; food for the body or breath for the soul; material clothing or immaterial raiment. To choose between such mutually interdependent realities is to resign oneself to the fragmentary. To embrace both, clinging to both body and spirit, time and timelessness, is to affirm wholeness, is to affirm the moral vision which sees both physical and metaphysical realities.

What we see, what we should see, is that in terms of moral vision, both Tzara and Lenin are blind. One glimmer of light to penetrate Tzara's monocle is his perception that art transcends or should transcend the materialistic, that 'without art man was a coffee-mill'. Against that glimmer are ranged his benighted beliefs that the artist is a special breed of person and 'without *him*, man would be a coffee-mill' (p. 47, my emphasis); that words are subject to arbitrary abuse; that sonnets are subject to capricious scissoring; that the entire human heritage of art from the Shakespearean to the Joycean, from Homer to Beethoven, is subject to contemptuous dismissal so that he can perversely and wrongly conclude that '*with* art, man – is a coffee-mill' (p. 47). By contrast, Lenin can see, as Tzara cannot, the 'beauty' of Beethoven's 'amazing, superhuman music', the laughter and tears which specific works of art can provide. But Lenin's blinkered ideological vision leads to his reductivist view of mankind as 'a sensational kind of material object'; his abuse of language, sanctioning the application of such jargon as 'economism, opportunism and social chauvinism' to such realities as 'trade unions, parliament and support for the war' (p. 75); and his willingness to subjugate all human emotion – from his personal exaltation by art to the anguish of peasants facing famine – to his ruthless impersonal dogma. Lenin wilfully blinds himself to any perception of the individual. If peasants starve, it will help to bring about the revolution. If music evokes a vision of human beings as miraculous, metaphysical creatures, you must wilfully close your eyes to such anarchist bourgeois individualism. Similarly, Tzara sees Carr as merely a capitalist puppet, a mere figure of a man instead of a real individual who did bleed in hopes of defending liberty and protecting 'boring little Belgians' from tyranny. Both Tzara and Lenin deny that the life of the average person is worthy, *even if* it does not advance art or social revolution, even if the individual is as ploddingly pedestrian as this particular Carr.

Contrasted with such beams obscuring the moral perception of Tzara and Lenin, the defects of moral vision in Joyce and Carr are mere motes. Capable of sweeping from Dublin to Troy in one glance, Joyce may be oblivious to such closer realities as clothes, the swings and roundabouts of political history, or even such ordinary human sentiments as patriotism, duty, and love of freedom. But Joyce's visionary glance is far-sighted in his celebration of art; his affirmation of a tradition of art stretching back to Homer; his association of writing with the dance and with immortality; his rejection of the need for art to change the world; and his praise of genius and subtlety, conscious craftsmanship and faithful stewardship of language. Focused on more immediate realities, Carr may be myopic in his middle-class fascination for fashion, his middle-brow taste in art, and his inordinately personal reaction to what he perceives as an affront by Joyce. But as a middle-class bourgeois, Carr accurately sees the importance of patriotism, love of freedom, hatred of tyranny, and – eventually – explains why 'Marx got it wrong'. As a middle-brow auditor of the arts, he defends the integrity of language against the mindless onslaughts of Tzara, recognises that art is of substantial though not supernal importance but that the artist is a mortal rather than some species of divinity, and senses that art 'gratifies a hunger that is common to princes and peasants' rather than merely being of utilitarian value in seeking to change society. And as an ordinary human being gifted with common sense, he accurately perceives that people are not merely 'a sensational kind of material object'; and recognises, percipiently in his own life, presciently in Stoppard's canon, that his 'feelings for Cecily', feelings which he is at pains to point out 'are genuine' may be more important than ideology, that love just might be the real thing.

So Carr is left at the end, saying that he learned three things in

Zurich: 'I wrote them down. Firstly, you're either a revolutionary or you're not, and if you're not you might as well be an artist as anything else. Secondly, if you can't be an artist, you might as well be a revolutionary . . . I forget the third thing' (pp. 98–9). Although Carr's closing speech has been brushed aside by several critics, implicit in the first two points Carr remembers is the answer to the germinal question that evoked *Travesties*. Can the artist and the revolutionary be one and the same person? Quite clearly the final words of *Travesties* answer in the negative. One is either an artist or one is a revolutionary. One is either a revolutionary or one is an artist. But a 'revolutionary artist'? That is a thing of nought. The very concept is not worth remembering. The first two points deny its very existence. 'I forget the third thing'. What is there to be besides being a revolutionary or being an artist? The third thing is to be Henry Carr, to be an ordinary human being; because even revolutionaries and artists are only Henry Carrs, only Leopold Blooms. When they attempt to assert the contrary, to destroy the Carr-ness in humanity, they become inhuman, self-contradictory, dangerous. Lenin *'wasn't Lenin then'*; nor is he ever the Lenin of history. Neither is Joyce the figure James Joyce, nor Tzara the Dadaist Tristan Tzara. That each person is like Bloom the hero of his own life, and yet each is an extraneous ordinary person, in spite of his achievements, is the third thing; and it binds the play together and caps the intricate vigorous unity of *Travesties*.

Far from revealing 'flaccidity of will, the weakening of moral sinew',[50] *Travesties*, like *Jumpers*, flexes a 'muscular intellectualism'[51] in its celebration of the human urge for immortality and art's gratification of that longing of the spirit. Far from being 'his blackest statement to date',[52] *Travesties* exudes a *joie de vivre*, a multi-lingual polyglot celebration of life from many tongues. In reshaping the mundane and ordinary into a lasting monument not just to his own intellect but to the mundane and ordinary, Stoppard's art at once emulates the extraordinary Joyce while exalting the ordinary Carr. Stoppard's Zurich, 'the still centre of the wheel of war' (p. 26), like T.S. Eliot's 'still point of the turning wheel', which it explicitly echoes, figures the interstices of mortality and immortality, the temporal and the timeless, the common sense of the ordinary citizen and the sensibility provided by art, the mutable realm of the flesh and the immutable realm of the spirit.

5

The Word Made Flesh:
Moral Action
in the Body Politic

For the first decade of his theatrical career, Tom Stoppard could expect to spend a substantial part of most interviews defending himself for not dealing with political realities in his plays. Tagged with a reputation for stylish stagecraft and erudite wordplay, Stoppard had to respond so often to the charge that his plays evaded 'real' issues, that he even attributes the genesis of a major play to the ubiquitous question: 'One of the impulses in *Travesties* is to try to sort out what my answer would in the end be if I was given enough time to think every time I'm asked why my plays aren't political.'[1] And yet – to paraphrase George in *Jumpers* – as though to defy reason, the question would not go away. Given Stoppard's sense of the primacy of moral issues, he could opine 'I'd like to write a play – say, *XYZ* – which would pertain to anything from a Latin American coup to the British Left, and probably when I've done it I'll still be asked why I don't write political plays'.[2]

But that was in 1974. By the end of the 1970s interviewers were no longer asking Stoppard that particular question. In the intervening years, Stoppard had pleaded the case of the Czechoslovakian Chartists within the pages of the *New York Review of Books*; been actively involved in the work of Amnesty International and the Committee Against Psychiatric Abuse; made page one headlines as the chairman of the 'Let Misha Go' campaign which called – successfully – for the release by Soviet authorities of the 13-year-old son of a Russian psychiatrist; enacted the role of Vaclav Havel's defence lawyer in a Munich re-creation of the trial of the Czech playwright for political dissidence; and used the forum of *The Sunday Times* to denounce British participation in the Moscow Olympics. Suddenly interviews were more likely to carry headlines like 'The Politicizing of Tom Stoppard'[3] or include questions about why he had become so overtly political.

82

With Stoppard's new outspokenness on public issues came a series of plays with contemporary political settings. However, the difference between Stoppard's 'political' plays and the ideological drama which has dominated much recent British theatre is greater than has usually been acknowledged. Joan FitzPatrick Dean argues that the two crucial distinctions separating Stoppard from such 'committed' playwrights as Wesker and Bond are that Stoppard's plays are highly theatrical rather than naturalistic and that his 'social and political concerns are not the favorites of liberal, intellectual circles'.[4] To be sure, in revealing the danger to free expression posed by Soviet intolerance of political dissidence (*Every Good Boy Deserves Favour*, 1977), by Czech suppression of philosophic debate (*Professional Foul*, 1977), by British trade unions' interruption of journalistic inquiry (*Night and Day*, 1978), and of totalitarian harassment of artistic expression (*Dogg's Hamlet, Cahoot's Macbeth*, 1979),[5] Stoppard has focused on such unfashionable topics as the abuses of the political left. However, we should not see Stoppard's plays on political topics as differing from most recent British political drama simply as the political right differs from the political left. Nor is such a difference limited to the fact that Stoppard writes political plays enlivened by theatrical experimentation and verbal grace.

Rather, Stoppard can be distinguished from the orthodox mainstream of British political drama because he does not conceive of the body politic as the ultimate frame of reference. Indeed, the conviction that human actions are to be judged against an absolute standard of morality rather than merely in terms of political effectiveness or social desirability undergirds Stoppard's outspokenness on the persecution of dissidents in the Soviet Union, in Czechoslovakia, and under other totalitarian regimes. His appeal to a moral order which transcends political ideology is perhaps most apparent in his impassioned 1980 appeal against British participation in the Soviet Olympics:

We have the chance to let it be known throughout the Soviet empire that contrary to appearances there is some bread we will not break with the saviours of Eastern Europe and Afghanistan, not to mention Greater Russia; that morality has not yet been stood on its head on planet earth, that for all the cultural and scientific exchanges, and for all the niceties of 'spheres of influence' and 'internal affairs', there is still a

decent way to govern people and an indecent way, that the
difference is not relative but absolute, and that when the USSR
and its clients have had their games and the bunting has been
taken down and the medals put on the mantlepiece and the
mantlepiece turned to dust, the difference will still be there
and still matter; we have this chance and, God help us, we
are going to pass it up.[6]

Writing in *The Sunday Times* about such an ostensibly political
topic as a British boycott of the Soviet Olympics, Stoppard
grounds his appeal on such apolitical bedrock as the existence
of morality, of a moral order which is not relative but absolute,
of moral values which transcend ideology, culture and time.

Similarly, Stoppard's plays are rooted firmly in his conviction
first reflected in *Jumpers* 'that all political acts have a moral basis
to them and are meaningless without it' ('Ambushes', p. 12).
In his 'political' plays Stoppard is applying those moral and
philosophical precepts which he had affirmed, albeit at a more
abstract level, in the earlier plays. Felicia Londré does well to
remind us – however briefly – that Stoppard 'has not deviated
in essence'[7] from the philosophy he expressed in his 1974 interview with *Theatre Quarterly*. Indeed, in that context he offered a
touchstone which is useful not only for *Jumpers* but for his more
recent work:

> the point is not to compare one ruthless regime against another
> – it is to set each one up against a moral standard, a consistent
> idea of what constitutes good and bad in the way human beings
> treat each other regardless of class, colour or ideology, and at
> least my poor professor in *Jumpers* got *that* right. ('Ambushes',
> p. 12)

Stoppard's 1972 play simultaneously faults the 'poor professor'
of moral philosophy for failing to enflesh the moral values he
perceives while affirming the truth of those values. And it is
the truth of those values first affirmed in *Jumpers*, a sense of
the reality of right and wrong, which informs Stoppard's more
recent 'political' plays.

However, these plays, on overtly social or political topics,
have been widely hailed as a fundamental departure from

Stoppard's previous drama. One London reviewer announced that in *Night and Day*, Stoppard 'abandons . . . fancy intellectual foot-work . . . to write a savagely serious drama . . . [which] makes all Stoppard's other plays look like so many nursery games'.[8] Such effusions simply state in the baldest form a misconception which has been voiced both in scholarly journals and in critical volumes. Noticing the wit but not the serious affirmation of moral absolutes in the earlier plays, noticing the serious concern with political issues but not the application of moral absolutes in the later plays, many critics have protested that the more recent plays are not even 'identifiable'[9] as the work of Stoppard.

Even such a perceptive critic as Kenneth Tynan ultimately goes astray by separating Stoppard's response to the Prague dissidents from the moral matrix of plays like *Jumpers*. By regarding Stoppard's actions and writings regarding the dissidents as tentative and inadequate steps toward political activism rather than seeing them as bodying forth the moral concerns of his earlier drama, Tynan leaves us with the belief that Stoppard's defence of transcendent moral values is simply a form of 'withdraw-ing . . . from the chaos'.[10] More recently Neil Sammells claims that Stoppard's plays beginning with *Night and Day* 'betray his distinctive gifts as a dramatist', 'deny his distinctive achievements as a dramatist' and put his work 'at the service of a political thesis which is at best self-contradictory and banal and, at worst, cyni-cal and dishonest'.[11] The thing to say about such charges is not that they are interesting or radical but that they are not true. Actually, Stoppard's heightened involvement in political issues is inseparable from his earlier moral perceptions.

Despite journalistic and academic announcements of his politi-cization, Stoppard protests that reports of his metamorphosis have been greatly exaggerated. 'That's just not the way it looks from my end of the telescope at all',[12] Stoppard says, 'There was no sudden conversion on the road to Damascus'.[13] Stoppard also denies any fundamental transformation within his plays: '*Jumpers* has got the same subject as *Professional Foul*',[14] he insists, 'both are about the way human beings are supposed to behave towards each other'.[15] Indeed, Stoppard maintains that even in his earlier plays an emphasis on the ethical always had political implications: 'a lot of my work connected with the same sort of areas of interest as more overtly social plays, but did so in much more generalised terms'.[16]

Such an insistence on the subservience of political con-
siderations to more important, more fundamental, and permanent
standards of right and wrong constitutes the distinguishing
characteristic of his 'political' plays. Whereas his earlier plays
affirm the abstract proposition that political acts must be judged
in moral terms, these plays subject specific identifiable regimes
to such moral scrutiny. Rather than radically departing from
his previous work, Stoppard is here applying, acting upon,
those moral and metaphysical affirmations which Eric Salmon
astutely commended to us as 'Faith in Tom Stoppard'. Further,
in these plays Stoppard also presents characters who come to
act upon those moral precepts which their predecessors had
only affirmed at a theoretical level. Ultimately we see that when
such characters do enact what they believe, their actions are not
depicted as pathetic protests against an absurd universe. Rather,
their actions frequently prove to be efficacious, capable of making
a real and tangible difference in the world which they confront. In
Stoppard's ostensibly political plays, that is, we see characters in
whose lives the word of moral precept becomes incarnate in the
flesh of moral action.

The discussion which follows will look first at the moral standards
by which actions are judged in each of the plays and secondly at
the ways in which those moral precepts gain the name of action.
In *Professional Foul*, Stoppard leads us to recognise the moral basis
of political acts by juxtaposing the abuses of the Czech regime
with a philosophical colloquium where debate, in part, is on the
existence of moral absolutes. The three British philosophers in
attendance are moral absolutist Chetwyn who affirms that ethical
principles possess objective, transcendent reality; an Oxbridge
ethics professor, Anderson, who argues for a human obligation to
adhere to ethical principles while denying that such principles are
given objective existence by a transcendent mandate; and Marxist
philosophical gadfly McKendrick who denies the existence both
of moral principles and the transcendent, 'reliable signposts on
the yellow brick road to rainbowland' (p. 85).

Though it is largely possible to delineate where Stoppard
stands in this debate, there is no doubt that the play – dedicated
'in admiration' 'To Vaclav Havel' – enlists the greatest respect

for both the personal plight and the philosophical position of a fourth intellectual, Pavel Hollar. Hollar's portrayal is the most fully rounded portrait in *Professional Foul*. We see him as a former student who trusts his mentors, a husband who is loved by his wife, a father who confides in his son (a 'good boy' who – like Sacha in *Every Good Boy Deserves Favour* – 'deserves a father', p. 29). Despite a Cambridge degree in philosophy, Hollar must now clean lavatories and in the course of the play is arrested and imprisoned for expressing ideas disapproved of by the State.

Hollar's philosophical position, made all the more poignant by his precarious circumstances, is that an individual possesses inherent rights, that such ethical standards are 'paramount' and are not subservient to State-defined correctness, and that 'the ethics of the State must be judged against the fundamental ethic of the individual' (p. 55). Stoppard echoes Hollar's words in his 1980 explanation to an interviewer that political ideology must be based on and judged by individual morality:

> However inflexible our set of beliefs, whether it's mine or the ayatollah's, however authentic their existence may be, the truth is that they owe their existence to individual acts between individuals, which themselves are derived from an individual's intuitive sense of what is right and wrong.[17]

Believing such moral standards are universally intelligible, Hollar supports his claim that a sense of what is right is inherent in all human beings by saying 'I observe my son for example' (p. 55). Hollar's appeal to the example of a child to demonstrate the intelligibility of moral absolutes has resonances through-out Stoppard's writings. Among the British professors at the colloquium, the philosopher who most nearly shares Hollar's sense of the universality of ethical standards is Chetwyn (who according to McKendrick believes 'that Aristotle got it more or less right, and St Augustine brought it up to date', p. 46). Faced with moral dilemmas which prove troublesome to clever philosophers, Chetwyn echoes Hollar in appealing to the ethical judgement of a child: 'A good rule, I find, is to try them out on men much *less* clever than us. I often ask my son what *he* thinks' (p. 79). The thought is picked up the next day by Anderson in his address when he says that the small child who cries 'that's not fair' is appealing to a sense of natural justice and that 'when, let us say, we are being persuaded that it is ethical to put someone in prison for reading or writing the wrong books, it is well to be reminded that you can persuade a man to believe almost anything provided he is clever enough, but it is much more difficult to persuade someone less clever' (p. 90). All of this precisely reiterates Stoppard's own explanation to an interviewer of all his 'political' plays:

> It seems to me that the point of view which these plays express is one which would be recognizable not merely to intellectuals but to an intelligent child – that something is self-evidently wrong.
>
> One of the things which complicates argument at the moment for me is that people are so clever that, paradoxically, they can be persuaded of almost anything. For example, if one were to say to an intelligent child the following: 'Life in East Germany is very agreeable, and there's a wall around it to keep people in,' the child would say, 'There's something wrong here.' But if you said it to a professor of political science or of political history, you'd have a much better chance of persuading him that what you said isn't nonsensical.[18]

If Hollar's appeal to the example of a child simply asserts the existence of innate rights as a self-evident – even an elementary – truth, Chetwyn's philosophical function within the play goes a step further to provide one explanation of the source of such an immutable standard. Twitting Anderson for ethical fastidiousness, McKendrick describes Anderson as 'a worse case than Chetwyn and his primitive Greeks' because Chetwyn actually *believes* in 'goodness and beauty' whereas 'you know they're fictions but you're so hung up on them you want to treat them as if they were God-given absolutes' (p. 78). However simplistic it may seem to McKendrick to believe that right and wrong ultimately have a divine genesis, it is the philosophic position which Stoppard confesses he has – reluctantly – been drawn to:

> I've always felt that whether or not 'God-given' means anything, there has to be an ultimate external reference for our actions. Our view of good behaviour *must* not be relativist. The difference between moral rules and the rules of tennis is that the rules of tennis can be changed. I think it's a dangerous idea that what

constitutes 'good behaviour' depends on social conventions –
dangerous and unacceptable. That led me to the conclusion,
not reached all that willingly, that if our behaviour is open to
absolute judgement, there must be an absolute judge.[19]

Whatever the playwright's personal attraction to Chetwyn's
belief in God as a progenitor of moral values, the protagonist
of *Professional Foul* – Professor Anderson – asserts that all human
beings have an obligation to adhere to moral standards whether
or not those standards have a divine genesis.[20] In his pivotal
address to the philosophy colloquium, Anderson quotes both the
American Constitution written by Founding Fathers who claimed
inalienable rights as the 'endowment of God', and the Constitution
of Czechoslovakia which of course makes no appeal to a divine
progenitor. Nevertheless, Anderson finds in both a 'consensus'
as to what constitutes an individual's right, what constitutes
fair and sensible treatment.[21] 'Is such a consensus remarkable?',
Anderson asks rhetorically, 'Not at all. If there is a God, we his
creations would doubtless subscribe to his values. And if there
is not a God, he, our creation, would undoubtedly be credited
with values which we think to be fair and sensible' (p. 89).
What clearly emerges from such a consensus is Stoppard's
overarching concern that good behaviour does not just consist
of 'club rules' which can be changed at will. Anderson enables
Stoppard to sidestep the question of whether moral absolutes do
or do not have a divine source while firmly maintaining that
such standards are universal, paramount, and immutable. While
Anderson's philosophical reservations about imputing objective
Platonic existence to ethics enables Stoppard to establish the
pre-eminence of moral values for theists and non-theists alike,
Stoppard's own pronouncements on the subject contain no hint
that the ethics on which we base our actions may be 'fictions'
which we should treat 'as if they were truths'. Instead, an axiom-
atic assertion of the immutable character of moral truth informs
Stoppard's pronouncements that the difference between 'a decent
way to govern people and an indecent way' is 'absolute' and will
endure the ravages of time.[22]
The absolute difference between a decent and an indecent
way of governing people is likewise the subject of Stoppard's
drama on the Soviet regime. In *Every Good Boy Deserves Favour* the
imprisonment and torture of Alexander for expressing a politically

unpopular truth is described not as 'inhumane' or 'antisocial' or even 'oppressive' but as 'wicked' (p. 35). With access only to a typescript of the play Kenneth Tynan quite accurately observed that '"E.G.B.D.F." rests on the assumption that the difference between good and evil is obvious to any reasonable human being'.[23] Even when Alexander's young son, acting out of an understandable human desire to have his father home, sounds the repeated refrain 'Papa, don't be rigid! Be brave and tell them lies!' (p. 35), Alexander bases his actions on a firm sense of what is right and wrong rather than what is politically expedient. To lie and say that barbaric treatment had been satisfactory, that the indecent is decent 'helps them to go on being wicked', Alexander tells his son, 'It helps people to think that perhaps they're not so wicked after all' (p. 35). The injunction not to be rigid runs like a leitmotif throughout the work. But it is the rigidity of absolute moral values which explains Alexander's actions. What the Soviets 'call their liberty', Alexander says, 'is just the freedom to agree/ that one and one is sometimes three' (pp. 34–5). Against a backdrop of such double-think, Alexander's refusal to condone wickedness and Sacha's school lessons come together in Alexander's insistence to his son that 'one and one is always two' (p. 36), that moral truths are as absolute as mathematical truths.

In *Professional Foul* and in *Every Good Boy Deserves Favour*, Stoppard attempts to demonstrate a universal consensus as to what constitutes fairness, goodness, ethical behaviour. Within the two works, Stoppard cites the American Constitution, the Czech Constitution, and the Soviet Constitution which all guarantee 'freedom of religious observance, of expression, of the press, and of assembly' (*Professional Foul*, p. 88; see also *EGBDF*, p. 29). However, by concentrating on the abuse of such ethical standards by the leftist regimes of the Soviet Union and Czechoslovakia, Stoppard has been accused by some of taking a 'reactionary' stance.[24] Stoppard's 1978 *Night and Day* raises the issues of freedom of expression and of the press in a drama which leads us to 'think about journalism on the level of social philosophy'.[25] As an exploration of the philosophic basis of political freedoms, *Night and Day* forms a coherent grouping with Stoppard's other 'political' plays. However, by dealing with British journalists of various political persuasions covering a Communist-supported insurrection in a mythical right-wing African country, Stoppard is able to dramatise abuses against free expression by ideological

adherents of both the right and the left. Thus, *Night and Day* reveals
– more clearly in some ways than any other play in his canon – that
what concerns Stoppard is not the comparison of one ruthless
regime with another but the universal moral standard which can
be brought to bear on each.

Further, while a moral standard derived from 'individual acts
between individuals' is applied to national and political issues in
all of his plays of the late 1970s, *Night and Day* both brings such a
standard to bear on journalism and deals – more extensively than
do the other plays – with individual acts between individuals. In
its more ambitious attempt to depict the female character, Ruth,
as well as in its presentation of the illicit attraction between Ruth
and the idealistic journalist Milne, *Night and Day* anticipates in
several important ways Stoppard's concerns in his more complex,
and more successful, exploration of love in *The Real Thing*.

Stoppard's title assumes a provocatively wide range of significances in the course of the play. Within the context of
the love story, the title *Night and Day* suggests the contrast
between consciousness and unconsciousness, between waking
and dreaming, between reality and fantasy. The title thus relates
to the elaborate exploration Stoppard makes between the public
words of Ruth and the private fantasizings of 'Ruth'. Indeed,
the principled young journalist Milne describes the realm of
erotic fantasizing as 'a parallel world. No day or night, no
responsibilities, no friction, almost no gravity' (p. 67). Like Annie
in *The Real Thing*, Ruth attempts to offer an apologia for adultery.
As opposed to such a fantasy world, Milne insists – in words
which roughly anticipate the stance of Henry – that in actuality
moral obligations and responsibilities are as real as the physical
realities of gravity or night and day. Thus, however attractive an
adulterous liaison with Ruth might be, the attempt to deny the
reality of guilt is – Milne insists – illusory. Although Ruth tries
to shrug off the 'post-coital remorse' she had experienced with
the flippant rhetorical question 'it's a bit metaphysical to feel guilt
about the idea of Geoffrey being hurt if Geoffrey is in a blissful
state of ignorance – don't you think?', Milne brings her up short
with the blunt reply, 'No'. 'You shouldn't try to make it sound
like a free ride', Milne explains, '"Geoffrey will never know and
I'm not his chattel so there's nothing to pay." There are no free
rides. You always pay' (pp. 68, 69).

Dismissing Ruth's sophisticated apologia for adultery, Milne

anticipates Henry's rejection of 'debonair relationships' as a
bogus substitute for the real thing. As in that later play, *Night
and Day* includes an extended scene which at first appears to
be taking place in real time and space and is only shown subsequently to have been imaginative. Unfortunately, the distinction
between waking reality and the fantasy scene in *Night and Day*
never became as clear as Stoppard had intended it.[26] Further,
Milne's ringing rejection of adulterous 'free rides' as a deceptive
fantasy is – we ultimately realise – not delivered in real time at
all but occurs after his death in a scene only imagined by Ruth.
Although some of the ideas Milne expresses may come to receive
much firmer support in *The Real Thing*, within *Night and Day* itself
it is very difficult to know how much weight to accord to ideas
which consist of Ruth's imaginings of what Milne might have
said. Nevertheless, in suggesting that extra-marital relationships
cannot be dismissed as a 'free ride' but are subject to immutable
standards of right and wrong, Stoppard's first serious attempt to
explore the nature of romantic love is linked thematically to his
exploration of the moral foundations of journalistic endeavour.

However, the contrast between the moral imperative of free
expression and various ideological imperatives which would
restrict the flow of information provides the fulcrum of *Night
and Day*. Despite Dean's assertion that *Night and Day* is an 'attack
against the entire journalistic system',[27] Stoppard has repeatedly
made clear that Milne's defence of free journalism and Guthrie's
blazing affirmation that information is light 'utterly speak for
me'.[28] 'No matter how imperfect things are', Milne says in words
which carry the ring of authorial endorsement, 'if you've got a
free press everything is correctable, and without it everything is
concealable' (p. 60). Stoppard is adamant in insisting not just that
he agrees with Milne but that 'what Milne says is true'. 'I mean it
is true', the playwright asserts, 'I believe it to be a true statement.
Milne has my prejudice if you like. Somehow unconsciously, I
wanted him to be known to be speaking the truth.'[29]

Ranged against the idealistic Milne are formidable adver-
saries of both the political right and the political left. President
Mageeba of Kambawe may be a virulent anti-Communist ready
to dispense death to any 'communist jackal' (p. 86). Veteran
journalist Richard Wagner may spout leftist rhetoric (the jargon
of 'the house Trots', p. 37) in championing trade unions which
issue the call 'workers of the world unite' (p. 93). But in the

course of the play we see that both Mageeba and Wagner are willing to violate the basic rights of others when their respective ideologies demand it. Rather than allow a non-union reporter to publish exclusive information from Kambawe in the London *Globe*, Wagner would close down publication 'in the country that began the whole idea of the right to publish' (p. 39). And rather than permit the publication of 'naked scepticism' about his anti-Communist regime, Mageeba has assured himself that the only English language newspaper in Kambawe will be 'responsible and relatively free'. 'Do you know what I mean by a relatively free press, Mr Wagner?' Kambawe's President Mageeba thunders, 'I mean a free press which is edited by one of my relatives' (p. 85). The line, which precedes Mageeba's slashing attack on Wagner, invariably gets a laugh. But back of the joke lies Stoppard's realisation that any attempt to rationalise a 'relatively free' press is just a semantic obfuscation for totalitarian control of information. The difference between free access to information and autocratic control of information is not, and can never be, relative. Indeed, the absolute nature of the gulf which separates on the one hand the illumination offered by the press, the beneficence of information which 'in itself, about anything, is light' and, on the other hand, the totalitarian repression of 'places where everybody is kept in the dark' (p. 92) is an unnoted significance of the play's title. The difference is not relative; the difference is absolute: the difference is that of *Night and Day*.

If *Night and Day* demonstrates the need not for a 'relatively free' press but for freedom of the press as a moral obligation which is absolute, *Dogg's Hamlet, Cahoot's Macbeth* turns to the absolute moral obligations for freedom of expression and freedom of assembly. Assembling in private homes to see underground, unauthorised performances of Shakespeare, the Czech actors and audience in *Cahoot's Macbeth* confront a repressive political regime which Stoppard's play and, implicitly, Shakespeare's play within the play, reveal as morally bankrupt. Banquo's condemnation of Macbeth proves specifically applicable to the Czech regime as Cahoot barks the words at the totalitarian inspector:

> Thou hast it now: King, Cawdor, Glamis, all
> As the weird sisters promised . . .
> . . . and I fear
> thou playedst most foully for't . . .

> . . . Yet it was said
> It should not stand in thy posterity . . .
>   (pp. 61, 62)

The inspector of course recognises the applicability of the condemnation – that the totalitarian regime's grasp of absolute political power through brute force is most foul and insupportable – and calls Cahoot's quotation of the Shakespearean text a violation of the law of slander. Shakespeare's *Macbeth*, that is, offers a moral matrix, a timeless standard against which human actions can be measured.

A sense of right and wrong, of absolute moral values, does not simply provide a basis for evaluation and judgement but a basis for action. In *Jumpers* the word of moral philosophy always remained separate, distinct from embodiment in the world of action. But in Stoppard's 'political' plays the perception of right and wrong is made manifest in right-acting: here the word of moral philosophy is made flesh in moral action. Further, when characters in recent Stoppard plays do act on the basis of moral principles, that action frequently proves effectual. Whether naïvely or not, the playwright who in *Jumpers* could reveal the inefficacy of correct belief when not enfleshed in moral action here celebrates the efficacy of moral action.

George Moore in *Jumpers* and Anderson in *Professional Foul* provide a most instructive comparison. Both are British moral philosophers with a rather tentative grasp on everyday realities. To be sure, Anderson's announced topic 'Ethical Fictions as Ethical Foundations' indicates, as Richard J. Buhr has shown,[30] that Anderson does not claim divine origin for moral values as does George. But both George and Anderson are ethicists, both are preparing to deliver scholarly disquisitions on ethics to a gathering of philosophers, both suffer from a sort of absent-minded bumbling, and in both cases such bumbling reveals a myopic inability to see beyond the narrow realm of philosophical argumentation. Anderson is initially oblivious to the realities of Pavel Hollar's plight in much the same way that George remains oblivious to the murder in *Jumpers*. Anderson begins the play, like George, hermetically sealed in his world of philosophical argumentation. In requesting that Anderson smuggle out a doctoral thesis advocating individual freedom, Hollar in essence turns to a philosophical colleague to plead – in the words of *Jumpers* – 'Professor – it's not right . . . Help!' But like George before him, Anderson – though an ethicist – refuses to take personal ethical action. Indeed, Anderson's excuse that such action would be a breach of good manners against the Czech government echoes George's own excuse, 'Well, this seems to be a political quarrel'.[31]

With the refusal of a philosophical ethicist to take immediate ethical action, *Professional Foul* thus begins where the 'Coda' of *Jumpers* concludes. '*Professional Foul* and *Jumpers*', Stoppard explains, 'can each be described as a play about a moral philosopher preoccupied with the true nature of absolute morality, trying to separate absolute values from local ones and local situations'.[32] However, unlike the earlier play, here the reality of Czech oppression and of Hollar's personal plight does come home to Anderson; the Oxbridge don does come to respond both to Hollar's personal plight and to his philosophical position. When Anderson does dare to respond personally, his efforts prove to be efficacious. Anderson does not just try to smuggle Hollar's manuscript out of Czechoslovakia; he accomplishes the task. One more voice will be heard: the thinking of one more individual from Eastern Europe will be given free expression in the West. Further, Anderson changes the address which he is to present at the Philosophy Colloquium by incorporating Hollar's thesis that the collective ethic espoused by the state must be judged against 'a sense of right and wrong which precedes utterance' (p. 90), a sense of what is right in one individual's dealings with another individual. And by virtue of its direct challenge to the existing political regime – Anderson quotes from the rights guaranteed by the Constitution of Czechoslovakia, thereby paralleling the approach of the real-life Czechs who drafted the historic Charter 77 – the very process of issuing a defence of the ethical basis for action becomes, itself, an example of ethical action.

Thus, whereas George's philosophising in *Jumpers* was always divorced from action, Stoppard is here able to portray the very act of delivering a philosophical address as being itself an act of moral courage. Indeed, Anderson's address stands at the structural centre of *Professional Foul* in much the same role that Stoppard had originally intended for George's address to the colloquium in *Jumpers*.[33] However, Anderson's address is not only dominating by virtue of its position in the play, it also serves as the synthesis of the play's entire range of ideas. From Hollar, Anderson accepts the primary thrust of his speech that the collective ethic must be based on the individual ethic. From Chetwyn, Anderson accepts the notion of natural justice which is apparent even to a child. From McKendrick, Anderson accepts [only] the premise that moral dilemmas do exist, but we should not see Anderson as endorsing the full range of McKendrick's views. Although McKendrick had argued that 'there aren't any principles in your sense' (p. 78), Anderson's chastened acknowledgement that 'there would be no moral dilemmas if moral principles worked in straight lines and never crossed each other' (p. 79) is conciliatory in tone but still maintains the conviction that however tangled there are moral principles. In a further synthesis of other ideas offered in the play, Anderson specifically rejects Stone's linguistic analysis approach which would hold that justice has no existence outside the ways in which we choose to employ the word. By moving beyond the paralytic philosophising of George, Anderson does not 'abandon' absolute moral principles as Buhr maintains.[34] Rather, by allowing his ethical values to become the foundations of his actions, he finds the moral courage to act upon that which he had previously only believed.

Professional Foul, as Stoppard describes it, depicts 'a man being educated by experience beyond the education he's received from thinking'.[35] Anderson's 'thinking' had led to his intellectual assent to ethical standards as 'fictions' but not to his visceral affirmation of the unbridgeable gulf between good and bad behaviour. Anderson has 'a perfectly respectable philosophical thesis', says Stoppard, 'and he encounters a mother and a child who are victims of this society, and it cuts through all the theory'. Like McFee witnessing the cold-blooded victimisation of Oates on the moon, Anderson is forced to realise that if this is what evil is really like his ethical fictions argument is up a gum-tree. 'I wanted to write about somebody coming from England to a totalitarian society', Stoppard explains, 'brushing up against it, and getting a little soiled and a little wiser'. But in becoming wiser, Anderson is not abandoning but is rather embracing at an experiential level the importance of absolute moral values. At the outset of the play 'Anderson produces his arguments about

why he shouldn't act', says Stoppard, 'and then what happens
is something extremely simple . . . he just brushes up against the
specific reality of the mother and the child, especially the child'.[36]
What happens in the course of the play is not that Anderson
abandons absolute moral values; rather he comes to abandon
dispassionate academic detachment as he recognises that the
irredeemable difference between right and wrong requires him
to act.

Whereas George in *Jumpers* does not act, and Anderson discovers in the course of *Professional Foul* his own capacity for
moral action, *Every Good Boy Deserves Favour* chronicles a person
who has already chosen a course of moral action before the play
begins. Alexander is a political prisoner in a mental hospital
because – to use a pun which runs throughout the work –
he did something 'really crazy': he had the nerve to tell the
truth. He had written a series of letters – 'To his superiors.
To the Party. To the newspapers' – saying that sane people
were put in mental hospitals. Although Alexander's dissent is
represented metaphorically within the symphonic *Every Good Boy
Deserves Favour* as a discordant note in an orchestrated society, it
is clear that his actions spring neither from non-conformist self-
indulgence nor from a pragmatic sense of what is feasible but from
a firm sense of moral right and wrong. The doctor tells Alexander
that he could be released if he would agree that he had been mad
and that his treatment has been satisfactory (p. 28). However, as
his nine-year-old son Sacha declares, 'Papa doesn't lie' (p. 24).
Stoppard explicitly voices his concern that moral values must
be incarnated in moral action in Alexander's declaration that
'There are truths to be shown, and our only strength is personal
example'. The line, contained in an earlier typescript of *Every
Good Boy Deserves Favour*, was perhaps deleted because it was too
explicit.[37] Celebrating an individual who adheres to a standard of
values higher than that of his society and who has the courage to
act upon those values, Stoppard here creates, for the first time in
his dramatic canon, a modern saint's play.

Surely, the affirmation that the repeated sounding of truth
– by however weak a voice – can ultimately disrupt the most
elaborately orchestrated lie is one of the strongest notes sounded

by *Every Good Boy Deserves Favour*. The stage may be awash in an ocean of red; the orchestra may fill both our field of vision and (when we are permitted) our hearing. Still, a single triangle – insistently struck – can prevail over the entire performance. The 'subversive triangle' played by nine-year-old Sacha repeatedly 'sabotages' the orchestra just as his guileless statements of truth – 'A plane area bordered by high walls is a prison not a hospital' – give the lie to the larger society.

More crucially we see that the Soviet attempts to orchestrate conformity are ultimately sabotaged by Alexander's insistent sounding of truth even in the face of imminent death. In the concluding scene the Soviet colonel who has taken charge of Alexander's case makes a brief appearance, asks Alexander a question appropriate for Ivanov, asks Ivanov a question appropriate for Alexander and promptly releases both men. Alexander, who steadfastly refuses to condone the unconscionable, is again free.

Lest such an ending appear facile in light of Soviet power, it is supported by Stoppard's own experiences. In early 1977 while Stoppard was writing *Every Good Boy Deserves Favour*, Vaclav Havel – a dissident Czech playwright – refused to quietly accept an exit visa and forced the Czech regime to face deporting him if they wished to get rid of him. On 7 February 1977 Stoppard wrote to *The Times* regarding Havel: 'The Czech Government now has to choose between two opposite embarrassments; to pursue the logic of repression, or to climb down.'[38] That historic choice which faced the actual Czech regime is precisely the choice which faces the Soviet regime in Stoppard's play. Alexander says of the Soviet authorities' response to his hunger strike: 'They don't like you to die unless you can die anonymously. If your name is known in the West, it is an embarrassment' (p. 24).[39]

However, Stoppard's elegantly brief resolution of *Every Good Boy Deserves Favour* has been perceived by several reviewers as a revelation of 'bureaucratic confusion'.[40] Although Stoppard insists that in the play as he wrote it 'the colonel knew exactly what he was doing', he acknowledges that at the play's première – a single performance in the Royal Festival Hall – 'it was apparent that a lot of people misunderstood the way that the last scene was played: they thought the colonel had made a mistake'.[41] When the play entered a second production at the Mermaid Theatre in June 1978, Stoppard staged the final scene differently 'to make sure that it was understood that the colonel understood what he was doing'.[42] But still some members of the audience did not understand. Protesting that 'I really thought we had it licked for the Mermaid', Stoppard confessed to a *Times* reporter in August 1978, 'I'm baffled that a substantial number of people still misunderstand the ending'.[43]

Although Stoppard does not mention all of the changes which were made in the way the last scene was staged, by the end of the Mermaid run in October 1978 the doctor was frantically gesticulating to call the attention of the colonel to the correct identities of the prisoners while the colonel was suavely – and quite deliberately – ignoring him. While changing the staging of the final scene, however, Stoppard made no textual changes for the Mermaid production. 'I didn't change the play', Stoppard insisted, 'it was just that we changed the way it was acted in order to make the play I wrote clearer'.[44] Despite Stoppard's tinkering with the scene to make sure that viewers would recognise that the colonel 'knew exactly what he was doing', despite Stoppard's repeated insistence in interviews published in 1978 and 1980 that anyone who fails to see that the colonel's actions are deliberate has simply 'misunderstood' the ending, critics have continued to bumble into the mistake that the colonel had merely bumbled into a mistake.[45]

Although Londré has corrected Cahn's egregious assertion that Alexander joins the orchestra,[46] she – like Cahn – fails to recognise that the Soviet colonel is aware of the identities of the two men he appears to confuse.[47] Such a misperception of the play has been widespread. 'Like many people seeing the first production at the Royal Festival Hall', Michael Billington confesses in his recent book, 'I myopically concluded that the Colonel himself was acting out of confusion'.[48] If Billington has distanced himself from his initial myopia, Corballis wilfully praises the advantages of being short-sighted. Despite being aware of Stoppard's repeated statements that the Colonel purposefully releases the prisoners, Corballis even maintains that a New Zealand staging in which the Colonel does make a mistake through 'stupidity and pride'' provides an 'interpretation [which] seems to me as effective as Stoppard's own'.[49] Such a line of reasoning both perversely ignores authorial intentions for the scene and is at odds with the tone of the rest of the play. If Alexander is simply released through bureaucratic confusion then we should simply laugh at the comic ineptness of the Soviet regime and dismiss Alexander's long years of heroic resistance as well-meaning but ineffectual. Such a play might be good for a few laughs – and Kennedy would have some basis for talking about a 'non-absurd vision of absurdity'[50] – but it would be fundamentally different from the work Stoppard wrote which is at once more menacing and more bracing than a farcical exposé of bureaucratic bungling.

In retrospect, it is possible to see Stoppard's preparation for the release throughout the play. In his second conversation with Ivanov, Alexander asserts that his transfer from the Special Psychiatric Hospital to a civil hospital 'means they have decided to let me go'. 'But it has to be done right', Alexander explains, 'They don't want to lose ground. They need a formula' (p. 25). The Colonel, a semanticist, is placed in charge of Alexander's case not because 'the powers in charge are seeking to control Alex's [sic] language and thereby to control his thinking'[51] but precisely because the Soviets are looking for a semantic 'formula' to save face while already preparing for capitulation. We learn first that the Colonel personally chose Alexander's cell-mate (p. 27) and then that the certifiably mad Ivanov (whose first name is Alexander) was chosen as a cell-mate for the political dissident Alexander (whose second name is Ivanov) precisely because their names are identical (p. 32). The confusion of names which enables Alexander's release is part of a deliberate attempt to find a formula for releasing a prisoner who has become an embarrassment. Such a release – when it does come – is not a fluke of confusion.[52] Precisely because the release is not a fluke, however, Billington concludes that 'the ending of the play is thus not a happy one and Bernard Levin was wrong to conclude that it triumphantly says "the gates of hell shall not prevail"'.[53]

Bernard Levin may have been overly sanguine in not acknowledging the continuing monolithic power of those gates but he was certainly right to recognise that an overriding purpose of the play 'is to call evil evil'.[54] Billington ignores the fact that a victory, even if a qualified victory, has been won. Stoppard's play shows the terrible cost to get even one prisoner released and after his release tens of thousands of human beings remain entrapped behind those gates. In 1980 Stoppard told an interviewer that *Every Good Boy Deserves Favour* 'ends with the prisoners being released, but it's not a particularly optimistic ending. It's based on the experiences of somebody I know, a friend of mine who was also released, because they found that they simply couldn't break him, and he was such an embarrassment that they really were dying to get rid of him and they were offering him all kinds of compromises. He wouldn't, he just didn't take any of them, and in the end they threw him out.'[55]

That Alexander's release is an occasion for celebration but not just for celebration is also clear from the dilemma which faces Alexander at the end of the play. Alexander's courageous refusal to recant – even at the risk of his own life – has forced the Soviets to back down. However the Soviet colonel, as Brassell rightly notes, 'ensures that Alexander's release is not obtained on his own terms'[56] by the deliberate use of a semantic equivocation. 'The final anguish', in the words of a *Times* reporter after interviewing Stoppard, is caused by Alexander 'having to decide whether to go along with that ploy in order to gain his freedom'.[57] That Alexander's release is a victory and an occasion for celebration is certainly true. But the ending of *Every Good Boy Deserves Favour* emphasises not the bureaucratic bungling of a comically inept empire but one limited victory – at great personal cost – over the sovereign and arbitrary power of an evil regime.

Just as Hollar in *Professional Foul* and Alexander in *Every Good Boy Deserves Favour* endanger their lives by freely expressing dangerous opinions, so in *Night and Day* we see journalists who endanger their lives in order to obtain and transmit information. Once again Stoppard is dealing with the philosophic basis of free expression and with the actual expressing of such an imperative in action. 'I was very interested in the idea of people risking their lives for what was, in the real world, a commercial enterprise', Stoppard says, 'After all, if you were selling Leyland cars, and you felt you could sell six Morris Marinas in Managua if you could just get through to the showroom . . . I mean, you wouldn't think, I'll get into a crouch and just run in a zig-zag manner to the Leyland dealer, and I'll sell six more Marinas. But a guy who's working for a newspaper, at the end of one of those lines of connection, is merely working for a different set of shareholders. In a sense. Obviously he's not.'[58] Stoppard is not just holding a moral mirror up to the suppression of free journalistic inquiry, he is also presenting individuals who act out their beliefs. Against insuperable odds, Milne in *Night and Day* does get the story and does get it out.

If information is light, Milne has probed the totalitarian regime of Mageeba with one more illuminating laser before his own life is snuffed out. Milne's willingness to act, his willingness to put his own life on the line 'in a sense confirms', Stoppard insists, 'the truth which he becomes a martyr to'.[59]

In *Dogg's Hamlet, Cahoot's Macbeth*, Stoppard returns to a question first raised in *Travesties*: 'whether an artist has to justify himself in political terms *at all*', 'whether the words "revolutionary" and "artist" are capable of being synonymous, or whether they are mutually exclusive, or something in between' ('Ambushes', pp. 16, 11). *Cahoot's Macbeth*, however, shows more clearly than ever before that while art need not be political, the two need not be mutually exclusive. Ironically, it is the totalitarian inspector who articulates most forcibly the moral and political power of art: 'The fact is, when you get a universal and timeless writer like Shakespeare, there's a strong feeling that he could be spitting in the eyes of the beholder' (p. 60). In demonstrating the incompatibility of universal and timeless art with a totalitarian political regime, Stoppard surely levels his primary attack at the moral and intellectual bankruptcy of totalitarianism. But the play also serves, implicitly, as a reply to those who have called for an overtly political theatre as the only way of demonstrating the social relevance of art. Because Stoppard defends such plays as *Jumpers* and *Travesties* which do not set out to rectify specific social problems, Philip Roberts has accused Stoppard of refusing 'to believe in the efficacy, in any sense, of theatre to affect anything, including an audience'. As opposed to the overt political statements of Edward Bond (which he prefers), Roberts sees Stoppard's defence of a universal and timeless art as creating a theatre which is 'diversionary and not central . . . a soother of worried minds and not an irritant'.[60]

Stoppard turns the tables on such critics in *Dogg's Hamlet, Cahoot's Macbeth* by showing the immediate political relevance of the moral matrix established by the timeless universal art of Shakespeare. In condemning the indirectness – the universality – of Stoppard's art, Roberts puts himself, ironically, in the position of agreeing with the chief of the totalitarian force: 'The chief says he'd rather you stood up and said, "There is no freedom in this country", then there's nothing underhand and we all know where we stand' (p. 60). As opposed to such overt political statements the universal art which Stoppard both celebrates and creates establishes a moral matrix from which to judge totalitarian repression. 'What we don't like', the inspector says, 'is a lot of people being cheeky and saying they are only Julius Caesar or Coriolanus or Macbeth' (p. 60).

The Czech troupe which performs *Macbeth* in the teeth of repression by Czech troops is not only engaged in the celebration of art but in an act of political dissidence. Further, they are – to use a word which has throughout Stoppard's drama acquired a depth of resonance – *acting*. As opposed to George who believes in moral values but does not take moral action, the Czech troupe's production of *Macbeth* at one and the same time constitutes artistic action, political action, and moral action. The philosophic word of moral truth is here enfleshed in moral action as surely as the words of Shakespeare are enfleshed in the living performance.

Correct though Salmon is in asserting the existence of 'Faith in Tom Stoppard',[61] such faith as exists in those earlier plays remains inert, unenacted. In Stoppard's subsequent plays that same faith in the spiritual nature of mankind and the moral nature of human behaviour becomes enfleshed in action. Thus in *Every Good Boy Deserves Favour* and in *Professional Foul*, in *Night and Day* and *Dogg's Hamlet, Cahoot's Macbeth*, the suppression of individual freedom is seen not as counter-revolutionary or anti-social or unpopular or inhumane but as simply, irredeemably wrong. In these plays the advocacy of a philosophic position has been replaced by the practical application of the philosophic position. But such a transformation from precept to praxis shows organic growth rather than violent uprooting within the body of Stoppard's work.

'Something which has preoccupied me for a long time', says Stoppard emphasising the continuity of his work, 'is the desire to simplify questions and take the sophistication out'. The irreducible core Stoppard is left with when he takes the sophistication out has 'to do with the morality between individuals'. And on such irreducible matters of morality, Stoppard asserts, 'I haven't been writing about questions whose answers I believe to be ambivalent. In *Every Good Boy* and *Professional Foul*, the author's position isn't ambiguous.'[62] In the moral philosopher's assertion of 'a sense of right and wrong which precedes utterance'; in the Russian dissident's insistence that moral absolutes are as immutable as mathematical laws; in the journalist's affirmation of free expression as a moral right which transcends the ideologies of both totalitarianism and union politics; in the actors' holding up Shakespeare as a timeless standard against which the acts of a regime can be judged – we see revealed Stoppard's affirmation of the primacy of moral values, the conviction that all political acts have a moral basis and must be judged in moral terms. Stoppard's characters, as well, demonstrate an organic continuity with, rather than a radical departure from their predecessors. In the British moral philosopher who comes to the aid of his Czech colleague, the Russian dissenter who holds fast to that which is true, the journalist who dies in the pursuit of the truth, the Czech actors who defy political repression by assembling to enact art, Stoppard creates characters in whom the philosophic tenets of moral belief become enfleshed in moral action, characters in whose lives the word becomes flesh.

6

'Not of the Flesh but Through the Flesh': Knowing and Being Known in *The Real Thing*

That Tom Stoppard's plays are neither imprecise nor obscurantist, that his ambiguities are intended neither to dazzle nor confuse but 'to be precise over a greater range of events', was perhaps the most signal contribution of Clive James's 1975 *Encounter* article: 'It is the plurality of contexts that concerns Stoppard: ambiguities are just places where contexts join.'[1] And in *The Real Thing* the interstices come between art and life. Stoppard's attempt, a breathtakingly ambitious one, is to deal at once with what is real in life, what is real in art, and what the real differences are between art and life. *The Real Thing* endeavours to distinguish the authentic from propagandistic imitations, the liveliness of the right words in the right order from the ham-fisted butchery of language, what endures as the marbled reality in an age that demands the poly-styrene, what endures as alabaster when the age demands plaster. But if the real thing exists in life and the real thing exists in art, the differences between life and art remain no less real. Indeed the very form of *The Real Thing*, opening as it does with a play within a play serves to dramatise the differences between reality and imaginative reality.

The contrast between the real and the imaginative accounts for the genesis not only of the play's form but for the emergence of a playwright as its protagonist. 'I've just finished a play', Stoppard told an American audience in March 1982, 'which is about a playwright – not for reasons of autobiographical megalomania'.[2] Rather, Stoppard continued, 'I wanted to write a play in which the first scene turns out to have been written by one of the characters in the second scene and consequently he had to be a playwright of course.'

As the curtain rises on that first scene, *The Real Thing* seems
the direct opposite of Stoppard's earlier plays. Whereas *Jumpers*
and *Travesties* begin with a 'pig's breakfast'[3] of incongruous,
seemingly random images, *The Real Thing* opens on a seemingly
straightforward domestic scene. At second glance, the plays
appear to be mirror images of each other. In *Jumpers* and *Travesties*
we gradually learn that the seemingly unreal opening scene is in
fact real; in *The Real Thing* we gradually learn that the seemingly
real is in fact imaginative, is a play within a play. But eventually
we should come to see – whether we begin with the seemingly
unreal and then learn that it is the real thing or whether we begin
with the seemingly real and then subsequently encounter the real
thing – that Tom Stoppard has been writing about real things for
quite some time now.

Even *Rosencrantz and Guildenstern are Dead* springs, as James
told us, from 'the perception – surely a compassionate one –
that the fact of their deaths mattering so little to Hamlet was
something which ought to have mattered to Shakespeare'.[4] If
such art is unarguably self-referential, what it is arguing for
is for a greater sympathy, and that in the sublimest of works,
for ordinary ramshackle humanity. At the heart of the extraordinary *Rosencrantz and Guildenstern* we find a celebration of the
merely ordinary. Just so, the bounding wit of *Jumpers*, endlessly
cartwheeling us from George's study to Dotty's bedroom, finally
leads us to see – as an urbane sophisticated world does not –
the validity of the insights of the ploddingly pedestrian George
who affirms the inherently moral nature of experience in the
real world; and to see – as George does not – the loneliness
and anguish of the pathetically real Dotty. In the intricately
erudite *Travesties* we find the ordinary decent consul Henry Carr
at the centre not only of the play's structure but of the play's
sympathy. If Joyce is celebrated, as he is, it is because his art
deals with the likes of Henry Carr, his art emerges from, even
immortalises, the real. Even more clearly, the more recent plays
deal with ordinary humanity in all their creatureliness: husbands
and wives, fathers and – again and again – sons. Just as George
in *Jumpers* may offer moral affirmations which are valid in theory
but which need to be demonstrated in practice, the tensions in
Professional Foul involve the disjunction between the realms of
Professor Anderson's abstract philosophising and the real world
of Pavel Hollar's wife and son. Stoppard has described the play

as an education by experience. Although Anderson may have 'a perfectly respectable philosophical thesis', Stoppard says, 'what happens is something extremely simple . . . he just brushes up against the specific reality of the mother and the child, especially the child'.[5] But in the disjunction between precept and practice, between moral abstractions and moral applications, there is not the absurdist assertion of a chaotic universe, nor the aesthete's withdrawal into sublimely stylish siren song, nor the obscurantist's perverse or inadvertent confusion. From the first, Stoppard's plays have depicted real people in real time and space rather than offering a surrealistic or absurdist vision of unreality.

The Real Thing's primary connection with the earlier plays is not just its verbal felicity (which many reviewers have noted) nor the naturalistic form which the play shares with *Night and Day*. *The Real Thing* – as remarkable for its emotional richness as for its wit – extends, deepens, and refines the concerns with which Stoppard has been dealing at least since *Jumpers*. Like *Jumpers*, *The Real Thing* depicts human experience as inherently, fundamentally moral. With equal clarity, the play affirms that the real thing exists in the realm of art and thus continues *Travesties'* concern with the difference between genuine and bogus art. Further, *The Real Thing* extends and deepens the concern in *Travesties* and *Dogg's Hamlet, Cahoot's Macbeth* over the connection between art and politics. If such plays as *Every Good Boy Deserves Favour* and *Professional Foul* narrowed the focus of the universal moral values adumbrated in *Jumpers* to an examination of the body politic and affirmed that 'the ethics of the State must be judged against the fundamental ethic of the individual' – that is, 'one man's dealings with another man' – *The Real Thing* narrows the focus still further precisely to the arena of one person's dealings with another person. Thus, the affirmation in *Jumpers* of moral absolutes; the apologia commenced in *Travesties* and continued in *Dogg's Hamlet, Cahoot's Macbeth* for art as a moral matrix; the application in *Every Good Boy Deserves Favour* and *Professional Foul* of moral judgement to the political arena; the assertion in *Night and Day* that corruption in language is connected with corruption in moral vision; all coalesce in *The Real Thing* with a deepened concern for the inherently moral commitment made between a man and a woman who know and are known by each other in the most intimate and most real of human relationships. Perhaps what *The Real Thing* most fundamentally shares with Stoppard's earlier plays is its assumption that reality exists, that life is meaningful, that the universe is not random or chaotic, that the difference between the real and the unreal, between the genuine and the artificial is knowable and that the real thing can be recognised.

Thus, if the opening causes the audience to experience disorientation, it also allows the audience to experience the shock of recognition. Hersh Zeifman's observation that the form of the play involves the audience viscerally in the questions being dealt with is undoubtedly correct.[6] We are taken in by that first scene. Indeed, it is not until some way into the second scene that we recognise the opening as having been a play within a play. But the point, surely, is that we can recognise the real thing when it comes along. If the play shows that appearances can be deceiving, that we may momentarily mistake the imaginative construct for actual reality, it also shows that we can recognise appearances for what they are – appearances. If it is sometimes difficult to tell the real from the ersatz, if the artificial can sometimes deceive us into believing it to be real, that in no way suggests that the real thing does not exist and cannot, upon discovery, be recognised.

The form of the play does not mystify, baffle, or confuse; it does not – as it is possible for a different sort of play to do – leave us up in the air as to which is the imaginative realm and which is actual experience, which is waking reality and which is the dream. Actually, in performance the play is surprisingly straightforward and easy to follow. Even the least sophisticated member of the audience would not emerge from Stoppard's play wondering if the opening scene about an architect were 'real' and the remaining two and a quarter hours constituted an elaborate play within a play. Perhaps, however, it must be ruefully noted that more sophisticated viewers may be taken in either by the play's form or by the sophistries which the play refutes. One of the things which complicates argument at the moment, as Stoppard has remarked elsewhere, 'is that people are so clever that, paradoxically, they can be persuaded of almost anything'.[7] Given the general level of academic twaddle about Stoppard as an 'absurdist', 'post-absurdist', or 'pan-parodist', we may yet encounter sophisticated academic nonsense about this play. Nevertheless, to emerge from *The Real Thing* with a sense that it is impossible to tell what is real and what is unreal within the play, one must be clever indeed.

Although disclaiming any autobiographical impulse behind the selection of a playwright as the protagonist for his play, Stoppard nevertheless reports that 'in the course of writing it, I found this man expressing some of the notions I have about writing', notions, he continued, 'which I probably will not disown in the near future'. Indeed, less than a week after finishing the play, Stoppard offered Henry's statements on writing to an American audience with the explanation that he would be 'reading them out as though they are mine'.[8]

The Real Thing's affirmation of art is rooted in a celebration of language, a celebration which extends Stoppard's previous concern that language not be subjected to the abuse of pedestrian cliché, political cant, or totalitarian obfuscation. Henry's role as guardian of the language at times takes the form of mere grammatical finickiness, the 'professional fastidiousness' of a playwright who corrects his guests' use of the gerund. However, when Henry objects to describing a conviction for arson as being 'hammered' by an emotional 'backlash',[9] he is not merely being pedantic. He is objecting to jargon which misrepresents real events, as well as objecting to the misuse of words in a mixed metaphor.

Such a concern for language extends the denunciation in *Night and Day* of both journalistic and political jargon, both the 'Lego-set language' of the London tabloids and the political cant of the trade unions. '"Betrayal" ... "Confrontation" ... "Management" ... My God, you'd need a more supple language than that to describe an argument between two amoebas', says Jacob Milne as he mimics the debased language which evicts 'ordinary English' when the 'house Trots' speak of a strike. More sweepingly, when the arsonist Brodie attempts to take up writing, Henry exposes the vacuity of his revolutionary rhetoric in what Roger Scruton rightly calls a 'masterly and devastating criticism of the radical butchery of language'[10]: 'I can't help somebody who thinks, or thinks he thinks, that editing a newspaper is censorship, or that throwing bricks is a demonstration while building tower blocks is social violence, or that unpalatable statement is provocation while disrupting the speaker is the exercise of free speech ... Words don't deserve that kind of malarkey' (p. 54). Eventually, however, Henry's celebration of words as 'innocent, neutral, precise, standing for this, describing that, meaning the other' not only affirms a connectedness between the word and the thing named but emerges as a sacramental view of language: 'I don't think writers are sacred, but words are' (p. 54).

Just as *Travesties* celebrates the 'immortality' of art 'that will dance for some time yet', *The Real Thing* celebrates the sacredness of words which can grant a form of immortality: 'If you get the right ones in the right order, you can . . . make a poem which children will speak for you when you're dead' (p. 54). Indeed, like *Travesties*, *The Real Thing* celebrates a non-propagandistic art, praises art which 'works' aesthetically whether or not it 'works' in terms of social utility, by, for example, securing the immediate release of prisoners. The two conceptions of art collide in the play's last scene in which Brodie sees a videotape of his own play in a version completely revised by Henry. When Annie, who had requested her husband Henry to rewrite Brodie's fumbling dialogue, says of the television play, 'It did work', Brodie – with no conception of how a play could 'work' aesthetically – asks uncomprehendingly, 'You mean getting me sprung?' 'No', Annie replies, 'I didn't mean that' (pp. 80–1). The difference between writing well and writing rubbish, between art which 'works' and plays 'which go "clunk" every time someone opens his mouth', springs not from the social or political importance of the subject ('something to write about, something real') or from the immediate social or political effect ('getting me sprung'), but from the liveliness or loutishness in the use of language, the carelessness or precision in putting words together.

The writer can 'get it right' or can fail to get it right. And the difference between the two is, in one of the memorable images of the play, as great as the difference between a cricket bat and a cudgel. 'This thing here', Henry says of the real thing, 'which looks like a wooden club, is actually several pieces of particular wood cunningly put together in a certain way so that the whole thing is sprung, like a dance floor' (p. 52). Both Henry's explanation of the intricate composition of the cricket bat (metaphorically 'well chosen words nicely put together') and his association of it with the dance recall Joyce's apologia in *Travesties* for art. By contrast, the turgid prose of Brodie's dialogue is a cudgel, 'a lump of wood of roughly the same shape trying to be a cricket bat, and if you hit a ball with it, the ball will travel about ten feet and you will drop the bat and dance about shouting "Ouch!" with your hands stuck into your armpits'. To demonstrate that the difference between the two (metaphorically the difference between 'good writing' and writing that is 'no good') is not just a matter of opinion, Henry points to Brodie's script and suggests that Annie try for herself: 'You don't believe me, so I suggest you go out to bat with this and see how you get on. "You're a strange boy, Billy, how old are you?" "Twenty, but I've lived more than you'll ever live." Ooh, ouch!' What Henry is suggesting, basically, is an education by experience. What he affirms, he argues, is not contingent on his skill in arguing, but is verifiable by experience, is – quite simply – true: 'This isn't better because someone says it's better', Henry insists, 'It's better because it's better' (p. 52).

Although *The Real Thing* continues to celebrate language, continues to associate complexity in composition and liveliness in writing with the dance, nevertheless implicit in the image of the cricket bat is a significant departure from some of Stoppard's previous descriptions of the genesis and purpose of art. If a cricket bat is 'for hitting cricket balls with', what, we may ask, is art 'for'? 'What we're trying to do', Henry explains, 'is to write cricket bats, so that when we throw up an idea and give it a little knock, it might . . . *travel*.' Art, as Henry explains it, is for launching ideas. Such a conception of art differs substantially from the much-quoted epigram Stoppard coined some years ago that 'plays are not the end-products of ideas, ideas are the end-products of plays'. More recently, however, when the quote came bouncing back to him from yet another interviewer, Stoppard tossed it aside as having 'the overstatement of most epigrams'. Indeed, that quip, Stoppard continued, 'of course . . . stopped being applicable round about the time I started writing *Jumpers*. There the play was the end-product of an idea as much as the converse.'[11] Just so, as Henry explains it, the idea seems to be pre-existent, to be already rolled up into, well, a ball, which the artist – if he wields his art lightly, forcefully, and well; if he avoids ham-fisted bludgeoning – can send soaring.

If Henry's explanation of the lofting of ideas demonstrates development in Stoppard's perspective on the genesis of art, Henry's reflections on the effect of art more profoundly clarify Stoppard's position from his treatment in previous plays of the connection between art and politics. Just as Tzara, in *Travesties*, could not change art into something it was not simply by abusing the word 'art', so in *The Real Thing* an artist cannot change 'politics, justice, patriotism' by trying to stick labels on them. However, Henry continues in clarification of what the artist can change, 'if you know this and proceed with humility, you may perhaps alter people's perceptions so that they behave a little differently at that axis of behaviour where we locate politics or justice' (pp. 53–4). Art, that is, can in some way effect social change toward justice. However, art is not useful in some kind of immediate way that gets Brodie free from prison next month. Rather, art is a civilising force, a humanising force, a 'moral matrix' as Stoppard told an interviewer in 1974, 'from which we make our judgments about the world'.[12]

If Joyce in *Travesties* affirmed art for art's sake, art completely removed from any kind of social or political obligations, art which exists in a separate realm where it 'will dance for some time yet and *leave the world precisely as it finds it*', Henry in *The Real Thing* affirms art which can both teach and delight, art which exists both in the realm of time and the timeless, the power of words with which an artist 'can nudge the world a little or make a poem which children will speak for you when you're dead'. Henry's climactic statement on art continues *Travesties'* affirmation that art need not be social, continues to see art as gratifying 'a hunger that is common to princes and peasants', or even children. However, the acknowledgement that art can 'nudge' the world, significantly, if modestly, extends Stoppard's claims for art. Social impact may not be art's major purpose; and art may not accomplish social change with immediate effect. Nevertheless, art need not leave the world precisely as it finds it; art can move the world, at least fractionally; and that movement can be in the direction of justice. Henry's climactic statements on art thus conflate a number of themes from the play. The world that is there to be nudged is real; a world in which people need to act with justice is inherently moral; and art, by faithfully reflecting the real world, can enable people to see the real world and their own actions with greater precision, to act with greater comprehension and clarity.

Thus, however distinct the plane of imaginative reality may be from reality, there are, finally, interconnections between them. There are points at which the aesthetic intersects the epistemo-logical and even the ethical. Distortions in one plane can lead to distortions in the other planes. Abuse of words in writing can lead to a warped vision of the real world, a bent toward seeing justice as fraud, property as theft, patriotism as propaganda, religion as a con trick (p. 53).[13] And such skewed perception of the real world can lead to the acting out of prejudice, to behaviour in the ethical plane which is likewise skewed. Thus clarity of artistic vision is not, finally, divorced from accuracy of epistemological perception or even from rightness of ethical action. Writing aright can lead, or can help lead, or – to put it as modestly as possible – can 'nudge' human beings 'a little' towards acting aright in the real world.

Stoppard's vision of the intersecting planes of the aesthetic, the epistemological, and the ethical may be intricate – and intricacy may characterise the art which bodies forth such complexity – but what it is not is chaotic. To abandon precision in epistemological perception of the real world is to make a 'mistake'; to abandon precision in moral vision is to manifest 'prejudice'; and to abandon precision in writing is to create works which do not square with the real world, works which do not even square with themselves, architectural follies which should be 'bridges across incomprehension and chaos' but which are in fact 'jerry-built', 'rubbish', incapable of supporting even their own clumsy weight.

If Stoppard's plays grow, or apparently grow, from the demand that art should be its own subject, they inevitably break through this new and alien and artificial turf and sink their roots into the timeless truth that the evanescent beauty of art can only blossom from the ordinary mundane soil of real life. Stoppard eschews the example of committed playwrights who 'grapple' with 'weighty' issues, argues James, 'not because he can't do what they can do, but because he can do what they can do so easily'.[14] Having demonstrated his mastery of the form, Stoppard finally leaves behind the inherently circular world of art which is merely self-referential for much the same reason.

Stoppard's is a paradoxical art. He writes cavortingly clever plays which wittily expose as effete the merely clever. He writes exuberantly risqué plays which ruefully reflect on human experience as ineluctably moral. He writes disarmingly stylish plays which expose the danger of mere style. He writes extraordinary plays which celebrate ordinary mundane human beings. He writes seemingly surreal plays that affirm the existence and the value of the real. In a farrago of words he affirms that the essential truths are simple and monolithic and precede language. And in one of the surpassing ironies of his paradoxical plays, Stoppard creates a self-referential work which celebrates that art which is mimetically rooted in its representation of

ordinary human experience, art which eschews the surreal for
the real.

Having established the contrast between real life and art in the
juxtaposition of scene one with scene two, having celebrated the
existence of the real thing in art in Henry's memorable contrast
of cricket bats with cudgels in the middle of the second act,
what remains as the ultimate concern of the play is the contrast
between the ersatz – however alluring or deceptive or temporarily
misleading – and the real thing in human relationships. 'Does
the word "love" mean anything at all?'[15] a character asks in a
1982 play by Harold Pinter. Stoppard's play asks a much harder
question. *The Real Thing* asks if commitment, fidelity, trust have
meaning even in a hedonistic environment which is as surfeited
with sensuality as 'this poncy business' of the theatre, even –
indeed – in a relationship which has its very inception in an
adulterous affair. *The Real Thing* asks if there can be affirmation of
commitment, fidelity, trust between lovers who were themselves
brought together by infidelity, the breaking of commitments, the
betrayal of trust.

Just as the play opens with two quite different scenes both
of which – initially – appear to be real; just as we are presented
with two characters who embody different views of writing; just
so *The Real Thing* presents us with characters who embody several different views of love and different views of the nature of
human relationships. Charlotte, Henry's first wife, discounts the
significance of love – romantic, marital, or even parental – from
her first appearance. Although she is primarily trying to insult
Henry's plays as unreal, there is also undisguised condescension
toward the whole notion of fidelity in Charlotte's assertion that
if Henry were to catch her with a lover his 'sentence structure
would go to pot, closely followed by his sphincter' (p. 22). Indeed,
in some of the coarsest language of the play, Charlotte describes
fidelity in a wife as merely a matter of having 'a stiff upper lip,
and two semi-stiff lower ones' (p. 21). She even jeers at Henry's
love for his daughter and describes parental love as abnormal,
saying that 'normal is the other way round' – normal, that is,
is the response of one who 'just can't stand the little buggers'
(p. 31). Ultimately Charlotte's view of relationships is articulated

in mercantile metaphors. 'There are', she asserts, 'no commitments, only bargains' (p. 65). If Charlotte dismisses relationships as 'bargains', Debbie puts a different price on relationships in her advocacy of 'free love'. Like her mother, Debbie contemptuously dismisses the necessity or significance of fidelity. Infidelity is 'a crisis' only if 'you want to make it' one, Debbie reasons, arguing that her boiler room trysts had shown her that sex is not 'secret and ecstatic and wicked and a sacrament' but, merely, 'turned out to be biology after all' (pp. 62, 63).

Whereas Charlotte and Debbie demonstrate a pragmatic devaluing of relationships, Annie – who marries Henry after both have divorced their first spouses – values commitment but sees it as negotiable. Certainly she is more willing than Henry to jettison a first marriage. However, she is intense in her affection, her love, for Henry and she sees their subsequent marriage as something more than a bargain, as a relationship involving a measure of commitment. But she does not equate love or commitment, necessarily, with fidelity. Having embarked on an adulterous affair with the actor Billy, Annie endeavours nevertheless to assert her continuing love for Henry. She says she has learned not to care about the affairs she had suspected Henry of having, and that while her affair with Billy may continue, it is quite separate from her relationship with Henry: 'You weren't replaced, or even replaceable.'

As opposed to such denials of the possibility of love, or of the need for love to be accompanied by marriage, or of the need for marriage to be accompanied by fidelity, Henry from the first affirms the insularity of passion, the significance of commitment, the value of fidelity. While Henry the playwright confesses that he does not 'know how to write love' because 'loving and being loved is unliterary', Henry the man can turn to Annie at the peak of an argument and say, however unliterarily, 'I love you so.' In performance the chemistry between Roger Rees and Felicity Kendal, the unselfconscious physical affection they share may provide compelling emphasis to Annie's response, 'I love you so, Hen.'

At least in part, however, the resonance of such an exchange is established precisely by the dialogue's unpolished simplicity. Scruton's description of Stoppard's dialogue as 'an exchange not of feelings, but of epigrams',[16] might well apply to the play within the play, the scene from *House of Cards* written by Henry.

But applied to *The Real Thing* Scruton's charge simply leaves out more than it includes. To fail to distinguish the verbal veneer of that first scene from the emotional richness of much of the rest of the play is to call attention only to the discussion of art and miss the immediate personal experience of love and betrayal, the offering of commitment and the discovery of infidelity which undergirds the fabric of the play. One of the most moving speeches of the play, Henry's anguished cry, restrained until after Annie has already departed for another adulterous rendezvous, 'Oh, please, please, please, please, *don't*' is scarcely aphoristic. Indeed, precisely what we do not get at the play's most emotional moments is what Henry and Charlotte identify as 'badinage', 'smart talk', sitting around 'being witty about place mats'. Even Henry's first act curtain speech, 'I love love', although – perhaps – impassioned, can scarcely be described as eloquent: 'I love having a lover and being one. The insularity of passion. I love it. I love the way it blurs the distinction between everyone who isn't one's lover. Only two kinds of presence in the world. There's you and there's them' (p. 44). Indeed, by having the climactic speech of act one couched in sentence fragments, Stoppard is deliberately undercutting the rhetorical possibilities of the moment.

While it may be true, as one academic has observed, that in Stoppard's play 'love speaks in many different tongues, with many different accents', it does not necessarily follow that it is impossible to tell 'which of them, finally, is "the real thing"'.[17] Such a view offers the sophisticated interpretation that while a Stoppard play might engage in elaborate theatre games, might recount the process of trying to define the real thing, it surely would not do anything quite so simplistic as to define the real thing, well at least – dear me – not in terms of the morality of sexual relationships.

Despite such critical reluctance to recognise anything but relativity, Stoppard asserts that when his characters speak on various sides of a question, one may be voicing a position which is not just more persuasive or more eloquent or more generally accepted, but is, quite simply, true. Of *Night and Day* Stoppard asserts, 'Ruth has got a gift for sarcastic abuse, but what Milne says is true'. 'I mean', Stoppard continues somewhat insistently, 'it is true. . . . I believe it to be a true statement. Milne has my prejudice if you like. Somehow unconsciously, I wanted him to be known to be speaking the truth.'[18] And such truths just might be surprisingly simple. A moment later Stoppard offers a blunt assessment of *Professional Foul*: 'it's to do with the morality between individuals.' 'Something which has preoccupied me for a long time', he continues, 'is the desire to simplify questions and take the sophistication out. A fairly simple question about morality, if debated by highly sophisticated people, can lead to almost any conclusion.'[19] When Stoppard takes the sophistication out, when he cuts through the sophistries and gets down to the real thing, what he finds is a question of 'the morality between individuals'.

Similarly, when *The Real Thing* cuts through the sophisticated badinage that 'little touches' can 'lift adultery out of the moral arena and make it a matter of style' the play leads us to a question about morality between individuals, a question about one person's dealings with another person in the most intimate of human relationships, a question that remains squarely in 'the moral arena'. But this matter of morality, the sophisticated observer may ask, it is still a question, *n'est-ce pas*? It is, how you say, an 'intellectual leap-frog'.[20] Skewering those who continue to find leap-frogging in his plays, Stoppard declares 'I can say that in the last few years I haven't been writing about questions whose answers I believe to be ambivalent. In *Every Good Boy* and *Professional Foul*, the author's position isn't ambiguous.'[21] Nor is it in *The Real Thing*.

Whatever Charlotte's gift for sarcastic abuse, whatever Debbie's gift for verbal sophistry, whatever Annie's gift for persuasive nonsense, we should eventually recognise the difference between the real thing and the bogus imitation as being as great as, well, the difference between a cricket bat and a cudgel. Indeed, like Brodie's attempt at playwriting, Charlotte's pronouncements on fidelity are undercut by their own 'crudity'. We discover, subsequently, that while married to Henry, Charlotte had embarked on an adulterous tour of the Home Counties with no fewer than nine different 'chaps'. 'I thought we'd made a commitment', Henry says in surprise, evoking Charlotte's disparaging comment that there are no commitments, 'only bargains'. Indeed, after Henry's marriage to Annie, we discover Charlotte is 'shacked up' with a real-life architect, has other affairs alongside that affair, and gives the architect the elbow when he objects. Charlotte may be an entrepreneur; but she's no bargain.

More persuasive, perhaps, is Debbie's advocacy of free love.

If sex is mere biology, relationships need make no pretence of even aspiring to fidelity: 'That's what free love is free of – propaganda.' Brodie's prose may be ham-fisted, whereas Debbie's phrase-making is 'flawless', 'neat'. But Henry faults both of them for using language to falsify reality: 'You can do that with words, bless 'em' (p. 63). What Debbie does with words is create 'sophistry in a phrase so neat you can't see the loose end that would unravel it. It's flawless but wrong. A perfect dud.' Henry demonstrates the ease of spinning out such phrases with a neat epigram of his own: 'What free love is free of, is love.' Later in the conversation Debbie unpops another pithy pronouncement: 'Exclusive rights isn't love, it's colonization.' Though he dismisses such a cleverty as 'another *ersatz* masterpiece', Henry's affection for his daughter is clear – as is his disapproval of her misuse of her gift for language – in saying she is 'like Michelangelo working in polystyrene' (p. 64). The scene does not, however, merely offer a battle of wits, a mock-epic exchange of epigrams. 'Don't write it, Fa', Debbie interrupts, 'Just say it.'

So Henry just says it. His daughter's glib devaluing of commitment prompts Henry's climactic statement on the nature of relationships – a statement which lacks eloquence or gloss or polish, but which for all that carries far greater weight than Debbie's 'polystyrene' philosophising: 'It's to do with knowing and being known. I remember how it stopped seeming odd that in biblical Greek knowing was used for making love. Whosit knew so-and-so. Carnal knowledge. It's what lovers trust each other with. Knowledge of each other, not of the flesh but through the flesh, knowledge of self, the real him, the real her, *in extremis*, the mask slipped from the face' (p. 63). Against such a standard, Debbie's burblings about free love and non-exclusive rights seem sophomoric, as, indeed, they are. Her glib sophistries are finally faulted, much as Charlotte's sardonic crudities, not merely as glib or wrong-headed or reductivist – though they are all of those – but because they are unreal. They lack reality.

Affirming a knowledge 'not of the flesh but through the flesh' Henry asserts that there is more to sex than just biology, more to a human being than meets the microscope, more to human actions than amoral glandular functions. Henry, that is, affirms human interaction, intimacy between 'the real him' and 'the real her' as inherently, ineluctably moral. Writing in 1977 on the ubiquitous attacks of relativists on objective truth and absolute morality, Stoppard declared his own belief in 'a moral order derived from Christian absolutes'.[22] Just so, more than Henry's language is derived from biblical Greek. Henry's view of relationships is derived from a biblical view of relationships: 'in pairs we insist that we give ourselves to each other. What selves? What's left?' Henry asks, 'A sort of knowledge. Personal, final, uncompromised. Knowing, being known. I revere that' (p. 63). From a sacramental view of language to a reverential view of relationships, *The Real Thing* continues to depict both life and the language which faithfully represents life as meaningful.

In contrast both to Charlotte's sardonic pragmatism and the trendy promiscuity that Debbie so glibly espouses, Annie demonstrates some degree of commitment. Even amid her affair with Billy, Annie maintains that she loves Henry, and tries to assure him that Billy is not a threat. However, her expectations that Henry should manifest 'dignity', should learn 'not to care', should 'find a part of yourself where I'm not important' are shown to be unrealistic. Just as *Professional Foul* shows a professor 'being educated by experience beyond the education he's received from thinking',[23] *The Real Thing* shows a writer being educated by experience beyond the education he's received from writing. Just as reality can cut through the seemingly seamless tissue that philosophers or professors are able to spin, so reality can cut through the seemingly seamless tissue that playwrights can weave. As a playwright, Henry has written about the discovery of infidelity and shown the cuckolded husband continuing to run on a witty line of banter. But when Henry the man discovers the infidelity of his own wife, he disclaims privacy, dignity and stagey sophistication: 'I don't believe in debonair relationships. "How's your lover today, Amanda?" "In the pink, Charles. How's yours?" I believe in mess, tears, pain, self-abasement, loss of self-respect, nakedness. Not caring doesn't seem much different from not loving' (p. 72). Rejecting the brittle stage banter of Noel Coward sophisticates, Henry also explodes Debbie's dicta on free love as simply sophisticated masks for indifference. What free love is free of is love because not to care is not to love.

Henry can swallow his pride; he can resist being 'pathetic' or 'tedious' or 'intrusive', but he cannot learn to 'not care'. The reviewer who came away with the impression that Henry 'comes to realise that exclusive rights to a person is not love'[24] got it, rather spectacularly, wrong. Henry quotes his daughter's

epigram but does so with bitter irony. 'We have got beyond
hypocrisy, you and I', Henry says, wryly hypocritical: 'Exclusive
rights isn't love, it's colonization.' 'Stop it – please stop it', Annie
interrupts, unable to endure the irony in Henry's voice. 'The
trouble is', Henry continues more straightforwardly, 'I can't *find*
a part of myself where you're not important. I write in order to
be worth your while and to finance the way I want to live with
you. Not the way *you* want to live. The way *I* want to live with
you' (p. 77). However eloquent Henry may be in defence of art,
he is quick to deny that his commitment to his art in any way
supersedes or is even separable from the commitments he makes
to relationships in real life. He is even willing to 'tart up Brodie's
unspeakable drivel into speakable drivel' if Annie wants him to.
We see in what sense this is a 'committed' playwright. Henry's
is a commitment not to causes or ideologies but to a person.
Although his memorable image of the cricket bat may be the
springboard for an articulate apologia for the real thing in art,
what finally matters to Henry more than art or even articulacy
is love – the genuine article, the real thing, however haltingly
expressed – in real life.

And yet, as right as Henry may be in the high view he takes of
love and commitment, he still needs to realise – in his own life –
something of the pain and the cost of that commitment. Despite
Scruton's charge that Stoppard 'does not portray characters,
who develop in relation to each other',[25] the play finally hinges
precisely on the transformation, the development, the growth we
see in both Henry and Annie. Henry, like George in *Jumpers*, may
have sound ideas but his words need to be lived out in the flesh
of experience. George may be absolutely right in his defence of
moral absolutes in *Jumpers* and yet be oblivious both to the pain
and suffering of his wife and to murder in his own house. Like
George, Henry needs to become more human, needs to experience
mess and pain and tears. Unlike George, Henry does. What Henry
has from the first been saying, 'I love you', is precisely the right
thing to say (though the smart-talking husband in *House of Cards*
never thinks to say it). But even if Henry – both as lover and as
writer – has been putting the right words in the right order, *The
Real Thing* at once celebrates the substance of the assertions Henry
has been making and demonstrates the need for something more
than assertion. The very rightness of Henry's words and the very
rightness of their order becomes a kind of verbal shield.

When circumstances force Henry 'to either drop his shield of words or risk losing the woman he loves' as one reviewer observed the day after interviewing Stoppard, Henry himself undergoes a transformation 'not because [Annie] demands it, but because, ultimately, he requires it of himself as both man and writer'.[26] What emerges from that searing experience is a person who demonstrates more of a capacity for pain than an aptitude for the apt use of gerunds; what emerges from his education by experience is, finally, a person who is more human. 'He starts out over-confident', says Roger Rees who created the role, 'but in the end he has to learn to deal with the true nature of a relationship'.[27] Because Henry 'grapples with the realities of "the real thing"', as one interviewer rightly notes, 'he comes of age as both a lover and writer'.[28] In the transformation, the metamorphosis, we see in Henry, Stoppard's play offers a ringing celebration of the possibility of growth, renewal and maturation.

But if the transformation in Henry demonstrates the need to go beyond ideas to action, the transformation in Annie demonstrates the essential soundness of Henry's ideas. Even if Annie's espousal of commitment without concomitant fidelity seems a more formidable position than either Charlotte's or Debbie's, the play does not leave such a view as just another option alongside Henry's conception of love. In a series of crucial revelations in the play's final scene Annie abandons such a position along with a number of other falsehoods. We learn first of all, that Brodie's ostensibly revolutionary offence had been wholly apolitical in motivation, had been performed, Annie says, with 'not an idea in his head except to impress me'.

Thus, for at least the second time in his career, Stoppard has written a play in which a shadowy Scot proves of pivotal significance. Just as *Jumpers* springs from George's attempts to compose a response to the philosophically radical McFee, so the putative political radical Brodie prompts Henry's response from the first scene. In both plays the off-stage Scot serves as the catalyst for an entire line of argument by the protagonist throughout the play, and then, at the penultimate moment of the play is discovered to be radically unlike what we had thought him to be. Further, such a radical alteration in our perception of him has the effect not of undercutting what the protagonist has been saying throughout the evening but of supporting, underscoring, reinforcing it. The posthumous revelation that McFee had rejected moral relativism, abandoned a materialist view of humankind, experienced a religious conversion, broken off an affair, and made plans to enter a monastery, does not go much further to support the theist affirmations of the moral absolutist George than Henry's position is supported by the revelation of Brodie, in the last scene, as a hooligan whose 'political' act of setting a fire on the Cenotaph had been prompted by a wholly apolitical desire, using the only means such an inarticulate lout had at hand, to impress a girl.

If the penultimate revelation of Brodie reaffirms all that Henry – as playwright – has said about writing, the ultimate revelation of a transformation in Annie reaffirms what Henry – as a lover – has said about love. The two long arcs of the play – the concern with writing and the concern with loving – thus meet and are resolved in the play's final scene. However much weight Henry's impassioned plea for commitment may have carried during the preceding scenes the play's affirmations are not, finally, based on Henry's words alone. In the closing scene, Annie, sick of the freedom – the licence – of her extramarital experimentation, rejects her adulterous involvement, recoiling from the prospect of another contact with Billy with a vehement 'No'. Moments later she turns to her husband and speaks six words. If Henry and Annie's reconciliation is almost 'wordless', as Scruton pejoratively describes it, we should recall, as Anderson says in *Professional Foul*, that 'the important truths are simple and monolithic. The essentials of a given situation speak for themselves, and language is as capable of obscuring the truth as of revealing it.' The simple and monolithic truth here is that the relationship of a husband and wife, a relationship bent to the breaking point, has been restored. The words are, merely:

ANNIE: I've had it. Look after me.
HENRY: Don't worry. I'm your chap. (p. 83)

But what has been exchanged is a world of feeling. And if the utter simplicity of Annie's words, if the expressiveness of her embrace, if the significance of her smile as she turns out the lights, if all this is not compelling, would it have been more compelling if they had discussed it? As the curtain descends on that luminous bedroom portal, the play ends not – as in Shakespearean comedy – with marriage as restoration, but – having attained the more mature vision of Shakespearean romance – with a restoration within marriage.

Just as we can tell the difference between a cricket bat and a cudgel, just as we can tell the difference between authentic artistry and the political hack-writing of Brodie, so we can tell the difference between ersatz pronouncements on love and the real thing, the difference between the real thing and bogus imitations in life. The real thing is real life as opposed to imaginative reality, actual experience rather than art. The real thing is love rather than, just, sex. The real thing is the word rather than the sophistry, the faithful use of language rather than the corrupt abuse of language into jargon. The real thing is art rather than its propagandistic imitation, writing that grows out of authentic human experience rather than doctrinaire posturing, the right words in the right order rather than ham-fisted rubbish. The real thing is the clear-sighted perception of politics, justice, patriotism rather than the obfuscation of prejudice. The real thing is the recognition of a relationship as a commitment rather than a mere bargain; the willingness to accept commitment in relationship rather than casualness in affairs; the fulfilment – and sometimes pain – of promise rather than the mere pleasure of promiscuity; costly love rather than free. And in facing the fact of infidelity, the real thing is the pain and nakedness of caring rather than a debonair front of witty repartee or the indifference of not caring.

The measure of Stoppard's achievement is not that he is able to depict the ecstatic passion of love, or the sweet pangs of unrequited love, or the attractiveness of illicit love, or – finally – even the agonies of betrayed love, though *The Real Thing* does all that. The measure of Stoppard's achievement is that he is able to depict and vivify and make compelling the enduring happiness – deeper than ecstasy if less spectacular, more satisfying than illicit love if sometimes less attractive, more profoundly moving than free love if more painful – of loving and being loved, knowing and being known, the giving and receiving of commitment, fidelity. If *Jumpers*, as Kenneth Tynan aptly observed, is unique in the theatre as 'a farce whose main purpose is to affirm the existence of God',[29] *The Real Thing* has its own uniqueness as a West End comedy of adulterous alliances – a play about 'infidelity among the architect class. Again' – whose main purpose is to affirm the vital importance of fidelity, yes even the vital importance, in the commitment which love entails, of being earnest. And if it seems even less likely in our time than in Wilde's that a playwright could affirm the importance of being earnest and be in earnest about it, could affirm fidelity and not be ironic or cynical or, merely, flippant about it, that too is a measure of Stoppard's achievement. Stoppard has the unmitigated audacity, the perfectly scandalous nerve – simply washing one's clean linen in public – to dedicate the text of his adulterous comedy to his wife; and while that sort of thing may not be enormously on the increase in London, Stoppard sends his audience streaming out into the West End night – the lyrics 'I'm a Believer' ringing in their ears – convinced that such dedication, 'For Miriam', just might, after all, be the real thing.

7

Particle Physics and Particular Persons: the Join Between Happenstance and Goodness in *Hapgood*

In a wonderfully evocative opening, *Hapgood* begins with a red dot moving about a map of London projected onto panels which fill the stage[1] while we eavesdrop – by means of a voiceover – on British espionage agents who have a blue Peugeot under surveillance as it traverses a Byzantine labyrinth of London streets. Stoppard, who used screens to dazzlingly theatrical effect in *Jumpers* by filling the stage with the projection 'in very big close-up' of Dotty's 'dermatograph',[2] expands the map of London before our eyes in ever-increasing close-up. As the supersleuths home in on their human prey with deadly accuracy, we can see not only major thoroughfares but side streets, tiny lanes, and finally the outlines and floor plans of individual buildings. Thus, in one dazzling stroke, *Hapgood* combines spy technology with stage wizardry to transform the entire audience into espionage agents following an electronic bleep. By the time the first person comes through the doors of the bathhouse which forms the set for the first scene we know that agents have been following him all around London. Or at least we *think* they have been following him all around London. Amid the multiple wordless exits and entrances of that first scene the audience may or may not catch on to the fact that the first person through the door, identified only as 'the Russian', has an identical twin who also enters and exits during the course of that scene. The twin Russians are but the first of a multiplicity of dualities which bifurcate *Hapgood*. Ridley, a British agent who may or may not have become a double agent for the Soviets, may or may not have an identical twin. Kerner, a Soviet agent who has become a double agent for the British, may or may not have become a triple agent and be again working for the Soviets. Hapgood, who is the British control agent in charge of Kerner, may herself have become a double agent working for the Soviets and may or may not have an identical twin sister.

Drawing a link between the ambiguities of human personality and the mysteries of the cosmos, suggesting a join between that which is random and that which is divinely ordered, between happenstance and goodness, the dualities of *Hapgood* embody dichotomies which permeate Stoppard's plays. From the outset of Tom Stoppard's career some observers have seen in his work the relativity of relatively everything. Other observers absolutely affirm Stoppard's affirmation of absolutes. Where Stoppard stood on such matters may in part have seemed to change depending on the position of the observer. On the one hand we have seen Tom Stoppard telling 'One Pair of Eyes' that 'Tom Stoppard Doesn't Know' and coining *bons mots* about having the courage of his lack of convictions. On the other hand we have heard Stoppard asserting that he is a moral absolutist and a theist who acknowledges that the important truths are universally apprehensible. Whether he is one or the other has been confusing enough to raise questions. Blair, the head of espionage in *Hapgood*, might be speaking to Stoppard himself in declaring to a double agent 'You're this or you're that, and you know which'.[3] David Gollob used a few more words in 1981 to try to confront the playwright with the issue: 'Now what I find so baffling is this: How does one reconcile this . . . this **idealism** with an opposite but more characteristic feature of your writing, which is the **relativism** of everything . . .'[4] *Hapgood* might very well serve as Stoppard's full-length answer to Gollob's question. If *Travesties* was Stoppard's answer to the question of why his plays were not political, *Hapgood* directly confronts the ambiguity at the heart of things and the difficulty of reconciling a sense of objective reality and moral absolutes with the complexities of experience.

As Stoppard has moved from the affirmation of moral absolutes to the application of those moral values in the world of experience, his vision has become increasingly subtle. The certainty in *Rosencrantz and Guildenstern are Dead* of a world beyond and the affirmation in *Jumpers* of moral absolutes are transformed when characters take action on those values in *Professional Foul*. In *Hapgood* (1988) Stoppard deftly demonstrates that he can indeed have it both ways, that he can dramatise the relativism of relatively everything while still affirming the morality inherent in human actions. *Hapgood* offers the response of the moral absolutist to randomness in the cosmos. Stoppard affirms that even a universe which is not only bafflingly intricate but unpredictably random may yet be presided over by a God who throws the dice. However, the complexities of *Hapgood* result from Stoppard's attempt to deal explicitly with the complexities of the cosmos. Clive James was the first to point out the parallels between Stoppardian theatrics and Einsteinian physics.[5] Intrigued by the analogies James drew in 'Count Zero Splits the Infinite', Stoppard has a decade later written a play which makes pivotal use not only of Einstein's theory of general relativity but also of quantum mechanics and the Heisenberg uncertainty principle. Now that Stoppard has explicitly attempted to encompass the vasty reaches of Einstein within his wooden O, we have even greater reason to recall James's caveat that puzzling ambiguities both in Einstein and Stoppard reflect not imprecision but the desire to be precise 'over a greater range of events'. Recognising the existence of relativity and uncertainty in the real world, Stoppard is no more interested in surrealistic imprecision than was Einstein.

The real world in *Hapgood* is stranger than we might have supposed, an inexhaustible source of wonder and awe. Unlike the imaginary but predictable world of the spy stories which Stoppard's physicist, Joseph Kerner, says he reads, the realities of the quantum world are freighted with unpredictability. It may be impossible to know simultaneously where an electron is and what it is doing because 'there is *no such thing* as an electron with a definite position and a definite momentum'. But such indefiniteness is not part of a muzzy, surreal dream. 'It's all done without tricks', Kerner insists, 'it's the real world' (p. 48).

And that real world, for Kerner and for Stoppard, evokes something approaching reverence. 'If your fist is as big as the nucleus of one atom', Kerner says, 'then the atom is as big as St Paul's, and if it happens to be a hydrogen atom then it has a single electron flitting about like a moth in the empty cathedral, now by the dome, now by the altar' (p. 49). Stoppard's analogy may, at first, just seem a memorable attempt to reflect the scale of the atom, an analogy for which the relationship between the size of a clenched fist and Queen Elizabeth Hall or Victoria Station might be equally apt. However, the values implicit in Kerner's choice of structures become clearer when he asserts 'Every atom is a cathedral'. Other structures might be to scale, but concert halls, train stations, or sports arenas would not adequately convey Kerner's – and Stoppard's – sense of awe at the mysteries of the quantum world.

Indeed, for Stoppard, awe at the mysteries revealed by quantum mechanics becomes not just a conundrum of physics but a mystery of metaphysics. 'I think that the choice of epigraph (Feynman) will irritate you', Stoppard wrote to theoretical physicist J.C. Polkinghorne in advance of the opening of *Hapgood*, 'and that the word "metaphysics" in scene five will infuriate you'.[6] The Feynman epigraph not only declares that the phenomenon of light being at once wave and particle is 'impossible, *absolutely* impossible, to explain in any classical way' but also asserts that 'in reality it contains the *only* mystery' (p. vii). Stoppard has Kerner echo Feynman directly when he says 'the only real mystery in physics' is 'the missing rung' in the 'straight ladder from the atom to the grain of sand': 'Below it, particle physics; above it, classical physics; but in between, metaphysics' (p. 49).

Although Stoppard includes in the theatre programme Polkinghorne's assertion that mathematical language can penetrate beyond 'the everyday dialectic of wave and particle' and leave the dual nature of light 'free of paradox for those in the know', Stoppard resolutely declines to number himself among those 'in the know' who purport to view the quantum world without a sense of awe. 'I think I understand your point', Stoppard responds to Polkinghorne, 'but it seems to me that in the case of quantum mechanics the difficulty is in reconciling the mathematical language with a commonsensical view of what is *possible*. Feynman who presumably understands the mathematics insists on being amazed and so do I, so please forgive me . . . '[7]

A sense of awe at metaphysical mystery seems inevitably if embarrassingly to impel Stoppard to an acknowledgement of divine mystery. In *Jumpers* George advanced causality as an argument for the existence of God, claiming 'that if an apparently endless line of dominoes is knocking itself over one by one then somewhere there is a domino which was *nudged*'.[8] Reflecting a world of probabilities rather than certainties, *Hapgood* advances, at least in passing, an even more challenging theism. The play intimates the existence of God not so much *despite* as *because of* the lack of causality and epistemological certainty in the universe. The uncertainties of quantum mechanics may have 'upset Einstein very much' as Kerner says, because 'it spoiled his idea of God', which, as Kerner quickly adds 'is the only idea of Einstein's I never understood'. Einstein, says Kerner, 'believed in the same God as Newton, causality, nothing without a reason, but now one thing led to another until causality was dead' (p. 49).

Insisting on being amazed by the metaphysics of reality, Stoppard aligns himself with the awe which Kerner expresses towards 'all the mystery in life' which 'turns out to be this same mystery, the join between things which are distinct and yet continuous, body and mind, free will and fate, living cells and life itself; the moment before the foetus. Who needed God when everything worked like billiard balls?' (pp. 49–50). Einstein may have found it impossible to believe in a God who threw dice and continued to believe 'in the same God as Newton'. But Kerner (and – implicitly – Stoppard) embraces a more difficult prospect, to accept the Heisenberg uncertainty principle, to accept that 'quantum mechanics made everything finally random' and yet affirm the existence of God. If Einstein refused to believe in a God who threw dice, Kerner says, 'He should have come to me, I would have told him, "Listen, Albert, He threw *you* – look around, He never stops"' (p. 49). Kerner implies that the wholly unpredictable uniqueness of the particular individual constitutes evidence for the existence of the divine. The argument recalls Stoppard's suggestion in *Jumpers* that the existence of a perfect infinite Creator is evidenced by the rationally inexplicable heights of His Creation. Is the creation of an Einstein a rationally cal-culable probability? Even the mathematics argues against it. The unlikelihood of such a 'chance' recalls Stoppard's rejection of the hypothesis 'that, given enough time, some green slime could write Shakespeare's sonnets'.[9] 'That strikes me as possible, but a very long shot', Stoppard counters, 'why back such an outsider?'[10]

For Stoppard it is unacceptably reductive to suppose that life can be reduced to 'an either-or'. The mystery of explaining how light can be both wave and particle becomes an image for the mystery of delineating the boundary between body and mind or between free will and fate. It is unacceptably reductive to say that one is *either* this *or* that, instead of being *both* this *and* that. In *Hapgood* the join is between happenstance and some overarching sense of enduring values. The indeterminacies of the subatomic world are reflected in the ambiguities of human identity, the presence of different 'selves' within the single self. Despite these mysteries, the play intimates that there are enduring values to be apprehended, that beyond whatever may hap there is that which is good.

Indeed the use of the first name in saying that God threw Albert (not, less personally, Einstein) points to a number of implications of the theology of personhood which the play at least throws out for consideration. Michael Billington's recognition of 'Stoppard's hint that there are, in the end, values worth preserving: that democracy is better than dictatorship, that love is a possibility and that . . . children anchor one in the real world'[11] begins to spell out the values implicit in the play. However, what the play affirms is not only democracy, love, and the importance of children, but, at a more fundamental level, the absolute value and worth of the individual human being. Just as Kerner may regard the electron with amazement and awe despite (or because of) the impossibility of penetrating its mystery, so the play leads us to view the individual person as being of ultimate, non-negotiable worth despite (or because of) the impossibility of penetrating the mystery of the individual self.

Indeed, although many reviewers talk about the play drawing parallels between quantum mechanics and espionage, the more basic parallel the play draws is between quantum mechanics and human identity. 'The trigger for the play', Stoppard says, 'was the notion that duality in particle physics had some sort of correspondence to duality in human personality'.[12] 'But a play about an idea has to be set inside a vessel, independent of it', Stoppard explains, 'Casting about for one, I thought of the world of espionage'.[13] Reviewers who supposed that Stoppard was trying to write a 'spy thriller' or that *Hapgood* is 'about' the 'appalling futility and idiocy of the superpowers' spying game'[14] have got the cart before the horse. 'The espionage thing', Stoppard insists, 'came second. It was just a consequence of looking for some sort of narrative which would try to exemplify the first thought'.[15]

Stoppard's first thought does not just apply to 'the looking-glass world of spies, double agents and defectors'[16] but to the looking-glass world one encounters each morning when confronting the person in the bathroom mirror. 'If there's a central idea', Stoppard explained to Michael Billington 36 hours after the play's first night, 'it is the proposition that in each of our characters – yours and mine are doubtless exceptions – the person who gets up in the morning and puts on the clothes is the working majority of a dual personality, part of which is always there in a submerged state'.[17]

Using quantum mechanics not just to explain espionage but to explain human identity, Stoppard suggests that each of us is our own double, that each of us is 'not so one-or-the-other' (p. 72) but somehow harbours our opposite within us. Just as the square root of sixteen is both four and minus four, so at the root of a single individual we may find two opposites – both priest and doubter, both patriot and traitor, both manager and rebel.

Although Hapgood, a title role memorably created by Felicity Kendal, has the espionage codename of 'Mother', she is also as it turns out, a mother. However, a sense of duality in human personality is not just reflected in Hapgood herself. Ideologically, Ridley may be a traitor who betrays Hapgood in her professional capacity as an MI5 intelligence officer. But personally he is 'potty' about Hapgood and eschews safety in order to risk everything for a chance that 'Hapgood and Ridley, Ridley and Hapgood' (p. 39) might be linked together not just in CIA suspicions but romantically. Blair knows nothing about science but expects to scrutinise individuals and gain results as objective and incontrovertible as experimental data. 'We're all doubles', the scientist Kerner tells Blair, 'Your cover is Bachelor of Arts first class, with an amusing incomprehension of the sciences, but you insist on laboratory standards for reality, while I insist on its artfulness' (p. 72). Kerner, magisterially played by Roger Rees, poses his own ambiguities.

Confronted by Blair, the grey flannel head of the British espionage unit, with evidence which seems to point toward his complicity with the Soviets, Kerner launches into an explanation of quantum mechanics. Whereas a Stoppard character in *Night and Day* had assured us that 'Information, in itself, about anything, is light',[18] Kerner raises questions about the very nature of light. Does light consist of waves or of particles? The objective reality of the phenomenon being observed alters depending on whether or not it is being observed. When the non-scientific Blair tires of Kerner's Heisenbergian uncertainties and tries to get back to the original question of whether Kerner is 'ours or theirs', Kerner remonstrates, 'I'm telling you but you're not listening' (p. 11). 'You want to know if I'm a wave or a particle', Kerner explains, but 'the act of observing determines the reality' (p. 12). That impossible reality – that light consists of waves if the experimenter looks for one phenomenon but of particles if he looks at it in a different way – becomes in *Hapgood* a metaphor both for the mysteries of the world of espionage and the even greater intricacies of the human personality.

In part the difficulty of distinguishing between this and that, of establishing unambiguous identification, is reflected in the use of names in the play. A sense of the significance of names and the subtle implications of the ways in which characters call each other by name permeates the play. Al Matthews's character is 'Ben' to Blair but 'Wates' to Hapgood even though he complains that being addressed by his surname 'doesn't sound friendly'. Hapgood calls Nigel Hawthorne's character 'Paul' but he is 'Blair' to Ridley. Being on a first name basis rather than using surnames is, of course, a way of being more personal rather than just professional in dealings with one another.

The contrast between being personal and professional is all the greater when what is used is not a surname but a codename. 'Do I have to keep calling you Mother? You can call me Ernest', Ridley tells Hapgood in an unsuccessful offer of greater intimacy. But when she remains silent, he resignedly accepts their impersonal social distance: 'Call me Ridley' (p. 43). Similarly, Hapgood talks in strictly professional terms when she uses the argot of espionage to describe Kerner as a spy under her control: 'Kerner is my joe – I run him'.[19] Joseph Kerner, however, stands the phrase on its head, using much the same words to invest himself not merely with a technical role but with a particular name: 'Yes, I'm one of your Joes. How is the little one?' (p. 46). Linking himself with the son who bears his name, Kerner uses the phrase to refer to himself and his son as persons rather than ciphers.

Eventually, however, the multiplicity of names points to the elusive nature of the very self. Kerner is a joe or Joe or Joseph or, as when Hapgood addresses him in the intimacy of his native Russian, Josef. The task facing Felicity Kendal in the title role is much more intricate. She is addressed by her MI5 subordinates at Half Moon Street by her espionage codename, 'Mother'. Although 'Hapgood is her own name', Blair tells Wates that in the absence of a Mr Hapgood, 'Mrs is a courtesy title' (p. 27) for the mother of a 10-year-old. Since her son, naturally enough, knows her as 'Mum' or 'Mother', she can send him 'a message from Mother' by way of the naïve Merryweather who supposes that phrase is part of a secret code. More personally, Mother, Hapgood, Mrs Hapgood is Elizabeth to Blair although she refuses to permit Ridley to use her

first name. Kerner, the Russian father of her son, has known her
and continues to know her as Yelizaveta (p. 49), by the Russian
diminutive Lilya (pp. 56, 60), or, more intimately, by the Russian
diminutive Lilya (pp. 56, 60). Well into the second act when
Hapgood disguises herself as her own twin we encounter 'Betty'
as a sisterly nickname for Elizabeth. Ridley joins the supposed
twin in referring to Hapgood as 'Betty' and quickly applies the
nickname of 'Auntie' to the twin instead of calling her by name
as Mrs Newton or Celia. However Hapgood's identify is in part
revealed in the person of her supposed twin. So when Ridley
addresses the person whom he thinks he knows and urges her
'Listen, by yourself' (p. 85), the advice is more complex than it
might sound. The task facing Felicity Kendal in the title role is to
create a single character who can be herself as Mother, Hapgood,
Mrs Hapgood, Mum, Elizabeth, Yelizaveta, Lilichka, Lilya, Betty,
Celia, Mrs Newton, or Auntie. Which is the real self? At least in
part, as Kerner explains regarding the dual nature of light as wave
and particle, the observer determines the reality.

Indeed, much within *Hapgood* looks like 'this' and like 'that'
simultaneously. When Ridley, a suspected mole in MI5, wants
Hapgood, whom he thinks is Hapgood's twin sister, not only to
pretend to be Hapgood on the telephone but to feign that she
is in pain over the loss of her son, he almost breaks her hand.
Stammering out a response to her son's supposed abductors on
the telephone, Hapgood sounds as if she's in pain. The reason
she *sounds* as if she's in pain is that she *is* in pain. But an
understanding of the cause of her pain will differ according to
the perception of the observer. The person listening on the other
end of the telephone to incoherent sobs might well surmise that
he is hearing the unfeigned agonising of a mother beside herself
with grief. In fact the agonising is unfeigned but only an observer
who had just seen Ridley use his own hand as a blade to chop
Hapgood across the knuckles would really know what made her
cry out with pain.

The dualities of the play hinge on numerous such phenomena
which simultaneously look like one thing and another. A double
agent passing genuine secret information to his Russian control
to string along the Soviets whom he is betraying is identical in
appearance to the triple agent passing genuine secret information to the Soviets whom he is serving. Ocular proof may be
determined by what one expects to see. Despite the similarity of

appearance of 'this' and 'that', what we discover is not so much
a conflict between appearance and reality. Talk of the contrast
between appearance and reality presupposes that a thing is not,
really, what it appears because, *really*, it is something else. Such
a line of reasoning is simply an expression of Blair's 'either-or'
mindset that a thing *is* one way *or* another. In fact, what we
discover is *not* so much that Kerner is *really* a triple agent rather
than a double agent. It's not that things are one way or another.
Things are not 'either-or', they are 'both-and'.

In one climactic confrontation Kerner 'confesses' that he
has turned and become a triple agent working for the KGB
because the Soviets had found out about and threatened his
son, Joe. Even though Hapgood herself protests that Kerner, 'a
physics freak and a maverick' who 'despises the Soviets' (p. 55)
would not have turned back to the Russian side, when we first
see the scene we may well suppose that Blair has indeed gotten
the goods on Kerner and that Kerner's revelation is a truthful
confession that he has become a triple agent. Immediately after
the scene, however, which culminates in the gut-wrenching realisation that the Soviets had abducted the 10-year-old boy, Hapgood
calmly places a telephone call to her son's boarding school,
speaks to one of his classmates and then chats with her son
about finding a misplaced key in his hamster's hutch. The boy
is fine, the Soviets have not touched him, and the scene we
had just witnessed in Hapgood's office was a 'play within a play',
a scene staged by Blair, Kerner, and Hapgood to ensnare the
traitorous double agent Ridley. Hapgood, and those of us in the
audience, recognise Kerner's supposed confession as a ploy, a
disarmingly effective piece of acting which is sufficiently con-
vincing to trap Ridley.

Only in the penultimate scene do we discover that Blair really
did have incriminating evidence against Kerner. In his climactic
confession in Hapgood's office, Kerner tells the truth, although
it is possible for observers to take it as not true but made up,
part of a 'magnificent' performance. Just so, when Kerner early
on talks to Blair about being both wave and particle his words
are truer than Blair can recognise at the time. Ostensibly, Kerner
is saying that a double agent who has 'given Georgi enough
information to keep him credible' (p. 12) will *appear* the same as
a triple agent giving Georgi secret information. But Blair insists
on going beyond appearances in his comment to Kerner late in

the play that 'you're this or you're that, and you know which' (p. 73).

Eventually we see that Kerner is not just wave and particle in terms of the way his actions might be seen by others, but that within himself he is deeply divided and, further, that such deep-seated division makes it impossible to label any of the central characters as just 'this' or just 'that'. Henry's assertion in *The Real Thing* that 'public postures have the configuration of private derangement' (p. 33) postulated that appearances can be deceiving, that an action might appear to be one thing whereas in reality it is something else. The uncertainty in *Hapgood* is more sweeping. Rather than an action being one thing or another, rather than a person being one way while seeming to be another, the uncertainty in *Hapgood* extends to the very essence of the person's being.

Hapgood herself exemplifies prudence, professionalism, and propriety. Felicity Kendal, who first dazzled Stoppard audiences when she went *On the Razzle*, and created the poignant role of Annie in *The Real Thing* before playing Dotty in the 1985 revival of *Jumpers*, here gives a towering performance in the most complex role Stoppard has ever written for a woman. Kendal's Hapgood is a ferociously intelligent, dauntingly competent manager always keeping a tight grip – both on herself and others – though her fist is gloved in the velvet of impeccably proper taste. In part, her identity is reflected in her language. Always holding herself in restraint, she says 'oh sugar' or 'fiddle' instead of any other words beginning with 's' or 'f'. Blair knows where she goes 'when the sugar hits the fan' and even the foul-mouthed American Wates recognises her aura of propriety enough to apologise when he uses language stronger than 'golly' in her presence (p. 31).

If it is obvious that the lady has taste, it is no less obvious that she has brains. In the office she can read decrypts from agents around the globe, while making decisions on actions to be taken, while simultaneously carrying on a conversation on another topic, while, as the *coup de grâce*, simultaneously playing a game of chess without a board. Intellectually she runs rings around CIA interloper Wates and commandingly orders the over-weening American to back off. The crowning touch, however, is her return to impeccable British manners. Having given Wates a verbal tongue-lashing, she then reveals that she had popped into Fortnum's to procure a lemon for the American's tea. A proper

British hostess as well as a brutal administrator, Kendal ends the scene – teapot in hand – brightly asking, 'Should I be mother?' (p. 39).

However, Hapgood, a.k.a. 'Mother', is also a mother, and whatever her managerial efficiency, her maternal intensity prompts her to break Secret Service rules when it comes to her son. Frustrated by Hapgood using the Downing Street one-to-one line to telephone her son, Blair finally explodes: 'For someone who's so safe you're incredibly, I don't know, there's a little anarchist inside you' (p. 63).

If Hapgood seems firmly in control, of herself, of her agents ('Kerner is my joe – I run him'), *Hapgood* demonstrates that she is not just what she appears. We get a glimpse of that anarchist when the prim, intellectual Hapgood pretends to be her own twin sister, a vulgar loquacious 'pot-head' who answers to the name of Celia (or, more usually, 'Auntie'). Ostensibly, Hapgood masquerades as her double in order to receive a message from the supposed abductors of her son while her superiors have her under surveillance elsewhere. More accurately, Hapgood plays her own double in order to reveal Ridley's duplicity. But playing her own double ultimately reveals to Hapgood not so much Ridley's duplicity as her own duality.

Talking to Hapgood but supposing her to be her own twin, Ridley reveals something of the ideological roots which make him a Soviet sympathiser. But Hapgood hears something else as well, discovering that Ridley really is 'potty about her'. Not realising that he's actually talking to her, Ridley says of Hapgood, 'I'll get her kid back for her but it's only personal' (p. 82). In retrospect we can see how Ridley took Hapgood's question 'so is it you and me or not?' (p. 61). By getting back the boy, he thinks he will get the girl. Hapgood suddenly realises that Ridley's continuing efforts to get her son back may, after all, not just be for the ulterior motive of passing secrets to the Russians but may be for the ulterior motive of pleasing her. His interest isn't just professional, it is personal. He even says (and now and again someone is telling the truth) that he likes kids. Hapgood's recognition of Ridley's concern for the boy is crucial enough that after opening night Stoppard added eight lines to show 'the precise point at which [Hapgood] moves from entrapment to warning and realises that the technical traitor is also the person most anxious to help her son'.[20] 'You're all right, Ernest', Hapgood says, perhaps articulating her own sudden realisation in the voice of her supposed twin, 'You're just not her type'. If Kerner says that he no longer loves her and Blair's interest in her has always been merely professional, Ridley offers ready access to someone whose interest is passionately personal, someone who would risk his own life to embrace her. However, it is only in the guise of her mythical twin that the fastidious Hapgood can bring herself to call Ridley by his first name, to ally herself with him against the professional responsibilities of her waking self, and to recognise that he is 'all right'. Calling him 'Ernie', Hapgood's *Doppelgänger* allies herself with Ridley, urging him to 'walk away', to 'open the box' (p. 82).

Whatever Hapgood's motivation may be, Ridley is sufficiently tantalised to make a sexual advance which Hapgood responds to in kind. '*Who the hell are you?*', Ridley asks as he pulls Hapgood from the bed and kneels over her on the floor. His blunt question, which implicitly calls into doubt the whole nature of human identity, resonates throughout the play. In the première production Felicity Kendal reached up to pull Iain Glen down to her so that she was not so much reciprocating as initiating the kiss. 'I'm your dreamgirl, Ernie – Hapgood without the brains or the taste' (p. 83) comes the reply as the two, intertwined on the floor, roll out of the downstage light into the midstage darkness in a long and lingering embrace. When Blair asks Ridley in the following scene, 'Surely you know Mrs Hapgood?' (p. 85), Ridley's reply – 'I know her sister better' – intimates that here, as in both *Jumpers* and *The Real Thing*, 'knowing' is to be understood in its biblical sense. However, the more basic question is not whether Ridley has known Hapgood or her sister but whether Hapgood knows herself and can acknowledge the side of herself which emerges only in the person of her supposed twin. By giving herself to Ridley she is embracing her own duality, recognising that there is a 'Hapgood without the brains or the taste' which is yet a part of an answer to the question '*Who the hell are you?*' (p. 83). Thus the play dramatises the process by which Hapgood comes to know her own duality.

'The play is specifically about a woman – Hapgood – who is one person in the morning but who finds that, under certain pressures, there is a little anarchist upsetting the apple-cart', Stoppard told Michael Billington just after the play's opening night, 'The central idea is that inside Hapgood One there is a Hapgood Two sharing the same body; and that goes for most of us'.[21] Having two

Hapgoods 'one inside the other', Stoppard told Kate Kellaway
of the BBC, 'is, as it were, offered as some kind of generalisation
about the human personality'. 'We all of us', Stoppard explained
to Kellaway, 'have, you know, a Stoppard Two and a Kellaway
Two who emerges under pressure'.[22]

'We're all doubles', Kerner tells Blair. No person, Kerner
continues in a speech which forms a crux of the play, is
just one thing or the other: 'The one who puts on the clothes
in the morning is the working majority, but at night – perhaps
in the moment before unconsciousness – we meet our sleeper –
the priest is visited by the doubter, the Marxist sees the civilizing
force of the bourgeoisie, the captain of industry admits the justice
of common ownership' (p. 72).

If a double agent is 'a trick of the light', if we're all doubles, if
the one who puts on the clothes in the morning is just the working
majority of a divided self, if light is both wave and particle, if the
universe itself is built with probabilities, what level of certainty
exists within the play? What of the realm of values? 'Yes, values',
as Blair asks Kerner, 'It's not all bloody computers, is it?' (p. 73).
While the play draws explicit comparisons between Western
democracy and the totalitarianism of the East, the differences
in political values of East and West seem less important than in
Professional Foul. Although Kerner argues that the West's 'moral
superiority lies in the fact that the system contains the possibility
of its own reversal' (p. 73), he says he could return to Russia and
live out the rest of his life under totalitarianism rather than in a
democratic system that he personally prefers.

However, Kerner seems to make a distinction between the
betrayal of a political system and the betrayal of a person.
Blair may oversimplify things too much by insisting to Kerner
that 'you're this or you're that' but when he tells Kerner 'I've
got one of my people working the inside lane on false papers
and if she's been set up I'll feed you to the crocodiles' (p. 73),
Kerner seems not so much moved by fear as by compassion for
the person. 'One of your *people*?' Kerner replies to Blair, 'Oh, Paul.
You would betray her before I would. My mamushka.' Although
Blair may perceive Kerner's statement as evidence of continuing
loyalty to the West, Kerner is actually saying that he places a
higher premium on not betraying a particular person – much
as he would protect his own mother – than on giving away
scientific secrets. Elsewhere Ridley dismisses the importance of

Kerner's scientific secret – the 'solution to the anti-particle trap' – in a devastating lampooning of the scientific implausibilities of any space defence system. Professor Leonardo Castillejo, a theoretical physicist at University College London, regarded Stoppard's explanation of one piece of anti-particle physics as 'a very nice side-swipe at President Reagan's Star Wars' although he thinks 'most people would miss the joke.'[23] While Ridley's speech effectively disarms Kerner's anti-particle trap of much military or political significance, Kerner seems to think not so much in terms of ideology as in terms of the responsibility he bears as an individual in dealing with other individuals. His position recalls the affirmation in *Professional Foul* that 'the ethics of the State must be judged against the fundamental ethic of the individual'.[24]

In *Hapgood* the join between ethical obligations to a group and ethical obligations to particular individuals forms the crucial nexus of the play. 'Don't take it personally', Blair tells Hapgood at the rugby pitch as he relays CIA suspicions of her joe, Kerner. 'Why would I? It isn't personal', Hapgood replies. 'This is personal', Hapgood says as her attention turns back to the field where her son is playing, 'Everything else is technical. You're personal sometimes; but not this minute which is all right' (p. 17). The contrast between the technical and the personal permeates the play and Blair invariably places a higher premium on the technical. His encouragement to Hapgood, 'Don't pack it in yet, I need you', prompts her rueful question, 'I suppose that's technical, is it?' But when Hapgood plaintively tells him 'I needed *you*', Blair makes his own values explicit as he says dismissively, 'No, no, that was only personal' (p. 24). He then turns to what he thinks matters, his expertise as a manager, when he adds, 'But you're going to need me now.'

Although the distinction between needing someone for personal or for technical reasons at first seems rather innocuous, it comes to be a matter of life and death. From the first Blair is inclined to say that needing someone else is 'only personal'. Blair can explain Hapgood's refusal to permit Wates or Ridley to be on a first-name basis with her as 'a sort of compliment' because it implies a professional relationship. Blair is equally adept at explaining the nuances of being personal or professional in calling one another by name as he is in explaining the difference between a 'friendly interview' and a 'hostile interview' (p. 52) because for him personal and professional are technical distinctions in the same way

that hostile interview and friendly interview are, for him, merely
technical terms in the spy business.

As opposed to Kerner's poignant concern for persons, the
urbane organisation man Blair is the prime exemplar in the
play of the elevation of corporate interests above any interest
in individuals. Polite, decorous, liberally educated as he may
be, Blair sees persons ultimately in terms of their instrumental
worth, as tools, chess pieces, to be used. But while he claims
that Hapgood calls him 'Paul' because 'we're friends' he does
not respond to her as a friend. Indeed, what Blair calls the 'little
anarchist' inside Hapgood may simply be the mother coming out
in 'Mother'. For the consummate organisation man anything as
personal as maternal feelings seems politically disruptive.

Breaking the rules, engaging in activities for personal rather
than professional reasons, taking action which could technically
be considered a professional foul, is a motif which is established
early in the play. For his part, Kerner breaks the rules by sending
his son chocolates – even if anonymously – and is incautious
enough to carry a picture of his son hidden in the lining of his
wallet ('a photograph, fingernail size, cut out with scissors, like
from a team photo . . . picture of a boy in a football shirt', p. 43).
However, it is not until the final scene – after Ridley's duplicity
has been exposed, after Ridley's twin has been taken into custody,
after Ridley himself has been fatally shot by Hapgood, after
Hapgood has returned to the rugby pitch where Kerner will have
a chance to see his son in person for the first time and perhaps
for the last time in his life – that we learn that Kerner in fact had
been telling the truth that the Russians really had found out about
Joe, that they had in fact got to Kerner, that Kerner had in fact
'turned' and had been functioning as a triple agent. Remembering
the visceral intensity of Kerner's confession of those very facts in
the Mousetrap scene in her office, Hapgood quietly observes with
some wonder, 'you made up the truth' (p. 88).

Although Kerner says that 'frankly, compared to the electron
everything is banal' (p. 48), the action of the play hinges on recognising that compared to the worth of an individual 10-year-old
boy everything is banal. Michael Billington rightly notes that the
moral centre in Stoppard's plays has, increasingly, tended to be
vested in children.[25] At the centre of the international intrigue
and intergalactic mysteries of *Hapgood* we have, finally, a little
boy. The cover of the Aldwych theatre programme is dominated

by the photograph of young Hapgood, its edges tattered where his father has torn it from a team picture, and meeting directly over the heart of the boy are a pair of rifle sights. By contrast, the Faber and Faber cover of *Hapgood*, showing two briefcases sitting beside three numbered booths, emphasises the legerdemain of the play's plot in the opening scene.[26] Where the book cover presents us with an intellectual conundrum, the theatre programme should help us to see that what lies at the heart of this play is the obligation of a parent to a beloved boy at risk.

Poised between Blair's elevation of 'the firm' at the expense of the personal and Kerner's elevation of the personal at the expense of leaking secrets to the Soviets, Hapgood herself is the pivot on which the play finally turns. For years Hapgood has adopted Blair's values hoping, in part, that their professional relationship will evolve into the personal. Ridley says that Hapgood has been 'getting her buzz out of running joes to please an old bastard who doesn't want her and never will'. Presented by Blair with the values of 'a racket which identifies the national interest with the interests of the officer class', Hapgood 'bought the whole lie and put it first, she *is* the lie' (p. 82). Although she remembers her relationship with Kerner in terms of love rather than any ulterior motives, she broke off that intensely personal relationship for professional reasons. Kerner was a 'prize double, a turned mole who would have been blown overnight if he was known to be the father' of her child. Faced with 'a choice between losing a daddy and losing a prize double', Hapgood denied her child a father for technical reasons. A loyal minion of MI5, which is 'in the mole business' not 'in the daddy business', Hapgood decided ten years ago to subordinate her personal needs and the needs of her son to the priorities of the 'business'.

In the intervening ten years she has tried to juggle her responsibilities to her son and the obligations she feels to 'the firm'. In her attempt to be a mother while continuing to be Mother, she cuts corners, breaks the rules, sends postcards to her son when she's in Vienna on a supposedly secret mission, gives her son the trip-code to telephone her on the Downing Street one-to-one red line, and – as Blair grumbles – uses 'an intelligence officer on government time to dispatch football boots around the Home Counties' (p. 63). But whatever Hapgood may provide for her son in the way of rugger boots, postcards, and maternal visits cannot assuage her painful awareness of what she has not given her son. 'She should have given him a daddy', Ridley says. And Hapgood herself has the painful sense that her fatherless child also does not have a mother much of the time because of the demands of her professional life.

The personal implications of her professional decision remain very much a live issue for Hapgood. One reason she put her son in boarding school is 'the male society thing, they're supposed to need that when they haven't got fathers' (p. 23). At her son's rugby pitch she asks Blair if he wants some tea saying that 'they lay it on for parents and he's entitled to two'. But if every good boy deserves a father, Hapgood is haunted by an awareness that the cost to her son of what he is missing may be real even if he can't articulate it: 'He got unhappy about something once when he was really little, he was crying, he couldn't tell me what it was, he didn't *know* what it was, and he said, "The thing is, Mummy, I've been unhappy for *years*"' (pp. 18–19).

The first act ends with Hapgood's tentative steps back to something truer than the falseness of the last ten years. Now that Kerner is 'blown', now that the prize double's 'career will be over', Hapgood tries to stammer out her personal need for him beyond his professional usefulness: 'I won't need you any more, I mean I'll need you again – oh, *sugar!* – you *know* what I mean – do you want to marry me? I think I'd like to be married' (p. 50). Hapgood's proposal to Kerner both expresses her own need for a husband and her son's need for a father: 'Won't you want to meet him now?'

Kerner acknowledges that he had loved her in the past but questions whether what was personal in their relationship a decade ago was ever separable from what was technical. As opposed to giving 'ourselves to each other' in a knowledge which Henry celebrated in *The Real Thing* as 'personal, final, uncompromised',[27] Kerner claims that Hapgood had always been the case-officer interrogating the spy: 'one day you switched off the hidden microphone and got pregnant' (p. 50). Despite Kerner's disclaimers, the directness and intensity of Hapgood's repeated claim 'I loved you, Joseph' (p. 50) lend credibility to her perception that their relationship had been more than just technical. Perhaps the observer determines the reality. But Hapgood's intense reaction to the news that Kerner really may return to Russia and the tenderness of the moment they share as Kerner comforts her in Russian, 'Milaya moya, rodnaya moya'

('My dearest, my loved one'[28]), makes it difficult to believe that their feelings for each other were *just* professional or *just* a thing of the past.

As in *The Real Thing*, some of the most deeply affecting moments are performed virtually wordlessly. In *The Real Thing* Roger Rees and Felicity Kendal could convincingly portray the reconciliation of husband and wife using just eleven words. In *Hapgood* there are no words at all as Kerner listens for the first time to the voice of his son. Although the stage directions say, merely, that 'Kerner gently takes the phone from [Hapgood] and listens to the phone for a few moments and then gives it back to her, and leaves the room' (p. 64), Stoppard participated in the rehearsal process both in London and Los Angeles and sanctioned a much more highly charged moment between Kerner and Hapgood for the première production. In performance Roger Rees hesitated for just a moment before listening, waiting until he has eye contact with Felicity Kendal – tacit recognition of their connection and relationship – before putting the receiver to his ear. In what follows, as William A. Henry rightly observes, 'The spellbound joy and agony on his face as he listens mutely on the telephone to the voice of the boy he can never claim as his, can scarcely even see, is the finest moment of performance in London'.[29] Although that description focuses on the father-son relationship, the scene as played spoke volumes, wordlessly, about the relationship between Hapgood and Kerner.

Ultimately the play hinges on Hapgood's moral decision as to whether 'being herself' is finally a matter of being professional or personal. Just as Kerner must decide between being a joe and being Joe, Hapgood must decide between being Mother and being a mother. Like George in *Jumpers* who thinks he's being good by being a good philosopher, Hapgood has prided herself for years on being a good espionage officer (in both senses of the word 'good' – she's skilful and she's on the side which has the right values). George needs to learn that it is not enough to try to prove moral absolutes but that he needs to embody them in his life and relationships. Similarly Hapgood, who first thinks of herself as being the good spy counteracting the bad spies, eventually comes to the conclusion that the values implicit in spying are the same for both sides. 'Telling lies' is her job, the way she can 'make a living' in a business where our side and their side come to seem as alike as plus and minus charges. Much as George needs to embrace an actual relationship with his wife rather than seeing goodness wholly in the abstract terms of a philosophical debate, Hapgood needs to embrace an actual relationship with her son rather than thinking that she can embody goodness by being on the right side in the spy business.[30]

All reality, according to Blair who articulates the values of the spy business, comes down to 'an either-or': 'It's them or us', Blair says, 'and we can't afford to lose' (p. 87). Although at first Blair can shrug off questions of liking children with the witticism that loving little boys has 'never been encouraged in the Service' (p. 15), by the end of the play we see more clearly just how high the Service looms in his thinking in a conflict between a professional goal and any personal consideration – even the safety of a child. Seeing the world in terms of 'an either-or', seeing the world as a contrast between 'us and the KGB' (p. 87), Blair deliberately uses Hapgood's son as political bait. Because he thinks it would be 'tricky doing the swap without a boy to swap' (p. 63), he exposes Hapgood's son to potential gunfire just so the late-night meet at the pool will 'look right' (p. 86).

Kerner says of the Soviets that they 'absolutely' would have taken his son. What the play eventually makes clear is that an 'either-or' mindset which supposes that it's either us or them results in there being very little difference between us and them. Both the Soviets and Blair are willing to sacrifice the rights and safety of the individual in order to secure a political advantage. In a play filled with uncertainties there is no equivocation whatsoever in Hapgood's climactic denunciation of Blair. Hapgood's pronouncement that she will 'never forgive' Blair for endangering her son, 'never ever', explicitly indicates her rejection of Blair's impersonal, technical scheme of values as immoral. Hapgood thus comes to the point where she makes the choice that Kerner has already made. Blair may suppose that 'one has to pick oneself up and carry on' because 'it's them or us'. But for Hapgood herself it's no longer going to be business as usual. If years before she had decided that it was more important to be 'in the mole business' than 'the daddy business', now she must decide whether she will continue in the 'Mother' business or the mother business. What she realises is that the job, the organisation, the institution is not worth it if it means putting her son at risk. The game is not worth the candle if it reduces persons to pawns.

Hapgood's decision to abandon a career which sees human

beings only in terms of instrumental worth is prompted both by her concern for her son and by her realisation of the moral cost to herself. Using people had been the name of the intelligence game, the *sine qua non* of 'Betty's job' as Ridley explains: 'Sometimes people die, or get stuck in *gulags* till their parents are dead and their kids have kids, so Betty can know something which the opposition thinks she doesn't know' (p. 81). 'They have forgotten their mortality',[31] Alexander says of his Soviet imprisoners in *Every Good Boy Deserves Favour*. The reality of killing people to get an advantage which may or may not be pyrrhic is brought home to Hapgood by personal experience. Ridley may be the 'technical traitor' but he is also the one 'person most anxious to help her son'.[32] Hapgood first sleeps with Ridley – the one man who is really 'potty' about her – and then later that night, in the line of duty, kills him. Her killing of Ridley is doubly important to her because she not only commits the ultimate act as Hapgood in killing a person but because she is killing a person whom she has known and been known by, a person who loves her. This awful act becomes a metaphor for her life as Hapgood. In her professional capacity, she responds to people more as a killer than as a lover or a mother. The sense of revulsion Hapgood feels for the whole enterprise she's been engaged in recalls Annie's revulsion in *The Real Thing* for the essentially unreal life she had been leading up to the final scene. If she fatally 'takes out' Ridley, she also takes herself out of the game professionally, announcing 'I'm out of it now' (p. 88). She confides to Kerner, the only person left with whom she has a relationship which is not just professional but personal, 'My career is over too.'[33]

The prim Hapgood and the vulgar Celia, the concerned mother and the managerial Mother, particle and anti-particle collide in the last moment of the penultimate scene in a verbal explosion of unprecedented magnitude: 'Who? Us and the KGB? The opposition! We're just keeping each other in business, we should send each other Christmas cards, (p. 87). Hurling her words at Blair (who thinks she never uses language stronger than 'Oh, fiddle'), Hapgood expresses her contempt in the strongest language she uses in the play. The only profanity to emerge from the lips of Hapgood,[34] as opposed to the words which proceed from 'Mother's' foul-mouthed 'sister', demonstrates that the decorum of the manager and the intensity of Celia are each sides of Hapgood herself.

The play ends with Hapgood, like Annie, turning away from the life she has been leading, seeking a restoration to values more real and enduring than those of the niche she has carved for herself, having all the brains and all the taste but treating life itself as a board game. But this play offers much less assurance that the pieces can be put back together, that the nuclear family can be restored once it has been split. Hapgood's last words to Kerner are 'How can you go? *How can you?*' (p. 89). Kerner starts to leave and gets as far as upstage left. What pulls him back is not so much Hapgood as the boy. When the game resumes, his interest 'is snagged'. In production Roger Rees crossed the stage moving all the way from a near-exit at upstage left until he was once again standing just behind Felicity Kendal downstage right. 'Come on St Christopher's!' Hapgood yells to her son's team, 'We can win this one!' As she glances back she discovers 'that Kerner is still there' and as she turns back to the game she 'comes alive' in a moment which is intensely moving as performed in the production Stoppard helped to rehearse. On most nights during the first production there were real tears on Felicity Kendal's cheeks which she wiped away as she cheered her son on 'Shove! – heel! – well heeled! – well out! – move it! – *move it, Hapgood*! – that's good – that's *better*!' (p. 89). The play ends with Kerner and Hapgood slightly apart but united in looking at that which unites them – one little boy who is flesh of their flesh and bone of their bone.

Given Hapgood's and Kerner's mutual discoveries in the final scene that they had both thrown over their careers because of the boy, Stoppard is presented with a perfect opportunity for a happy ending. The Hapgood who asks Kerner 'How can you go? *How can you?*' is very different now than when she asked Kerner 'Do you want to marry me? I think I'd like to be married' (p. 50). In confronting her own capacity to kill as well as to give life, and in choosing the personal over the professional, she emerges as a more broken, more human person. But if reconciliation hovers as a possibility in the final scene, Stoppard resists any storybook ending in which the girl gets her chap, the little boy gets a daddy, and Joseph gets his jo and his son. Stoppard leaves us with the sense that putting the pieces back together will involve on-going adjustments and tensions and may, finally, prove impossible.

Whether Kerner goes back to Russia or not is a question the play does not resolve. We don't find that out any more than we find out who killed McFee in *Jumpers*. According to Roger Rees, maybe Kerner does not stay at the rugby pitch or maybe he stays for the rest of his life or maybe he stays for two days.[35] The ending of the play is intentionally ambiguous. Perhaps Kerner gives up his career and stays in order to be a father to his son; perhaps he gives up his freedom and spends the rest of his life in the hands of the Soviets so that his son will no longer be at risk. And yet while it may be impossible to say that any single action is 'right', it is still possible to say that one action is better than another, that there is still, to use a phrase from *Jumpers*, 'the sense of comparisons being in order'.[36] Just as it is possible in *Jumpers* to compare the actions of Scott and Oates on the moon with the actions of their historical namesakes in Antarctica, in *Hapgood* the young boy serves as a touchstone against which to measure the actions of Hapgood and Kerner and Blair. Whether Kerner's morally ambiguous decision to value his son above the secrecy of his scientific ideas can be considered good, his concern for the boy is better than the inhuman indifference of Blair. However, Hapgood's self-sacrificial willingness to value the personal above the technical, her willingness to abandon her own career in order to embrace a relationship with her son, demonstrates an altruism which differs fundamentally, absolutely, from the actions of Blair who deliberately puts the boy in harm's way, using the boy as a pawn in order to capture a more powerful piece.

The alternative, the choice, is to avoid viewing persons in terms of instrumental worth. That is why the statement 'Kerner is my joe – I run him' is so objectionable. Altogether apart from the need to disassociate oneself from the faceless role of being a joe is the need to dissociate oneself from the exploitative role of seeing persons just as joes to be run. Having finally decided that she is going to leave the spy game, that she is going out now and may be gone for some time, Hapgood concludes the play with an action which happens to be good. The play leads us to see that she has chosen that which is good and to hope that Kerner too will make the better choice of being a father rather than a 'physics freak', of valuing particular persons more highly than particle physics. In the final moment of the play Hapgood and Kerner, Elizabeth and Joseph, stand side by side, their hands touching the bench, ostensibly looking straight out at their son, but also looking straight out at the audience in a moment where the immensity of moral choice becomes palpable on both sides of the proscenium. If the moment leads us to long for Joseph to stay, it also confronts us with our own capacity to choose. If we can recognise the worth of a son, the value of love and the importance of a commitment to particular persons, perhaps this play written for a son – an intellectual *tour de force* dedicated to 'Oliver with love' – can lead us to recognise our own responsibility for choosing between that which is technical and that which is personal, our own responsibility for choosing how we will value particular persons.

What Stoppard leaves us with is the certainty that there are moral problems, that we are responsible for our choices however freighted with ambiguity they may be, and that there is an enduring sense of goodness, an enduring sense of right and wrong even if the ambiguities of particular contexts make such choices difficult. Although *Hapgood* invites us to recognise the impossibility of plucking out the mystery of an individual, the conclusion of the play leads us to acknowledge that what is right and what is wrong comes down to the matter of how one individual treats another individual and to see that the person is more important than the business, however lofty the aims of that business may be. Finally, the play leads us to see that even if it may be difficult or impossible to say that one action is absolutely right, it is possible when comparing an altruistic action and an exploitative action to recognise the difference and to say absolutely, using the final words of *Hapgood*, 'that's good – that's *better!*'

8

Moral Absolutes
and Mortal Contexts

When interviewed just 36 hours after the opening of *Hapgood*, Stoppard found himself being asked – again – about his political identity as a playwright. Given *Hapgood*'s exploration of the indeterminacies of the subatomic world and of human personality, some viewers might have expected that now, finally, Stoppard would avoid answering a political question in terms of morality. However, despite the ambiguities and indeterminacies of *Hapgood*, Stoppard's response to the familiar question was neither indeterminate, nor ambiguous, nor – to anyone who has followed his career – unfamiliar. 'I still believe', Stoppard told Michael Billington on 10 March 1988, 'that if your aim is to change the world journalism is a more immediate, short-term weapon. But art is important in the long-term in that it lays down some kind of matrix of moral responsibility'.[1] Reiterating a view of art which he has been articulating since 1974, Stoppard continues to affirm an open and direct connection between art and morality. Looking for a bridge, a join, between the timeless realm of moral absolutes and the time-bound realm of human behaviour, Stoppard finds that the play just might be the thing. Stoppard's affirmation of art as inherently moral continues to be far removed both from the orthodox mainstream of contemporary British playwrights and from the critical orthodoxies of academe. As a result, it has taken some time for sophisticated observers to discern the power of plays which ordinary audiences have, all along, found moving. Stoppard's recognition of a disparity in responses to *Hapgood* may apply to other plays as well: 'My impression is that your ordinary punter has less trouble with it than some of our critics.'[2]

Not until 1987 did Anthony Jenkins provide a sustained refutation of the accusation that Stoppard is heartlessly cerebral, a charge which has followed Stoppard throughout his career.[3] Michael Billington reiterates that particular charge throughout his 1987 book, declaring that 'what one looks for, in vain, are

the common human emotions of love, hate, jealousy, private
pain or any revelation of what men and women are like when
alone'.[4] But less than a year later Billington reversed field. After
insisting in 1987 that the 'recurrent flaw' of the plays was 'a
curious detachment from human passions', Billington in 1988
could acknowledge that 'in *Jumpers* – more in the Aldwych
revival than the original Old Vic production – you felt the
pain of a marriage audibly splintering'.[5] Noting that Stoppard's
plays 'have been analysed as if they were intellectual conceits',
Billington now concedes that 'I suspect they only work because
of their emotional ground-base.'[6] Well, the world does turn and
the whirligig of time does bring in its revisions. But Billington's
later insights, expressed in two paragraphs while writing up an
interview with Stoppard, display a sounder judgement than the
repeated charges of detachment which permeate his book.

However, Stoppard must bear responsibility for some of the difficulty viewers have experienced in coming to terms with his plays.
If he has always been clever, he has frequently been too clever by
half, as he himself has sometimes conceded. While denying that
for him style is an end in itself, he admits that stylistic virtuosity
though 'merely the means' sometimes obscures the more sub-
stantive end he has in mind. Although Stoppard insists that he
is 'not a writer who doesn't care what things mean and doesn't
care if there isn't any meaning', he acknowledges that 'despite
myself I *am* a kind of writer who doesn't give a fair crack of the
whip to that meaning'.[7] Since Stoppard contrives 'to inject some
sort of interest and colour into every line',[8] he glosses his serious
concerns in layers of confection until 'the plays tend to give an
impression of effervescence and style and wit for their own sake
and thereby obscure what to me is the core of the toffee apple'.[9]
As a result, plays which are *vastly* entertaining may be thought to
be *merely* entertaining. Striving to contrive the perfect marriage of
farce with the comedy of ideas, he sometimes fails to husband
his wit. The perhaps homely idea which he would espouse is
sometimes upstaged in a scintillating *tour de force*.

Stoppard may be right that *Jumpers* both 'works as a funny
play' and 'makes coherent . . . a fairly complicated intellectual argument'.[10] However, amid the bounding gymnasts and
rebounding wit, many viewers may have enjoyed the revelation
of professorial ineptitude and secretarial pulchritude while finding
the play to be 'philosophically opaque'. Even if Stoppard himself

thinks that 'opacity would be a distinct failure in that play',[11] enough viewers have been mesmerized by its shimmering surface that any light the play may shed on the question of moral absolutes has been perceived, if at all, rather dimly. *Travesties* and *Hapgood* offer even more problematic instances in which the play comes close to being a casualty of its own conceptual intricacy. Stoppard's impulse to discount criticism that *Hapgood* is 'incomprehensibly baffling' by noting that the play did not lose its audience in preview and opening night performances does not satisfactorily answer the objection. One has to be clever indeed to emerge from *The Real Thing* purporting to believe it impossible to tell what is real from what is unreal within the play. By contrast it is much easier for the ordinary punter to find Stoppard's spy thriller thrilling without recognising that Hapgood really does not have a twin sister, that Hapgood really has not been functioning as a double agent, or that Kerner really has become a triple agent. And those realisations are just the most basic underpinnings of the plot. The intricacies of the play's exploration of the dual nature of light, of quantum mechanics, and of the metaphoric relevance of quantum mechanics to human personality are of a different order of complexity altogether. With *Hapgood* Stoppard may be in no danger of losing the rapt attention of his audience in a play which brilliantly exploits the argot and milieu of the espionage world fleshed out on the Aldwych stage by the passionate acting of Felicity Kendal, Roger Rees, and Nigel Hawthorne. But viewers may remain intrigued without ever being enlightened. Simply getting the plot straight may require more than one viewing; perception of the full scope of Stoppard's concerns may require even more. Once again the shimmering Stoppardian surface remains compelling; once again Stoppard's serious concerns would be illuminating if seen; but between the two falls, if not the shadow, at least a certain translucence.

Although Stoppard has always insisted that a play is an event rather than a text, he continues to struggle with Peter Wood – who has directed every full-length play since *Jumpers* – over how explicitly a play should lay bare its concerns in its brief hour upon the stage. 'Peter is an advocate for the audience and tries to make the play work for an imaginary spectator called Rupert', says Stoppard, 'who he believes was the bear of little brain. It's no good my telling him that was actually Pooh'.[12] For his part, Wood says he 'took refuge in an imaginary character called Rupert, so that I could say "Yes, I absolutely understand this, but I don't think Rupert does."' The tension between playwright and director, says Stoppard, has 'to do with *my* reluctance to be over-explicit and *his* fear that the audience isn't being given enough information. I like to get the shock of finding things out, and in some cases Peter saves me from their *never* finding out'. And in yet other cases, even Wood's efforts do not salvage the situation and the audience never does find out. 'I'm constantly aware that you can't do in a play what you can in a book', Wood says, 'turn back the page to find out what has happened to make this happen.'[13] With *Hapgood*, compelling though it may be as spectacle, enough members of the audience – not just the bear of little brain – found it impossible on first viewing to follow the Byzantine intricacies of the play that Stoppard began rewrites for the American production even before the play had closed in London.[14] A play may be an event rather than a text, but with a Stoppard play it may be necessary to turn back the page as well as to view the event in order to arrive at an eventual understanding. However, if it is a criticism of Stoppard that his plays require repeated viewings, it is also true that his plays reward repeated viewings. Although Stoppard continues to affirm that 'the best art has more effect on our moral sensibilities',[15] his plays continue to reflect his reluctance to be over-explicit, even if it means the audience never finds out some things about the way the plays reflect his long-held moral and theological beliefs. Nevertheless, such concerns permeate his entire canon. The emotional ground-base of the plays rests on a bedrock of morality.

Indeed, from the first Stoppard has seen social and political events in the larger context of timeless moral absolutes; or, to describe the same matrix from a different angle, he has responded to the timeless within the context of temporal events. Even while confessing in 1968 that as a writer he had no 'social objective' to declare, Stoppard acknowledged that 'one thing that had an enormous effect on me was the evidence at the trial of the people who killed three Civil Rights workers at Meridian, Mississippi. I couldn't get out of my head the awful fact of those murders; but I couldn't begin to write about that kind of a subject in real terms.' But if Stoppard's reaction to the 'real social stuff which makes headlines' did not lead to 'the slightest desire to write about it on its own terms', what were the terms of Stoppard's response? 'I think what I would write about if I ever got to the subject at all would be the fact that I was so personally revolted and disturbed by the cold-blooded killing of those three people that I'd like to get the people who did it and cold-bloodedly kill them.'[16]

From the first, that is, Stoppard is unable to deal with political events in terms which are, merely, political. From the first, Stoppard's response to the 'real social stuff which makes headlines' is in implicitly moral terms. The actuality of murder by others prompts the recognition of his own propensity for evil. Stoppard is unable to accuse smugly. If he accuses, it is with the same recognition as Solzhenitsyn that the world is not divided between 'evil people' somewhere out there and 'the rest of us' but that 'the line dividing good and evil cuts through the heart of every human being'.[17] The gulf between Stoppard and a 'committed' political playwright like Edward Bond should be apparent. In a play like *The Woman* (1978) Bond has little difficulty in distinguishing between 'them' and 'us', between those 'evil people' who have insidiously been oppressors and the rest of us who may – the play dramatises approvingly – be able to throw off our oppressors through such a politically necessary step as cold-blooded murder.

For his part, Stoppard has returned to such issues throughout his career. *Rosencrantz and Guildenstern are Dead* demonstrates, as Clive James rightly says, that the fact of the courtiers' deaths mattering so little to Hamlet should have mattered to Shakespeare. *Jumpers* hinges on George's obliviousness to politically expedient murder both on the moon and in his own house. *Travesties* deals, in part, with an ideological imperative which convinces Lenin that 'we've got to *hit* heads, hit them without mercy, though ideally we're against doing violence to people'.[18] In Stoppard's later plays we see the totalitarian fruit, of both the right and the left, which grows from such ideological roots. And in *Hapgood*, Stoppard shows a defender of democracy who is willing to expose a young boy to gunfire in order to catch a suspected traitor, thereby fighting totalitarianism by adopting the enemy's chillingly amoral tactics. But such attempts to find ideological sanction for a mortal to proceed as an avenging angel are always exposed as inadequate. If Stoppard accuses, it is with the recognition that both accuser and accused are subject to the same standard, a standard not based on political expediency or ideological imperative, a standard which reveals that the moral weight of the phrase 'cold-blooded' applies no matter whether it's one of 'us' or one of 'them' who thinks himself justified in killing his fellow man.

However, talk of a moral 'matrix' implies the complexity of context. As Stoppard moves from the affirmation of moral absolutes in his earlier plays to the more applied context of his later plays, the word of moral principle is incarnated in the flesh of moral action. Such a movement from precept to praxis is by no means simple. As Anderson acknowledges at the end of *Professional Foul*, 'ethics is a very complicated business'. If as W.H. Auden tells us, the words of the poet are modified in the guts of the living, it may seem impossible in the welter of actual experience to recognise anything of the timeless among whatever is begotten, born and dies.

But if Stoppard insists on examining an action in its context, he rejects the temptation to suppose that all moral judgement is relative. As *Professional Foul* demonstrates, we may have to know the context to understand the significance of Anderson putting Hollar's manuscript in McKendrick's briefcase or the significance of saying 'You ate well'. But if we need to examine the context of an utterance to appreciate the significance of a word, that does not give us a licence to skew language so that 'words are taken to stand for opposite facts, opposite ideas',[19] to pronounce 'justice is a fraud, property is theft . . . patriotism is propaganda, religion is a con trick'.[20] Just so, if we need to examine the context of an action to appreciate its morality, that does not give us a licence to claim that cold-blooded murder is 'instinctive', 'rational', and 'natural'[21] as Archie once claimed or that 'justice has no existence outside the ways in which we choose to employ the word'.[22] Ethics may not be 'a ghostly Eiffel Tower constructed of Platonic entities'[23] but the importance of discerning the difference between what is just and what is unjust still looms large in Stoppard's canon and one who cannot tell the difference between treating other persons with kindness or with cruelty is, in terms of moral vision, myopic. However complex the interstices may be between the timeless and the temporal in his plays, it is imperative to recognise that Stoppard etches a moral matrix in which the horizontal plane of human experience and the vertical plane of timeless absolutes are both essential. To suppose that his plays can be discussed just in terms of the abstract word of moral precept or just in terms of the flux of human experience is to see only one dimension of the matrix.

Indeed, starting with Rosencrantz and Guildenstern's apprehension of a world beyond their ken, Stoppard's plays have always demonstrated a sense of the numinous beyond the phenomenal. Although acknowledging that few statements go unrebutted, Stoppard vowed that he was 'not going to rebut' his declaration that 'one thing I am sure about is that a materialistic view of history is an insult to the human race'.[24] Starting from that premise, Stoppard's plays have never insulted the human race. Instead his plays pervasively dramatise human beings as not just materialistic entities but moral and spiritual beings. Rosencrantz and Guildenstern intuit that actions in the world they inhabit must signify something other than the redistribution of wealth; George recognises there must be something more in him than meets the microscope; *Travesties* acknowledges a human hunger for something immaterial, a hunger which is common to princes and peasants; *Professional Foul* celebrates 'human rights' as inherent; *The Real Thing* affirms that in committing themselves to each other a couple shares a knowledge 'not of the flesh but through the flesh'; and in *Hapgood* we come to recognise the non-negotiable worth of the individual human being.

Further, there is always in Stoppard the sense that the behaviour of these moral and spiritual creatures is subject to judgement, that there is a fundamental difference between using someone and treating someone as a person, and that the difference between decent and indecent treatment of others is not relative but absolute. Starting with such bit players as Rosencrantz and Guildenstern, the roll call of the disenfranchised, the powerless, the exploitable in Stoppard's canon includes Dotty in *Jumpers*, Carr in *Travesties*, Pavel Hollar in *Professional Foul*, Alexander in *Every Good Boy Deserves Favour*, the dissidents in *Cahoot's Macbeth*, Annie in *The Real Thing*, the boy in *Hapgood*. In each case, however, the human propensity to exploit the exploitable, to treat human beings with inhuman indifference as if they were objects to be used, is exposed as morally culpable. From George turning a deaf ear to his wife's (and Clegthorpe's) calls for help in *Jumpers* to Blair's treatment of life as a boardgame in which small boys are mere pawns, Stoppard's plays consistently lead us to recognise that some actions are morally culpable while other actions are 'not

more useful, or more convenient, or more popular, but simply
pointlessly *better*.[25]

Finally there is the suggestion, though never a sense of
certitude, that these moral beings whose behaviour is subject to
absolute judgement are in all probability not merely human beings
but human creatures, that they are endowed with certain inalienable rights not merely by each other but by their Creator, and that
God, in all probability, is. While Rosencrantz and Guildenstern
merely apprehend the numinous, *Jumpers* – as Kenneth Tynan
rightly described it – is unique in the theatre as 'a farce whose
main purpose is to affirm the existence of God'.[26] Calling *Jumpers*
'a theist play',[27] Stoppard shares George's conviction as well as
his embarrassment at arguing for the existence of both God
the Creator and God the progenitor of moral values. Stoppard
distances himself from theistic affirmations in *Professional Foul*
where Anderson affirms the 'consensus about an individual's
rights' shared both 'by those who invoke God's authority' and
by those who do not while clearly indicating that he does not
invoke divine authority himself. But if there is a straight line from
George's embarrassment to Anderson's equivocation, a quantum
leap separates George's apologia for God as the great un-nudged
nudger of 'an apparently endless line of dominoes' from Kerner's
sense that even the uncertainties of the sub-atomic world impel
him to share Einstein's belief in God: 'Who needed God when
everything worked like billiard balls?'[28]

It is impossible to predict where Stoppard is heading next; playwrights, like physicists and electrons, do not work like billiard
balls. But if it was impossible to predict in mid-career what direction Einstein would take next, it was nevertheless possible to recognise that however wide his intellect may have ranged, Einstein's
concern was to describe, account for, and come to terms with the
real world – however mysterious and awe-inspiring it may be –
rather than make up some fantasy of his own. Stoppard is a realist
in something of the same sense as is Einstein. Just so, the world
of Stoppard's plays is neither surrealistic nor absurdist, however
much such words and concepts may run round in academic
circles. He starts from the belief that the world is real and his
concern is to describe, account for, and come to terms with the
nature of behaviour and the validity of ideas in the real world. In
order to examine the way light travels it may be necessary to set
up a series of refracting mirrors. Similarly, Stoppard may at times

reflect reality not merely by holding the mirror up to nature but by creating an entire hall of mirrors. In *Squaring the Circle* with its multiple versions of events in the confrontations of Solidarity with the Czech government and the Catholic church, it may be impossible finally to say which of the versions is true. But if that 1984 film for television, like much of Stoppard's work, deals in probabilities rather than certainties, it does not deal in impossibilities.

If we cannot know what is coming next from a playwright who 'ultimately . . . would like to have done a bit of absolutely everything' and has always found it 'very hard to turn down offers to write an underwater ballet for dolphins or a play for a motorcyclist on the wall of death',[29] it may yet be possible to observe the energy and momentum of his work. Stoppard's plays, cunningly put together in a certain way so that the whole thing is sprung, will continue to be written with élan, verve, and verbal complexity. But even if the plays are 'intellectual extravaganzas',[30] the core of the toffee apple, the nucleus around which Stoppard's wit and verbal panache and visual high jinks revolve is a recognition of the numinous beyond the phenomenal, of the inextricable link of the mortal and the moral. Thus, Stoppard will not depict human life as a dog-eat-dog power struggle in a world devoid of any sense of the possibility of altruism.

The world of spying in *Hapgood* may at first glance seem like an amoral Pinteresque power struggle; but even there Stoppard affirms the worth of the individual human being and the possibility of self-sacrifice for another. 'The events of the play', says Simon Jones who appeared as Blair in the Los Angeles production, bring Hapgood 'to a more solid realization' that what is both 'real' and 'important' in life are 'straightforward ordinary human relationships' ('Morning Edition', National Public Radio, 12 April 1989). After his weeks of rehearsal with Stoppard in preparation for the play's American première, Jones was echoing concerns which Stoppard has voiced throughout his career. 'I try to be consistent about moral behaviour',[31] Stoppard avers. We can expect such an attempt to continue. And Stoppard's concern for the inherently moral dimension of human behaviour relentlessly impels him towards recognition of a realm which is explained not merely by physics but by metaphysics.

What is reflected in the multiple mirrors of Stoppard's drama is a world which he, like Einstein, recognises as real even as he stands with open-mouthed awe before its mysteries. After eighteen years

of directing Stoppard's work, Peter Wood told an interviewer for
National Public Radio that '*Hapgood* offers the richest example to
date of the playwright's favorite theme'. 'There's no doubt about
it', Wood declares, 'faith is a prerequisite where mankind is
concerned'. If quantum mechanics only predicts probability,
if realities are not 'all bolted together' in a rigidly monumental
Eiffel Tower (as Anderson says of ethics in *Professional Foul*), that
very incertitude may not diminish but may actually increase one's
sense of the ineffable. 'If you cannot say that scientific thinking
is any longer absolutely reliable, if you're going to say that at the
centre of all mathematical thinking there is a dangerous, anarchic,
random element', explains Wood, 'then in a kind of way we're
back to the old situation aren't we?' That old situation, a concern
as old as humankind, echoes through the corridors of Stoppard's
canon, according to Peter Wood, though never more tauntingly
than in *Hapgood*: 'Are we sure there is no God, says the play. *Are we
sure?*' 'And if there is one', Wood adds, 'is He somebody with the
most immense sense of irony?' ('Morning Edition', National Public
Radio, 12 April 1989). What Stoppard sees, what he offers to those
who have eyes to see, is a vision of human beings as moral and
spiritual creatures who inhabit a cosmos which is both real and
freighted with mystery. The reality Stoppard perceives is that
human beings are not just organisms but spiritual beings, that
events cannot be explained by logical positivists because there is
a moral dimension to experience that defies scientific replication.
In this sense, indeed, there is mystery beyond the clockwork and
a sense of metaphysics beyond the physics. But it is the mystery
of the moral and spiritual depth of experience.

Notes

CHAPTER 1: ART AS A MORAL MATRIX

1. Lewis Funke, *Playwrights Talk about Writing: 12 Interviews* (Chicago: Dramatic Publishing, 1975), p. 228.
2. Tom Stoppard, a lecture at the National Theatre, London, 15 November 1984.
3. Tom Stoppard, 'The Language of Theatre', a public lecture at the University of California at Santa Barbara, 14 January 1977; recording: UCSB Library Special Collections.
4. Oleg Kerensky, *The New British Drama: Fourteen Playwrights since Osborne and Pinter* (London: Hamish Hamilton, 1977), p. 170.
5. Tom Stoppard, 'But for the Middle Classes', review of *Enemies of Society*, by Paul Johnson, *Times Literary Supplement*, 3 June 1977, p. 677.
6. Harold Hobson, 'A Fearful Summons', *Sunday Times*, 16 April 1967, p. 49.
7. Peter Lewis, 'How Tom Went to Work on an Absent Mind and Picked up £20,000', *Daily Mail*, 24 May 1967, p. 6.
8. Clive Barnes, 'Theater: *Rosenkrantz* [sic] *and Guildenstern Are Dead*, *New York Times*, 17 October 1967, p. 53.
9. Irving Wardle, 'Theatre: A Grin without a Cat', *The Times*, 22 June 1968, p. 19.
10. Philip Roberts, 'Tom Stoppard: Serious Artist or Siren?' *Critical Quarterly*, 20 (Autumn 1978), pp. 85, 87.
11. Thomas R. Whitaker, *Tom Stoppard* (London: Macmillan; New York: Grove Press, 1983), p. 6.
12. Whitaker, *Tom Stoppard*, p. 9.
13. Whitaker, *Tom Stoppard*, pp. 10, 32, 22.
14. Tim Brassell, *Tom Stoppard: An Assessment* (London: Macmillan; New York: St. Martin's Press, 1985), pp. 15–16.
15. Kenneth Tynan, 'Withdrawing with Style from the Chaos', *New Yorker*, 53 (19 December 1977), pp. 41–111; repr. in Kenneth Tynan, *Show People: Profiles in Entertainment* (New York: Simon and Schuster, 1979), pp. 44–123.
16. Brassell, *Tom Stoppard: An Assessment*, p. 17.
17. Tom Stoppard, 'Ambushes for the Audience: Towards a High Comedy of Ideas', *Theatre Quarterly*, 4, no. 14 (May–July 1974), p. 12: hereafter cited in my text as 'Ambushes'.
18. Stoppard, 'But for the Middle Classes', p. 677.
19. Stoppard, 'But for the Middle Classes', p. 677.
20. Kerensky, *The New British Drama*, p. 170.
21. Kerensky, *The New British Drama*, p. 170.

22. Kerensky, *The New British Drama*, p. 170.
23. Mel Gussow, 'Stoppard's Intellectual Cartwheels Now With Music', *New York Times*, 29 July 1979, sec. 2, p. 22.
24. Tynan, 'Withdrawing with Style from the Chaos', pp. 41–111; repr. in *Show People*, pp. 44–123.
25. Roberts, 'Tom Stoppard: Serious Artist or Siren?' p. 91.
26. Roberts, 'Tom Stoppard: Serious Artist or Siren?' p. 85.
27. Tynan, 'Withdrawing with Style', p. 102; repr. in *Show People*, p. 112. More recently Michael Billington offers a more temperate statement of the same charge: 'What Stoppard doesn't acknowledge is the power of art to unsettle and unnerve or to alter our vision of reality' *Stoppard the Playwright* (London and New York: Methuen, 1987), p. 103.
28. A.C.H. Smith, 'Tom Stoppard', *Flourish* [The RSC Club news-sheet], issue one, 10 June 1974, n. pag.
29. Milton Shulman, 'The Politicizing of Tom Stoppard', *New York Times*, 23 April 1978, sec. 2, p. 3.
30. Hugh Hebert, 'A Playwright in Undiscovered Country', *Guardian*, 7 July 1979, p. 10.
31. Ronald Hayman, *Tom Stoppard*, 4th ed. (London: Heinemann, 1982), p. 137.
32. Andrew K. Kennedy, 'Tom Stoppard's Dissident Comedies', *Modern Drama*, 25 (December 1982) 469.
33. Kennedy, 'Tom Stoppard's Dissident Comedies', p. 470.
34. Eric Salmon, 'Faith in Tom Stoppard', *Queen's Quarterly*, 86 (Summer 1979) 216.
35. Tom Stoppard in interview with David Gollob and David Roper, 'Trad Tom Pops In', *Gambit*, 10, no. 37 (Summer 1981), pp. 10, 11.
36. Hugh Hebert, 'A Playwright in Undiscovered Country', *Guardian*, 7 July 1979, p. 10.
37. Shulman, 'The Politicizing of Tom Stoppard', p. 3.
38. Gussow, 'Stoppard's Intellectual Cartwheels', p. 22.
39. Ronald Hayman, 'Second Interview with Tom Stoppard: 20 August 1976', *Tom Stoppard*, 4th ed., p. 139.
40. Tom Stoppard, a lecture at the National Theatre, London, 15 November 1984.

CHAPTER 2: *ROSENCRANTZ AND GUILDENSTERN ARE DEAD*

1. Tom Stoppard, *Travesties* (London: Faber and Faber, 1975), p. 37.
2. Tim Brassell, *Tom Stoppard: An Assessment* (London, Macmillan: New York: St. Martin's Press, 1985), p. 55; hereafter noted parenthetically in my text as Brassell.
3. Tom Stoppard, 'Ambushes for the Audience: Towards a High Comedy of Ideas', *Theatre Quarterly*, 4, no. 14 (May–July 1974), p. 11, hereafter cited in my text as 'Ambushes'; Ronald Hayman, 'Second Interview with Tom Stoppard: 20 August 1976'; *Tom Stoppard*, 4th

ed. (London: Heinemann, 1982), p. 139; Mel Gussow, 'Stoppard's Intellectual Cartwheels Now with Music', *New York Times*, 29 July 1979, sec. 2, p. 22.

4.   Lewis Funke, *Playwrights Talk about Writing: 12 Interviews* (Chicago: Dramatic Publishing, 1975), p. 221.

5.   Jon Bradshaw, 'Tom Stoppard, Nonstop: Word Games with a Hit Playwright', *New York*, 10 (10 January 1977), p. 50.

6.   Ronald Hayman, 'Profile 9: Tom Stoppard', *New Review*, 1 (December 1974), p. 20.

7.   Janet Watts, 'Tom Stoppard', *Guardian*, 21 March 1973, p. 12.

8.   John Dodd, 'Success Is the Only Unusual Thing about Mr. Stoppard', *Sun*, 13 April 1967, p. 3.

9.   Joost Kuurman, 'An Interview with Tom Stoppard', *Dutch Quarterly Review of Anglo-American Letters*, 10 (1980) 51.

10. Funke, *Playwrights Talk about Writing*, p. 221.

11. Although Joseph E. Duncan recognises the crucial difference that 'while Beckett's characters face interminable waiting, Stoppard's face sudden and inexplicable change', he continues to read the play as 'revealing an absurdist universe' ('Godot Comes: *Rosencrantz and Guildenstern Are Dead*', *Ariel*, 12 [1981] 57, 63). Less helpful is the observation by Richard Corballis that while *Rosencrantz* 'may look derivative', we should eventually see that 'beneath this Beckettian veneer lie the customary Beckettian problems'. Although well aware of Stoppard's rejection of existentialism as neither 'attractive or plausible', Corballis insists that 'most critics have been happy to plump for the existential label' (*Stoppard: The Mystery and the Clockwork* [Oxford: Amber Lane Press; New York: Methuen, 1984], pp. 33, 36, 47, 48). This shaky argument is sufficiently compelling to Corballis that he chooses, contentedly, to plump along with the rest.

12. Ruby Cohn, 'Tom Stoppard: Light Drama and Dirges in Marriage', in C.W.E. Bigsby (ed.), *Contemporary English Drama*, Stratford-Upon-Avon Studies, no. 19 (London: Edward Arnold; New York: Holmes & Meier, 1981), p. 114.

13. Jim Hunter, *Tom Stoppard's Plays* (London: Faber and Faber, 1982), p. 170.

14. William E. Gruber, '"Wheels within wheels, etcetera": Artistic Design in *Rosencrantz and Guildenstern Are Dead*', *Comparative Drama*, 15 (Winter 1981-82) 308; hereafter noted parenthetically in my text as Gruber.

15. Oleg Kerensky, *The New British Drama: Fourteen Playwrights since Osborne and Pinter* (London: Hamish Hamilton, 1977), p. 170.

16. Giles Gordon, 'Tom Stoppard', *Transatlantic Review*, no. 29 (Summer 1968), p. 20.

17. Brassell, *Tom Stoppard: An Assessment*, pp. 66, 47.

18. Jim Hunter, *Tom Stoppard's Plays*, pp. 139–40.

19. Tom Stoppard, *Rosencrantz and Guildenstern are Dead*, rev. ed. (London: Faber and Faber, 1968) p. 7; hereafter noted parenthetically in my text.

20. Jonathan Bennett, 'Philosophy and Mr Stoppard', *Philosophy*, 50 (January 1975) 8.

21. Stoppard's peacock story is conflated from three of his numerous retellings: 'One Pair of Eyes: Tom Stoppard Doesn't Know' (television documentary), London: BBC 2, 7 July 1972, transcript housed in the BBC Script Library, pp. 5–6; Bradshaw, 'Tom Stoppard, Nonstop', p. 50; 'An Evening with Tom Stoppard' (a question-and-answer session at the American Conservatory Theatre), San Francisco, 27 March 1977, transcript housed in the ACT offices, p. 5. For other accounts see Kenneth Tynan, 'Withdrawing with Style from the Chaos', *New Yorker*, 53 (19 December 1977), p. 41, repr. in Kenneth Tynan, *Show People: Profiles in Entertainment* (New York: Simon and Schuster, 1979), p. 45; Sylvie Drake, 'Stage Notes: Tom Stoppard–The Entertainer', *Los Angeles Times*, 12 December 1974, sec. 4, p. 26; Janet Watts, 'Tom Stoppard', *Guardian*, 21 March 1973, p. 12; Richard Natale, 'I'm Always Chasing Peacocks', *Women's Wear Daily*, 27 April 1972, p. 12.

22. 'An Evening with Tom Stoppard', 27 March 1977, p. 5.

23. Mel Gussow, 'Stoppard Refutes Himself, Endlessly', *New York Times*, 26 April 1972, p. 54.

24. Rodney Simard, 'The Logic of Unicorns: Beyond Absurdism in Stoppard', *Arizona Quarterly*, 38 (Spring 1982) 37–44.

25. Jim Hunter, *Tom Stoppard's Plays*, p. 139.

26. Tom Stoppard, *Jumpers*, 2nd. ed. (London and Boston: Faber and Faber, 1986), p. 60.

27. Tom Stoppard, lecture at the National Theatre, London, 15 November 1984.

28. As recorded in the prompt script for *Rosencrantz and Guildenstern Are Dead* housed in the National Theatre, London; cf. text: 'We'll be free', p. 72.

29. The survival of art is emphasised in the ending Stoppard wrote for a 1978 radio version of *Rosencrantz and Guildenstern are Dead*. Although retaining Horatio's final speech from *Hamlet* as the closing lines of Stoppard's play, the radio version ends as '*Horatio's voice is fading and being overtaken by the elemental sounds of wind and water, and then the creak of the player's cart and the player's distant voice urging, "Onward!!"*' Transcript housed in the BBC Drama Script Library.

30. National Theatre prompt script for *Rosencrantz*, p. III-21, cf. text, p. 95.

31. National Theatre prompt script for *Rosencrantz*, p. III-21, cf. text, p. 95.

32. Peter J. Rabinowitz, '"What's Hecuba to Us?": The Audience's Experience of Literary Borrowing', in Susan R. Suleiman and Inge Crosman (eds), *The Reader in the Text: Essays on Audience and Interpretation* (Princeton, N.J.: Princeton University Press, 1980), pp. 241–63.

33. Jill Levenson, 'Views from a Revolving Door: Tom Stoppard's Canon to Date', *Queen's Quarterly*, 78 (Autumn 1971) 436.

34. Rabinowitz, '"What's Hecuba to Us?"', p. 257.

35. Hersh Zeifman, 'Tomfoolery: Stoppard's Theatrical Puns', in *Yearbook of English Studies*, 9 (1979), p. 206.

36. Zeifman, 'Tomfoolery', p. 207.

37. Zeifman, 'Tomfoolery', p. 206.

38. Michael Billington, *Stoppard the Playwright* (London and New York: Methuen, 1987), p. 35.

39. Tom Stoppard to Stanley Eichelbaum, '"Call me the thinking man's farceur"', *San Francisco Examiner*, 11 December 1974, p. 69.

40. Funke, *Playwrights Talk about Writing*, p. 221.

41. Kerensky, *The New British Drama*, p. 170.

42. Funke, *Playwrights Talk about Writing*, p. 228.

CHAPTER 3: *JUMPERS*

1. Perhaps Tarzan's swinging descent onto the *Jumpers* stage should – like Captain Scott's – be described as a re-entry. As part of the original script 'And Now The Incredible Archibald Jumpers', Tarzan rehearsed for the 1972 production, survived the shortening of the title to *Jumpers*, and actually was allowed to swing for two nights on the Old Vic stage. However, during previews prior to the opening night in January 1972 the decision was made that Tarzan had to go. Although he left his mark on the rehearsal script preserved at the National Theatre, Tarzan never appeared in any published version of the play or in any production. Between his disappearance from the Old Vic stage on 28 January 1972 and his blood-curdling re-entry at the Aldwych on 1 April 1985, Tarzan had gone out and had been gone for some time.

2. G.B. Crump, 'The Universe as Murder Mystery: Tom Stoppard's *Jumpers*', *Contemporary Literature*, 20 (Summer 1979) 356; Eric Salmon, 'Faith in Tom Stoppard', *Queen's Quarterly*, 86 (Summer 1979) 215; Salmon, p. 215; Crump, p. 354.

3. Kenneth Tynan, 'Withdrawing with Style from the Chaos', *New Yorker*, 53 (19 December 1977), p. 44; repr. in Kenneth Tynan, *Show People: Profiles in Entertainment* (New York: Simon and Schuster, 1979), p. 53.

4. Tom Stoppard, 'Ambushes for the Audience: Towards a High Comedy of Ideas', *Theatre Quarterly*, 4, no. 14 (May–July 1974), p. 7; hereafter cited in my text as 'Ambushes'.

5. Tynan, 'Withdrawing with Style', p. 85; repr. in *Show People*, p. 93.

6. Mel Gussow, 'Stoppard's Intellectual Cartwheels Now With Music', *New York Times*, 29 July 1979, sec. 2, p. 22.

7. Tim Brassell, *Tom Stoppard: An Assessment* (London: Macmillan; New York: St. Martin's Press, 1985), p. 132.

8. Crump, 'The Universe as Murder Mystery', pp. 366, 368.

9. Tom Stoppard in 'A Conversation' with Peter Wood in the programme for the National Theatre's 1976 production of *Jumpers*,

n. pag; 'First Interview with Tom Stoppard: 12 June 1974', in Ronald Hayman, *Tom Stoppard*, 4th ed. (London: Heinemann, 1982), p. 5; Tom Stoppard, 'The Language of Theatre', a lecture delivered at the University of California at Santa Barbara, 14 January 1977; Stoppard, 'A Conversation', n. pag.

10. Mel Gussow, '*Jumpers* Author is Verbal Gymnast', *New York Times*, 23 April 1974, p. 36.

11. Tom Stoppard, *Jumpers*, 2nd ed. (London and Boston: Faber and Faber, 1986), p. 12. Quotations hereafter noted parenthetically in my text are from this revised 1986 edition. Material contained only in the first two printings of the first edition of *Jumpers* (London: Faber and Faber, 1972) will be identified as '1972 text'. The third and subsequent printings of the first edition – identified by the author's 'Postscript (February 1973)', p. 11 – incorporated revisions made in the course of the original National Theatre production at the Old Vic. Material contained in this state of the text will be identified as '1973 text'.

12. Tom Stoppard, 'But for the Middle Classes', review of *Enemies of Society*, by Paul Johnson, *Times Literary Supplement*, 3 June 1977, p. 677.

13. Stoppard, 'But for the Middle Classes', p. 677.

14. Lucina P. Gabbard identifies Stoppard's advice with Archie's and asserts that the play ridicules morality ('Stoppard's *Jumpers*: A Mystery Play', *Modern Drama* 20 [March 1977] 95, 88). Mary R. Davidson concurs that Archie 'is not an unsympathetic character' ('Historical Homonyms: A New Way of Naming in Tom Stoppard's *Jumpers*', *Modern Drama*, 22 [September 1979] 310).

15. Crump, 'The Universe as Murder Mystery', p. 368.

16. Michael Billington, *Stoppard the Playwright* (London and New York: Methuen, 1987), p. 90.

17. Tom Stoppard to Oleg Kerensky, *The New British Drama: Fourteen Playwrights since Osborne and Pinter* (London: Hamish Hamilton, 1977), p. 170.

18. Quoted by Mel Gussow, 'Stoppard Refutes Himself, Endlessly', *New York Times*, 26 April 1972, p. 54.

19. Prior to Stoppard's 1973 decision to shorten the Coda by deleting the appearance of Captain Scott, Archie defended the murder as 'instinctive', 'rational', and 'natural' (1972 text, p. 84). With Stoppard's decision to retain Captain Scott in the 1985 Aldwych production, Archie's defence of the cold-blooded murder as 'your natural response to a pure situation' (p. 74; 1972 text, p. 84) was restored to the script.

20. Stoppard, 'But for the Middle Classes', p. 677.

21. John A. Bailey, '*Jumpers* by Tom Stoppard: The Ironist as Theistic Apologist', *Michigan Academician*, 11 (Winter 1979) 248; repr. in Harold Bloom (ed.), *Tom Stoppard*, Modern Critical Views (New York: Chelsea House, 1986), p. 41.

22. I agree with Bailey that 'Here, for once, George is no longer mannered, or ridiculous, but speaks with eloquent authority –

and Stoppard, one senses, speaks with him' (p. 248; repr. Bloom, p. 42). But Bailey places so much weight on that phrase 'for once' that he can eventually conclude 'that jumping also refers to life, that for Stoppard living is jumping, from one position to another, finally from life to death' (pp. 249–50; repr. Bloom, p. 43).

23. Tom Stoppard to Kerensky, *The New British Drama*, p. 170.
24. Tom Stoppard to Kerensky, *The New British Drama*, p. 170.
25. Richard Corballis, *Stoppard: The Mystery and the Clockwork* (Oxford: Amber Lane Press; New York: Methuen; 1984).
26. Corballis, *The Mystery and the Clockwork*, p. 15.
27. Quoted by Gussow, 'Stoppard Refutes Himself', p. 54. Two years later Stoppard expresses the identical affirmation to Gussow, '*Jumpers* Author', p. 36.
28. Quoted by Gussow, '*Jumpers* Author', p. 36 (my italics).
29. See Kathleen Halton's interview with Stoppard ([American] *Vogue*, 15 October 1967, p. 112), in which he anticipates the consequences of landing on the moon.
30. Gabrielle Robinson, 'Nothing Left but Parody: Friedrich Dürrenmatt and Tom Stoppard', *Theatre Journal*, 32 (March 1980) 90–1. Michael Hinden commits much the same error in '*Jumpers*: Stoppard and the Theater of Exhaustion', *Twentieth Century Literature*, 27 (Spring 1981) 1–15. Citing the murders in the play, Hinden asserts: 'Evidence is lacking in such a world to support either of George's intuitions, that of a "God of Goodness to account for moral values" or that of a "God of Creation to account for existence". The old philosophy George clings to is a ladder that cannot support much weight' (pp. 10–11). Hinden implies, rather naïvely, that if a God of goodness exists humankind would be incapable of murder. But George never predicates divine perfection on the existence of human perfection.
31. Brassell, *Tom Stoppard: An Assessment*, p. 127.
32. The inhumanity of George's actions should give us pause when we encounter Susan Rusinko's observation that 'the philosophical gymnasts – Archie, McFee, and Clegthorpe – with their relativistic, intuitional, pragmatic ethics . . . contrast sharply with George's failed philosophy but decent behavior' (*Tom Stoppard* [Boston: Twayne, 1986], p. 43). Rusinko gets it wrong on just about all counts. Archie and McFee are not the intuitionist philosophers; George is. George's philosophy does not fail in the play; but his inhuman indifference to Dotty displays a behaviour which is anything but 'decent'.
33. In the interest of brevity, Stoppard reluctantly deleted the appearance of the astronaut from the initial production of *Jumpers*; see his note dated February 1973 (1973 text, p. 11). However Stoppard restored Scott to the 1985 Aldwych production of *Jumpers*; see his note in the 1986 revised edition of the play, about changes 'made for the 1984 [sic] production' (p. 5).
34. Billington, *Stoppard the Playwright*, p. 87.
35. Gabrielle Robinson, 'Plays Without Plot: The Theatre of Tom Stoppard', *Educational Theatre Journal*, 29 (March 1977) 47.

36. For the 1985 Aldwych production, Stoppard retained the form of Henry II's famous question but updated the last words. In this most recent version Archie intones 'Will no one rid me of this copper's nark!' (p. 76).

37. For the 1985 Aldwych production, Stoppard deleted the line because he thought 'the line was unnecessary and made an obvious point of something that the audience would already have grasped'. The deletion came much to the chagrin of at least one American academic according to an account Stoppard provided to Clare Colvin ('The Real Tom Stoppard', *Drama*, 43, no. 161 [1986], p. 10).

38. Clive James, 'Count Zero Splits the Infinite', *Encounter*, 45 (November 1975), pp. 71, 70.

CHAPTER 4: *TRAVESTIES*

1. Ronald Hayman, 'First Interview with Tom Stoppard: 12 June 1974', *Tom Stoppard*, 4th ed. (London: Heinemann, 1982), p. 12.

2. Tom Stoppard, *Travesties* (London: Faber and Faber, 1975), pp. 18–19; hereafter cited parenthetically in my text.

3. Mel Gussow, 'Stoppard Refutes Himself, Endlessly', *New York Times*, 26 April 1972, p. 54.

4. Janet Watts, 'Tom Stoppard', *Guardian*, 21 March 1973, p. 12.

5. Tom Topor, 'Lunch with a Playwright', *New York Post*, 10 April 1974, p. 64.

6. Mel Gussow, '*Jumpers* Author Is Verbal Gymnast', *New York Times*, 23 April 1974, p. 36.

7. Tom Stoppard, 'Ambushes for the Audience: Towards a High Comedy of Ideas', *Theatre Quarterly*, 4, no. 14 (May–July 1974), p. 16; hereafter cited in my text as 'Ambushes'.

8. Hersh Zeifman, 'Tomfoolery: Stoppard's Theatrical Puns', in *Yearbook of English Studies*, 9 (1979), p. 213.

9. Andrew K. Kennedy, 'Natural, Mannered, and Parodic Dialogue', *Yearbook of English Studies*, 9 (1979), p. 50; Rodney Simard, 'The Logic of Unicorns: Beyond Absurdism in Stoppard', *Arizona Quarterly*, 38 (Spring 1982) 37; Andrew K. Kennedy, 'Tom Stoppard's Dissident Comedies', *Modern Drama*, 25 (December 1982) 469; Gabrielle Robinson, 'Plays without Plot: The Theatre of Tom Stoppard', *Educational Theatre Journal*, 29 (March 1977) 37.

10. Eric Salmon, 'Faith in Tom Stoppard', *Queen's Quarterly*, 86 (Summer 1979) 215, 229.

11. David Camroux, 'Tom Stoppard: The Last of the Metaphysical Egocentrics', *Caliban* (Toulouse), 15 (1978) 86.

12. The voices in the chorus are those of John William Cooke, 'The Optical Allusion: Perception and Form in Stoppard's *Travesties*', *Modern Drama*, 24 (December 1981) 525; Gabrielle Robinson, 'Nothing Left but Parody: Friedrich Dürrenmatt and

Tom Stoppard', *Theatre Journal*, 32 (March 1980) 85-94; Michael Hinden, '*Jumpers*: Stoppard and the Theater of Exhaustion', *Twentieth Century Literature*, 27 (Spring 1981) 1–15; Carol Billman, 'The Art of History in Tom Stoppard's *Travesties*', *Kansas Quarterly*, 12, no. 4 (Fall 1980), p. 47; Kennedy, 'Dissident Comedies', p. 469; Simard, 'Logic of Unicorns', p. 37.

13.   In March 1977 while in San Francisco for the American Conservatory Theater production of *Travesties* Stoppard chatted with interviewers at a press luncheon and met with an ACT audience for a question-and-answer session which was billed as 'An Evening with Tom Stoppard'. A tape recording and partial transcript of the latter as well as various newspaper accounts of the former are preserved in the ACT archives. Stoppard's assertions in the above paragraph of his personal stance largely come from this material.

Stoppard's statements occur, respectively, in Robert Taylor, 'Tom Stoppard's Plays Are More Than Just "Clever Nonsense"', *Oakland Tribune*, 17 April 1977, p. 2; 'An Evening with Tom Stoppard', 27 March 1977; Ronald Hayman, 'First Interview', *Tom ᷉oppard*, p. 10; Stanley Eichelbaum, 'So Often Produced, He Ranks ᷉ith Shaw', *San Francisco Examiner*, 28 March 1977, p. 24; Bernard Weiner, 'A Puzzling, "Traditional" Stoppard', *San Francisco Chronicle*, 29 March 1977, p. 40; Taylor, 'More Than Just "Clever Nonsense"'; Barbara Bladen, 'Playwright Sees Plays as "Rational"', *San Mateo Times*, 29 March 1977, p. 29; Kenneth Tynan, 'Withdrawing with Style', p. 108; Eichelbaum, 'So Often Produced'; Taylor, 'More Than Just "Clever Nonsense"'; C.E. Maves, 'A Playwright on the Side of Rationality', *Palo Alto Times*, 25 March 1977, p. 16.

14.   Coppélia Kahn, '*Travesties* and the Importance of Being Stoppard', *New York Literary Forum*, 1 (Spring 1978) 196.

15.   Allan Rodway, 'Stripping Off', *London Magazine*, 16 (August/September 1976), p. 68.

16.   Eichelbaum, 'So Often Produced, He Ranks with Shaw'.

17.   In 'The Event and the Text', a public lecture at San Diego State University, San Diego, California, 4 November 1981, Stoppard partially translated the speech having first admonished the audience, only half-kiddingly, not to relay the French translation to any actor playing Tzara.

18.   Tzara's putative nonsense is printed as four lines in the published version of *Travesties*. Tynan published the above translation of the last two lines in 1977 ('Withdrawing with Style', p. 101; repr. *Show People*, p. 110). In 1981 Ruby Cohn ventured a translation of lines 1 and 4 but reported that she was stumped by lines 2 and 3 ('Tom Stoppard: Light Drama and Dirges in Marriage', in C.W.E. Bigsby [ed.], *Contemporary English Drama*, Stratford-upon-Avon Studies, no. 19 [London: Edward Arnold; New York: Holmes & Meier, 1981], p. 117). The first published translation of all four lines was offered by Felicia Hardison Londré, who, however, appears to mistranslate (see the following footnote) the first two lines:

> *Il est énorme, s'appelle Tzara,*
> *Qui déréchef se hâte. Hilare nonpareil!*
> *Il reste à la Suisse parcequ'il est un artiste.*
> *'Nous n'avons que l'art,' il déclara!*

> He is larger-than-life, is called Tzara,
> Who rushes headlong once again. Peerless jokester!
> He stays in Switzerland because he is an artist.
> 'We have only art!' were his words.

(*Tom Stoppard* [New York: Ungar, 1981] pp. 72, 168)

19. The RSC Archives at Stratford-upon-Avon preserve both a prompt book and a stage manager's script from the 1974 Aldwych production. In the prompt book, which seems to be the earlier of the two versions, Tzara's first words appear as follows:

> Ell ate enormous appletzara
> key dairy chef's hat he'll learn oomparah!
> Ill raced alas whis-
> pers kill later nut east,
> noon avuncular ill day Clara!

In the stage manager's copy, a typescript prepared by Fraser & Dunlop, the five-line arrangement above is lost:

> Eel ate enormous appletzara
> key dairy chef's hat he'll learn
> oomparah!
> Ill raced alas
> whispers kill later
> nut east
> noon avuncular ill day Clara!

Although the prompt book substitutes 'Ell' for 'Eel' as the first word (perhaps a typographical error), its arrangement of words on the page seems much more authoritative. The prompt script provides a five-line limerick structure with a rhyme on 'appletzara', 'oomparah', and 'Clara' and a slant rhyme on 'whis-' and 'east'.

Jim Hunter was the first critic to recognise Tzara's words as 'the play's first limerick – in *French*'. Although he differs with Londré on both the first and second lines, even he puts a question mark after the second line:

> *Il est un homme, s'appelle Tzara*
> *Qui des richesses a-t-il nonpareil (?)*
> *Il reste à la Suisse*
> *Parce qu'il est un artiste*
> *'Nous n'avons que l'art', il déclara.*

He is a man called Tzara
who has unparalleled talent
He stays in Switzerland
Because he is an artist
'We have only art,' he declared.

(*Tom Stoppard's Plays* [London: Faber and Faber, 1982], p. 240).

20. Kahn, 'The Importance of Being Stoppard', p. 192.
21. Tom Stoppard, *The Real Thing*, rev. ed. (London and Boston: Faber and Faber, 1984), pp. 53, 54; hereafter cited parenthetically in my text.
22. For this understanding of the contrast between Tzara's and Cecily's treatments of words, I am indebted to the insights of Jay Hochstedt offered while he was an undergraduate at Westmont College.
23. Hayman, 'Profile 9: Tom Stoppard', *New Review*, 1 (December 1974), p. 20.
24. Charles Marowitz, 'Tom Stoppard – The Theater's Intellectual P.T. Barnum', *New York Times*, 19 October 1975, sec. 2, p. 5.
25. Craig Werner, 'Stoppard's Critical Travesty, or, Who Vindicates Whom and Why', *Arizona Quarterly*, 35 (Autumn 1979) 231.
26. Weiner, 'A Puzzling, "Traditional" Stoppard'.
27. Robert Taylor, 'More Than Just "Clever Nonsense"'; 'An Evening With Tom Stoppard', 27 March 1977.
28. Gussow, 'Stoppard Refutes Himself, Endlessly', p. 54.
29. Marowitz, 'The Theater's Intellectual P.T. Barnum', p. 5.
30. Taylor, 'More Than Just "Clever Nonsense"'.
31. Watts, 'Tom Stoppard', p. 12.
32. Howard D. Pearce, 'Stage as Mirror: Tom Stoppard's *Travesties*', *MLN*, 94 (December 1979) 1156.
33. Cooke, 'The Optical Allusion', pp. 527, 536; Margaret Gold, 'Who Are the Dadas of *Travesties*?' *Modern Drama*, 21 (March 1978) 64.
34. Cooke, 'The Optical Allusion', p. 536.
35. Pearce, 'Stage as Mirror', p. 1154.
36. Gussow, '*Jumpers* Author Is Verbal Gymnast', p. 36.
37. Tom Stoppard, 'But for the Middle Classes', review of *Enemies of Society* by Paul Johnson, *Times Literary Supplement*, 3 June 1977, p. 677.
38. Stoppard confirmed to Kenneth Tynan that he concurs in Carr's definition of an artist ('Withdrawing with Style', p. 80; repr. *Show People*, p. 90).
39. Richard Ellmann, 'The Zealots of Zurich', *Times Literary Supplement*, 12 July 1974, p. 744.
40. Daniel Henninger, 'Theater: Tom Stoppard and the Politics of Morality', *Wall Street Journal*, 1 February 1980, p. 17.
41. Kennedy, 'Dissident Comedies', p. 470; Robinson, 'Plays without Plot', p. 43; Cooke, 'The Optical Allusion', p. 527.
42. Stoppard, 'But for the Middle Classes', p. 677.
43. Stoppard, 'But for the Middle Classes', p. 677.
44. Watts, 'Tom Stoppard', p. 12.

45. Salmon, 'Faith in Tom Stoppard', p. 224.
46. Tynan, 'Withdrawing with Style', pp. 102, 85; repr. *Show People*, pp. 112, 93-4.
47. Tynan, 'Withdrawing with Style', p. 110; cf. *Show People*, p. 121.
48. For this comparison of Carr and Joyce, I am happy to acknowledge my indebtedness to the insights of former student Jay Hochstedt.
49. Gussow, '*Jumpers* Author', p. 36; A.C.H. Smith, 'Tom Stoppard', *Flourish* [The RSC Club news-sheet], issue one, 10 June 1974, n. pag.
50. Harold Clurman, 'Theatre', *Nation*, 221 (22 November 1975) 540.
51. Salmon, 'Faith in Tom Stoppard', p. 232.
52. Gerald Weales, 'The Stage: *Travesties*', *Commonweal*, 103 (13 February 1976) 114.

CHAPTER 5: THE 'POLITICAL' PLAYS

1. Ronald Hayman, 'First Interview with Tom Stoppard: 12 June 1974', *Tom Stoppard*, 4th ed. (London: Heinemann, 1982), p. 2.
2. Tom Stoppard, 'Ambushes for the Audience: Towards a High Comedy of Ideas', *Theatre Quarterly*, 4, no. 14 (May–July 1974), p. 13; hereafter cited in my text as 'Ambushes'.
3. Milton Shulman, 'The Politicizing of Tom Stoppard', *New York Times*, 23 April 1978, sec. 2, pp. 3, 27.
4. Joan FitzPatrick Dean, *Tom Stoppard: Comedy as a Moral Matrix* (Columbia: University of Missouri Press, 1981), pp. 88–9.
5. Tom Stoppard, '*Every Good Boy Deserves Favour: A Play for Actors and Orchestra*' and '*Professional Foul: A Play for Television*' (London: Faber and Faber, 1978); Tom Stoppard, *Night and Day*, 2nd ed. (London: Faber and Faber, 1979); Tom Stoppard, *Dogg's Hamlet, Cahoot's Macbeth* (London: Faber and Faber, 1980). Quotations from these editions will be noted parenthetically in my text.
6. 'Tom Stoppard on the KGB's Olympic trials', *Sunday Times*, 6 April 1980, p. 16.
7. Felicia Hardison Londré, *Tom Stoppard* (New York: Frederick Ungar, 1981), p. 142.
8. John Barber, 'Newspaper Drama is Year's Best New Play', *Daily Telegraph*, 10 November 1978.
9. The term comes from Ronald Hayman who remonstrates that if *Professional Foul* had been presented pseudonymously it would scarcely have been 'identifiable' as Stoppard's work (*Tom Stoppard*, 4th ed., London: Heinemann, 1982, p. 137). Although Hayman offers perhaps the most extreme denial of the continuity of Stoppard's drama, other critics emphasise the change in Stoppard's material while virtually ignoring the moral matrix which continues to figure as the pattern in his carpet. See Victor L. Cahn, *Beyond Absurdity: The Plays of Tom Stoppard* (Rutherford, N. J.: Fairleigh Dickinson

University Press, 1979); Michael Hinden, '*Jumpers*: Stoppard and the Theater of Exhaustion', *Twentieth Century Literature*, 27 (Spring 1981) 1–15.

J.L. Styan argues that Stoppard's 'career in flighty Pirandellian theater gamesmanship has taken a turn toward the serious' ('High Tide in the London Theatre: Some Notes on the 1978–79 Season', *Comparative Drama*, 13 [Fall 1979] 255) and Joan FitzPatrick Dean concurs that these plays 'turn from the frivolous and farcical' in a clear 'departure from his work prior to 1975' (*Comedy as a Moral Matrix*, pp. 86, 87). Such criticism not only overstates the transformation in Stoppard's art by failing to recognise the stature of the earlier plays, it also fundamentally misperceives the significance of Stoppard's newly 'political' plays.

10. Kenneth Tynan, 'Withdrawing with Style from the Chaos', *New Yorker*, 53 (19 December 1977), pp. 41–111; repr. in Kenneth Tynan, *Show People: Profiles in Entertainment* (New York: Simon and Schuster, 1979), pp. 44–123.

11. Neil Sammells, *Tom Stoppard: The Artist as Critic* (London: Macmillan, 1988), pp. 122, x, 142.

12. Robert Berkvist, 'This Time, Stoppard Plays It (Almost) Straight', *New York Times*, 25 November 1979, sec. 2, p. 5.

13. Shulman, 'The Politicizing of Tom Stoppard', p. 3.

14. Berkvist, 'This Time', p. 5.

15. Hugh Hebert, 'A Playwright in Undiscovered Country', *Guardian*, 7 July 1979, p. 10.

16. Hebert, 'A Playwright in Undiscovered Country', p. 10.

17. Daniel Henninger, 'Theater: Tom Stoppard and the Politics of Morality', *Wall Street Journal*, 1 February 1980, p. 17.

18. Henninger, 'Tom Stoppard and the Politics of Morality', p. 17.

19. Oleg Kerensky, *The New British Drama: Fourteen Playwrights since Osborne and Pinter* (London: Hamish Hamilton, 1977), p. 170.

20. Nevertheless, given the rather peremptory dismissal of 'club rules' it is a clear implication of Anderson's speech that if humans *do* have rights which are not fictions, then God exists. He is, thus, similar to George in asserting that belief in the reality of moral absolutes leads to belief in God.

21. Stoppard may not be as philosophically precise as he might be in using 'right' and 'rights' virtually interchangeably. Indeed, philosophy dons upon first seeing *Professional Foul* noted that Stoppard was 'perhaps not quite so good at philosophy itself but terribly good at philosophers' ('Dons Wave Play On', *Times Higher Education Supplement*, 30 September 1977, p. 5). But while one might wish to draw a more precise philosophical line between what is right and what are rights, Stoppard certainly does not see a diametric opposition between moral right and human rights as argued by Richard J. Buhr, 'Epistemology and Ethics in Tom Stoppard's *Profession Foul*', *Comparative Drama*, 13 (Winter 1979–80) 320–9.

22. 'Tom Stoppard on the KGB's Olympic Trials', *Sunday Times*, 6 April 1980, p. 16.

23. Kenneth Tynan, 'Withdrawing with Style', p. 46; cf. *Show People*, p. 57. Tynan was perhaps the earliest commentator to note the affirmation of moral absolutes in both *Jumpers* and *Every Good Boy Deserves Favour* ('Withdrawing', pp. 85, 46; repr. *Show People*, pp. 93, 57). But Tynan saw any change in Stoppard's plays or personal beliefs as tentative and inadequate steps towards politicization rather than the organic outworking of Stoppard's earlier affirmation of moral absolutes. Noting 'signs' that 'history' was 'forcing Stoppard into the arena of commitment' ('Withdrawing', p. 45; repr. *Show People*, p. 57), Tynan presented Stoppard's political actions and writings as reactions to external stimuli rather than seeing the more recent work as bodying forth the concerns of Stoppard's earlier drama.

24. Dean, *Comedy as a Moral Matrix*, p. 88.

25. Tom Stoppard quoted by Berkvist, 'This Time', p. 5.

26. Although Stoppard told Nancy Shields Hardin that his 'idea was to stage it as though it was absolutely real . . . and then for the revelation to be retroactive', he admitted that 'I must say that it hasn't always succeeded in the case of the audiences for *Night and Day*'. In April 1979 Stoppard said he was still tinkering with the scene because 'Some people weren't quite sure . . . afterwards whether it was a fantasy or not. Although there was no way it couldn't be one. Even some of the original reviews referred to the scene as though it actually happened' ('An Interview with Tom Stoppard', *Contemporary Literature*, 22 [Spring 1981] 159–60).

27. Dean, *Comedy as a Moral Matrix*, p. 101.

28. Berkvist, 'This Time', p. 5; see also Hebert, 'A Playwright in Undiscovered Country', p. 10; and Nancy Shields Hardin, 'An Interview with Tom Stoppard', p. 159.

29. David Gollob and David Roper, 'Trad Tom Pops In', *Gambit*, 10, no. 37 (Summer 1981), p. 15.

30. Buhr, 'Epistemology and Ethics', pp. 321–2.

31. Tom Stoppard, *Jumpers* (London: Faber & Faber, 1973 text), p. 85.

32. Gollob and Roper, 'Trad Tom Pops In', p. 7.

33. Although stepping on the tortoise had always been intended as *Jumpers'* first act curtain with the second act consisting of the colloquium itself, Stoppard said that by the time his characters had finished talking, two hours had gone by and George's address had to be relegated to the 'Coda'.

34. Buhr, 'Epistemology and Ethics', p. 328. Buhr is surely incorrect in implying that McKendrick speaks for Stoppard. McKendrick is identified as a Marxist (p. 48), an empiricist (p. 60), a pragmatist (p. 85) and a self-aggrandizing careerist who is not above a swift kick in the kneecap on the way up the academic ladder (p. 85). McKendrick in short recapitulates the values of the jumpers which Stoppard so utterly condemned in his earlier play.

35. Gollob and Roper, 'Trad Tom Pops In', p. 8.

36. Gollob and Roper, 'Trad Tom Pops In', pp. 8, 9, 8.

37. Tynan, 'Withdrawing with Style', p. 46; repr. *Show People*, pp. 56–7.

38. Tom Stoppard, 'Czech Human Rights', *The Times*, 7 February 1977, p. 15.

39. The conviction that actions by people in the West can make a difference motivated Stoppard's own efforts on behalf of a good boy who deserved a father. Having served as international chairman of the 'Let Misha Go' committee, Stoppard told reporters that the boy's release demonstrated that 'for the Soviet leaders, silence is golden'. 'They can be forced to move by public protest', he said, 'The lesson is that the people in the Kremlin want us to shut up. If the only way they can get us to shut up is to let someone out, they let them out' ('Russians Free Exiled Doctor's Mother and Son', *Daily Telegraph*, 26 April 1979, p. 1).

40. Peter Stothard, review of *Every Good Boy Deserves Favour*, *Plays and Players*, 24 (September 1977), p. 33.

41. Joost Kuurman, 'An Interview with Tom Stoppard', *Dutch Quarterly Review of Anglo-American Letters*, 10 (1980) 53.

42. Kuurman, 'An Interview with Tom Stoppard', p. 53.

43. Martin Huckerby, 'Arts Diary: KGB to Blame in the End', *The Times*, 17 August 1978, p. 12.

44. Kuurman, 'An Interview with Tom Stoppard', p. 53.

45. Joan FitzPatrick Dean's 1981 assertion that 'only through the ineptitude of Colonel Rozinsky . . . is Alexander released' (*Comedy as a Moral Matrix*, p. 96) is clearly incorrect. More ambiguously Thomas Whitaker refers to the ending as 'sly bureaucratic confusion' but finds that the Colonel's 'reputed "genius" is hard to distinguish from stupidity' (*Tom Stoppard* [London: Macmillan; New York: Grove Press, 1983], pp. 142, 138). By contrast, Jim Hunter rightly recognises that 'Stoppard did not intend any ambiguity: the Colonel is *pretending* to make an error' (*Tom Stoppard's Plays* [London: Faber and Faber, 1982], pp. 246–7). Tim Brassell adds the further insight that the Colonel's 'underhand' device 'ensures that Alexander's release is not obtained on his own terms' (*Tom Stoppard: An Assessment* [London: Macmillan; New York: St. Martin's Press, 1985], p. 186).

46. The assertion by Victor L. Cahn, *Beyond Absurdity: The Plays of Tom Stoppard* (Rutherford: Fairleigh Dickinson University Press, 1979), p. 147, is corrected by Felicia Hardison Londré, rreview of *Beyond Absurdity*, *Comparative Drama*, 14 (Summer 1980) 199.

47. Londré, *Tom Stoppard*, pp. 152–5.

48. Michael Billington, *Stoppard the Playwright* (London and New York: Methuen, 1987), p. 114.

49. Richard Corballis, *Stoppard: The Mystery and the Clockwork* (Oxford: Amber Lane Press; New York: Methuen, 1984), p. 111.

50. Andrew K. Kennedy, 'Tom Stoppard's Dissident Comedies', *Modern Drama*, 25 (December 1982) 470.

51. Cahn, *Beyond Absurdity*, p. 146.

52. Dean's repeated assertions that the release comes about 'only through the ineptitude of Colonel Rozinsky', that such inept confusion 'is the only thing that saves them from the Soviet

system', simply miss the point (Dean, *Tom Stoppard*, pp. 96, 95). As recently as 1986 Susan Rusinko was still arguing that since the Colonel 'in his confusion' released the two prisoners 'the conclusion one can draw is that repressive institutions, if they fall, may do so from the weight of their own bureaucratic bungling'. According to Rusinko, Rozinsky is described to Alexander as 'not a psychiatrist but a doctor of philosophy'. Rusinko not only misses *the point* of Rozinsky being a philologist; she misses *the fact* that he is 'a doctor of philology'. 'In the bungling of the minor officials', Rusinko opines in her terminal comment on the play, 'the dead language is heavy indeed'. (Rusinko, *Tom Stoppard* [Boston: Twayne, 1986], pp. 81, 83).

53. Billington, *Stoppard the Playwright*, p. 114.
54. Bernard Levin, 'The Shining Truth of Tom Stoppard', *Sunday Times*, 18 June 1978, p. 38.
55. Kuurman, 'An Interview with Tom Stoppard', p. 53.
56. Brassell, *Tom Stoppard: An Assessment*, p. 186.
57. Huckerby, 'KGB to Blame', p. 12. The bittersweet nature of a victory over Soviet power was made clear again in 1986 when the Soviets released Anatoly Shcharansky. Stoppard commemorated Shcharansky's release by organising an all-day vigil outside the National Theatre to read one after another the names of tens of thousands of Soviet Jews who have been denied exit visas and are retained in Russia against their will.
58. Hebert, 'A Playwright in Undiscovered Country'. p. 10.
59. Gollob and Roper, 'Trad Tom Pops In', p. 15.
60. Philip Roberts, 'Tom Stoppard: Serious Artist or Siren?', *Critical Quarterly*, 20 (Autumn 1978), pp. 85, 91.
61. Eric Salmon, 'Faith in Tom Stoppard', *Queen's Quarterly*, 86 (Summer 1979) 215–32.
62. Gollob and Roper, 'Trad Tom Pops In', pp. 16, 17.

CHAPTER 6: *THE REAL THING*

Clive James, 'Count Zero Splits the Infinite', *Encounter*, 45 (November 1975), pp. 71, 70.
2. Tom Stoppard, 'The Event and the Text', a lecture in conjunction with the Third International Conference on the Fantastic, Boca Raton, Florida, 13 March 1982.
3. Ronald Hayman, 'First Interview with Tom Stoppard: 12 June 1974', *Tom Stoppard*, 4th ed. (London: Heinemann, 1982), p. 12.
4. James, 'Count Zero Splits the Infinite', p. 74.
5. Tom Stoppard in interview with David Gollob and David Roper, 'Trad Tom Pops In', *Gambit*, 10, no. 37 (Summer 1981), p. 8.
6. Hersh Zeifman, 'Comedy of Ambush: Tom Stoppard's *The Real Thing*', *Modern Drama*, 26 (June 1983) 141.
7. Interview with Daniel Henninger, 'Theater: Tom Stoppard and

the Politics of Morality', *Wall Street Journal*, 1 February 1980, p. 17.

8. Stoppard, 'The Event and the Text', Boca Raton, Florida, 13 March 1982.

9. Tom Stoppard, *The Real Thing*. Copyright © 1982 by Tom Stoppard. 2nd rev. ed. (London and Boston: Faber and Faber, 1984), pp. 33, 34; further quotations will be noted parenthetically in my text.

10. Roger Scruton, 'The Real Stoppard', *Encounter*, 60, no. 2 (February 1983), p. 46.

11. Stoppard, 'Trad Tom Pops In', p. 10.

12. Tom Stoppard, 'Ambushes for the Audience: Towards a High Comedy of Ideas', *Theatre Quarterly*, 4, no. 14 (May–July 1974), p. 14.

13. The passage dealing with patriotism, religion and royalty appeared in the 1982 first edition (p. 54), was deleted when the text was reprinted with revisions in 1983, but was restored in 1984 when the text was reprinted with further revisions (p. 53). The passage does not appear in the first American edition, also published by Faber and Faber in 1984 (p. 52).

14. James, 'Count Zero Splints the Infinite', p. 74.

15. Harold Pinter, 'Family Voices', *Other Places*, 1982.

16. Scruton, 'The Real Stoppard', p. 47.

17. Zeifman, 'Comedy of Ambush', p. 148.

18. Gollob and Roper, 'Trad Tom Pops In', p. 15.

19. Gollob and Roper, 'Trad Tom Pops In', p. 16.

20. Stoppard, 'Ambushes for the Audience', p. 7.

21. Gollob and Roper, 'Trad Tom Pops In', p. 17.

22. Tom Stoppard, 'But for the Middle Classes', review of *Enemies of Society*, by Paul Johnson, *Times Literary Supplement*, 3 June 1977, p. 677.

23. Gollob and Roper, 'Trad Tom Pops In', p. 8.

24. John Barber, *Daily Telegraph*, 17 November 1982; repr. in *London Theatre Record*, 2, no. 23 (1982), p. 634. More recently Richard Corballis seems to perpetuate the same misimpression in *Stoppard: The Mystery and the Clockwork* (Oxford: Amber Lane Press; New York: Methuen; 1984), p. 146.

25. Scruton, 'The Real Stoppard', p. 47.

26. Vicki Sanders, 'Stoppard Delivers the "Real Thing"', *Miami Herald*, 30 January 1985. In *Performing Arts* microfiche, 11 (February 1985) card 78: D12.

27. Roger Rees to Patrick Ensor, 'An Actor at the Sheepdog Trials', *Guardian*, 12 November 1982, p. 9.

28. Vicki Sanders, 'He Makes You Want to Listen', *Miami Herald*, 29 January 1985. In *Performing Arts* microfiche, 11 (February 1985) card 78: D11.

29. Kenneth Tynan, 'Withdrawing with Style from the Chaos', *New Yorker*, 53 (19 December 1977), p. 85; repr. in Kenneth Tynan, *Show People: Profiles in Entertainment* (New York: Simon and Schuster, 1979), p. 93.

CHAPTER 7: *HAPGOOD*

1. *Hapgood* opened at the Aldwych Theatre, London, on 8 March 1988 and had its first American production at the Doolittle Theatre, Los Angeles, in April 1989. Although both productions were directed by Peter Wood, Tom Stoppard was fully involved in rehearsals both in London and Los Angeles. The projection onto panels of an expanding map of London was added during rehearsals for the Aldwych production and was retained for the Los Angeles production.
2. Tom Stoppard, *Jumpers* (London: Faber and Faber, 1972 text), p. 82.
3. Tom Stoppard, *Hapgood*. Copyright © 1988 by Tom Stoppard. (London and Boston: Faber and Faber, 1988), p. 73; hereafter noted parenthetically in my text.
4. David Gollob and David Roper, 'Trad Tom Pops In', *Gambit*, 10, no. 37 (Summer 1981), p. 16.
5. Clive James, 'Count Zero Splits the Infinite', *Encounter*, 45 (November 1975), pp. 68–76.
6. Tom Stoppard, 'Some Quotes and Correspondence', *Hapgood* theatre programme, London: Aldwych Theatre, March 1988, p. [11].
7. Tom Stoppard, 'Some Quotes and Correspondence', p. [11].
8. Tom Stoppard, *Jumpers*, 2nd ed. (London and Boston: Faber and Faber, 1986), p. 20.
9. Mel Gussow, '*Jumpers* Author is Verbal Gymnast', *New York Times*, 23 April 1974, p. 36.
10. Mel Gussow, 'Stoppard Refutes Himself, Endlessly', *New York Times*, 26 April 1972, p. 54.
11. Michael Billington, 'Tricks of the Light', *Guardian*, 9 March 1988, p. 17.
12. Tom Stoppard in interview with Kate Kellaway, 'Review', BBC-TV (13 March 1988).
13. Tom Stoppard in interview with Peter Lewis, 'Quantum Stoppard', *Observer Magazine*, 6 March 1988, p. [58].
14. Steve Grant, review of *Hapgood*, *Time Out*, 16 March 1988; Charles Osborne, review of *Hapgood*, *Daily Telegraph*, 10 March 1988; both reviews are reprinted in *London Theatre Record*, 7, no. 5 (28 March 1988), pp. 279, 280.
15. Tom Stoppard in interview with Kate Kellaway, 'Review', BBC-TV (13 March 1988).
16. Tom Wilkie (science correspondent), review of *Hapgood*, *Independent*, 23 March 1988, repr. *London Theatre Record*, 7, no. 5 (28 March 1988), p. 293.
17. Michael Billington, 'Stoppard's Secret Agent', *Guardian*, 18 March 1988, p. 28.
18. Tom Stoppard, *Night and Day*, 2nd ed. (London: Faber and Faber, 1979), p. 92.
19. Tom Stoppard, *Hapgood*, revised script used in performance, June and July 1988, cf. text, p. 17.

20. Billington, 'Stoppard's Secret Agent', p. 28.
21. Billington, 'Stoppard's Secret Agent', p. 28.
22. Tom Stoppard in interview with Kate Kellaway, 'Review', BBC-TV (13 March 1988).
23. Professor Leonardo Castillejo as quoted by Adam Edwards, 'Criticism Takes a Quantum Leap', *Mail on Sunday*, 20 March 1988, p. 16.
24. Tom Stoppard, *Professional Foul* (London: Faber & Faber, 1978), p. 55.
25. Billington, 'Tricks of the Light', p. 17.
26. Again, as with *The Real Thing* the theatre programme points to the emotional heart of the play while the cover of the Faber and Faber text emphasises dispassionate detachment. Whereas the dust jacket of *The Real Thing* shows receding stage proscenia emphasising the contrast between levels of imaginative reality in the play, the image of *The Real Thing* which the theatre programme gives us is a man and a woman kissing.
27. Tom Stoppard, *The Real Thing*, 2nd rev. ed. (London and Boston: Faber and Faber, 1984), p. 63.
28. Roger Rees, interview with author, London, 16 June 1988.
29. William A. Henry III, 'London's Dry Season', *Time*, 132 (18 July 1988), p. 73.
30. I am indebted to my colleague David Downing for this comparison to *Jumpers* and for emphasising the central significance of Hapgood's final decision in the structural economy of the play.
31. Tom Stoppard, *Every Good Boy Deserves Favour* (London: Faber and Faber, 1978), p. 29.
32. Billington, 'Stoppard's Secret Agent', p. 28.
33. As performed in the Aldwych Theatre production, June 1988.
34. The text contains two moments in the first scene of act two where Hapgood says 'damn you' (p. 53) and 'damn well' (p. 55) and a passage late in scene six where she says 'Christ, Paul' (p. 87). The deletion of those six words in performance prepares us to find her final words in the penultimate scene (p. 87) to be all the more unexpected.
35. Roger Rees, interview with author, London, 16 June 1988.
36. Tom Stoppard, *Jumpers*, 2nd ed., p. 46.

CHAPTER 8: MORAL ABSOLUTES AND MORTAL CONTEXTS

1. Michael Billington, 'Stoppard's Secret Agent', *Guardian*, 18 March 1988, p. 28.
2. Billington, 'Stoppard's Secret Agent', p. 28.
3. Anthony Jenkins, *The Theatre of Tom Stoppard* (Cambridge, London, New York: Cambridge University Press, 1987).
4. Michael Billington, *Stoppard the Playwright* (London and New York: Methuen, 1987), p. 61.

5. Billington, *Stoppard the Playwright*, p. 56; Billington, 'Stoppard's Secret Agent', p. 28.
6. Billington, 'Stoppard's Secret Agent', p. 28.
7. Jon Bradshaw, 'Tom Stoppard, Nonstop: Word Games with a Hit Playwright', *New York*, 10 (10 January 1977), p. 51.
8. Tom Stoppard, 'Ambushes for the Audience: Towards a High Comedy of Ideas', *Theatre Quarterly*, 4, no. 14 (May–July 1974), p. 6.
9. Bradshaw, 'Tom Stoppard, Nonstop', p. 51.
10. Stoppard, 'Ambushes for the Audience', pp. 7–8.
11. The criticism by one of Stoppard's interviewers and Stoppard's response occur in 'Ambushes for the Audience', p. 13.
12. Billington, 'Stoppard's Secret Agent', p. 28.
13. The discussion between Tom Stoppard and Peter Wood is found in Ronald Hayman, 'Double Acts', *Sunday Times Magazine*, 2 March 1980, p. 29.
14. Charles Champlin, 'Fryer's Finale: A Milestone at the Ahmanson', *Los Angeles Times*, 8 September 1988, sec. 6, p. 1.
15. Mel Gussow, 'The Real Tom Stoppard', *New York Times Magazine*, 1 January 1984, p. 28.
16. Tom Stoppard, 'Something to Declare', *Sunday Times*, 25 February 1968, p. 47.
17. Aleksandr Solzhenitsyn, *The Gulag Archipelago*, vol. 1 (New York: Harper, 1973), p. 168.
18. Tom Stoppard, *Travesties* (London: Faber and Faber, 1975), p. 89.
19. Stoppard, *Travesties*, p. 39.
20. Tom Stoppard, *The Real Thing*, 2nd rev. ed. (London and Boston: Faber and Faber, 1984), p. 53.
21. Tom Stoppard, *Jumpers* (London: Faber and Faber, 1972 text), p. 84.
22. Tom Stoppard, *Professional Foul* (London and Boston: Faber and Faber, 1978), p. 90.
23. Stoppard, *Professional Foul*, p. 89.
24. Stoppard, 'Ambushes for the Audience', p. 13.
25. Stoppard, *Jumpers*, 2nd ed. (London and Boston: Faber and Faber, 1986), p. 45.
26. Kenneth Tynan, 'Withdrawing with Style from the Chaos', *New Yorker*, 53 (19 December 1977), p. 85; repr. in Kenneth Tynan, *Show People: Profiles in Entertainment* (New York: Simon and Schuster, 1979), p. 93.
27. Tom Stoppard to Oleg Kerensky, *The New British Drama: Fourteen Playwrights since Osborne and Pinter* (London: Hamish Hamilton, 1977), p. 170.
28. Stoppard, *Jumpers*, 2nd ed., p. 20; Stoppard, *Hapgood* (London and Boston: Faber and Faber, 1988), p. 50.
29. Tom Stoppard to Jon Bradshaw, 'Tom Stoppard, Nonstop', p. 51.
30. Tom Stoppard to Dan Sullivan, 'Stoppard: Getting the Right Bounce', *Los Angeles Times*, 2 June 1986, sec. 6, p. 6.
31. Tom Stoppard to Mel Gussow, 'Stoppard's Intellectual Cartwheels Now With Music', *New York Times*, 29 July 1979, sec. 2, p. 22.

Bibliography

Although Stoppard has been described as a dream interviewee speaking in eerily quotable sentences, he protests that he is becoming increasingly reluctant to grant interviews. But while Stoppard has insisted again and again that he does not like to be interviewed, he has overcome his reluctance often enough to grant a few hundred interviews in the course of his career. A former journalist himself, he has usually been more willing to be questioned by members of the press than by denizens of the groves of academe. Although Stoppard has been attracting increasing critical attention, many of the most helpful insights into his plays are contained in those interviews which have appeared in publications ranging from *Time Out* in London to the *Wall Street Journal* to the *Palo Alto* (California) *Times*. In the following bibliography I have been highly selective in listing critical articles about Stoppard while attempting to be much more comprehensive in listing both articles by Stoppard and interviews with Stoppard.

ARTICLES BY STOPPARD

'A Very Satirical Thing Happened to Me on the Way to the Theatre Tonight', *Encore*, 10 (March-April 1963), pp. 33–6.

'Just Impossible'. Review of 'The Impossible Years'. *Plays and Players*, 14 (January 1967), pp. 28–9.

'A Case of Vice Triumphant'. Review of 'The Soldier's Fortune'. *Plays and Players*, 14 (March 1967), pp. 16–9.

'The Definite Maybe'. *Author*, 78 (Spring 1967), pp. 18–20.

'Something to Declare'. *Sunday Times*, 25 February 1968, p. 47.

'Confessions of a Screenwriter'. *Today's Cinema*, 3 February 1969, p. 5.

'I'm Not Keen on Experiments'. *New York Times*, 8 March 1970, sec. 2, p. 17.

'Joker as Artist'. Review of *Magritte* by Suzi Gablik. *Sunday Times*, 11 October 1970, p. 40.

'Childbirth'. [British] *Vogue*, 128 (May 1971), p. 54.

'In Praise of Pedantry'. *Punch*, 14 July 1971, pp. 62–3.

'Orghast'. Review of 'Orghast' by Ted Hughes. *Times Literary Supplement*, 1 October 1971, p. 1174.

'Yes, We Have No Banana'. *Guardian*, 10 December 1971, p. 10.

'Playwrights and Professors'. *Times Literary Supplement*, 13 October 1972, p. 1219.

Review of *A Supplement to the Oxford English Dictionary, Volume 1, A-G*. *Punch*, 13 December 1972, pp. 893–4.

'Acting out the Oil Game'. *Observer*, 8 September 1974, p. 24; 'The Miss UK Sales Promotion', 15 September 1974, p. 27; 'Disaster in

Bangladesh', 22 September 1974, p. 27; 'Festival of Soap Opera', 29 September 1974, p. 28 [Television reviews].

Introduction in *Glyn Boyd Harte: A Spring Collection*. London: Thumb Gallery, 1976.

Article on the National Theatre controversy raised by Max Hastings, *Evening Standard*, 30 September 1976. Cited by Peter Hall, *Peter Hall's Diaries: The Story of a Dramatic Battle*, edited by John Goodwin, London: Hamish Hamilton, 1983, p. 260.

'Czech Human Rights'. Letter to the Editor. *The Times*, 7 February 1977, p. 15.

'Dirty Linen in Prague'. *New York Times*, 11 February 1977, sec. 1, p. 27.

'The Face at the Window'. *Sunday Times*, 27 February 1977, p. 33.

'But for the Middle Classes'. Review of *Enemies of Society* by Paul Johnson. *Times Literary Supplement*, 3 June 1977, p. 677.

'Prague: The Story of the Chartists'. *New York Review of Books*, 24, no. 13 (4 August 1977), pp. 11–15.

'Journalists' Closed Shop'. Letter to the Editor. *The Times*, 11 August 1977, p. 13.

'Human Rights in Prague'. Letter to the Editor. *The Times*, 17 October 1977, p. 13.

'My Friends Fighting for Freedom'. *Daily Mail*, 20 October 1977, p. 6.

'Looking-Glass World'. *New Statesman*, 28 October 1977, pp. 571–2.

'Nothing in Mind'. *London Magazine*, 17 (February 1978), pp. 65–8.

'A 15-Year Wait for Nureyev's Mother'. Letter to the Editor co-signed by Alan Ayckbourn, Sir John Gielgud et al. *Daily Telegraph*, 17 March 1979, p. 20 [Available on microfilm, *The Times*, 17 March 1979].

'Leftover from Travesties'. *Adam International Review*, 42, no. 431–3 (1980), pp. 11–12.

'Tom Stoppard on the KGB's Olympic Trials'. *Sunday Times*, 6 April 1980, p. 16.

'Borisov's Brief Freedom'. Letter to the Editor. *Sunday Times*, 15 June 1980, p. 12.

'Previous Non-convictions'. Letter to the Editor. *The Times*, 3 November 1980, p. 13.

'Prague's Wall of Silence'. Open letter to President Husák of Czechoslovakia. *The Times*, 18 November 1981, p. 10; repr. as 'Open letter to President Husák' in George Theiner (ed.), *They Shoot Writers, Don't They?*. London: Faber and Faber, 1984, pp. 57–9.

'Wildlife Observed: The Galapagos: Paradise and Purgatory'. *Observer Magazine*, 29 November 1981, pp. 38–51.

Is it True What They Say about Shakespeare? International Shakespeare Association Occasional Paper No. 2. Oxford: The University Press, 1982.

'Lech's Troubles with Chuck, Bruce and Bob'. On *Squaring the Circle*. *The Times*, 31 May 1984, p. 14.

'Arrests in Prague'. Letter to the Editor co-signed by Charles Alexander et al. *The Times*, 4 October 1986, p. 9.

'Human Rights'. Letter to the Editor. *The Times*, 13 February 1987, p. 17.

'Going to Bat for Britain'. *House & Garden*, 159 (November 1987), pp. 22–30.

'Some Quotes and Correspondence'. Letter about *Hapgood* to nuclear physicist J. D. Polkinghorne with Polkinghorne's reply. In the Aldwych Theatre *Hapgood* production programme, 8 March 1988, London, n. pag.

LECTURES

Elsa Chapin Memorial Lecture, Lobero Theater, Santa Barbara, Calif., 8 December 1974. Partial transcript included in Sylvie Drake, 'Stage Notes: Tom Stoppard – The Entertainer'. *Los Angeles Times*, 12 December 1974, sec. 4, p. 26.

'The Language of Theatre', a public lecture at the University of California at Santa Barbara, 14 January 1977. Recording: UCSB Library Special Collections. Partial account included in Kenneth Tynan, 'Withdrawing with Style from the Chaos', *New Yorker*, 19 December 1977, pp. 44–111; repr. in *Show People: Profiles in Entertainment*. New York: Simon and Schuster, 1979, pp. 44–123.

'Gleanings from London: Tom Stoppard', transcript of a lecture and question-and-answer session, *Readers Theatre News* (San Diego State University), 4, no. 2, Spring 1977, pp. 3–4.

'An Evening with Tom Stoppard', a public question-and-answer session at the American Conservatory Theater, San Francisco, 27 March 1977; tape recording and partial transcript housed in the ACT archives.

Clark Lectures, Cambridge University, February 1980. Partial transcript contained in Philip Gaskell, '*Night and Day*: The Development of a Play Text', in Jerome J. McGann (ed.), *Textual Criticism and Literary Interpretation*, Chicago and London: University of Chicago Press, 1985, pp. 162–79.

'The Event and the Text', a public lecture at San Diego State University, San Diego, Calif. Videotape: Media Library, SDSU, 4 November 1981.

'The Event and the Text', a lecture in conjunction with the Third International Conference on the Fantastic, Boca Raton, Florida, 13 March 1982.

'What Makes a Play Play', a public lecture at Rice University, Houston, Texas, 22 October 1982; partial account included in Eric Gerber, 'Life Imitates Art with Playwright Tom Stoppard Center Stage', *Houston Post*, 23 October 1982; In *Performing Arts* microfiche, vol. 9 (November 1982), card 39: A13.

'Platform Performance', a public lecture and question-and-answer session sponsored by the National Theatre, London: Lyttleton Theatre, 15 November 1984.

'Direct Experience', The Dawson-Scott Memorial Lecture at the London PEN Writers' Day, London: South Bank Centre, 23 March 1985. Introduction by Harold Pinter. Panel discussion chaired by Francis King, with questions from the floor; panel participants: Arthur Miller, Fay Weldon, Harold Pinter, Tom Stoppard and Malcolm Bradbury. Recording: National Sound Archive.

Darwin lecture, Cambridge, 1986. Partial account by Valerie Grosvenor Myer, 'Stoppard on the Bard', *Plays and Players*, no. 386 (February 1986), p. 6.

'The Event and the Text', The Whidden Lectures, McMaster University, Hamilton, Ontario, 24–6 October 1988. Stoppard presided at a question-and-answer session on 25 October and gave an informal talk on 26 October. For a transcript of the 24 October lecture see Tom Stoppard, 'The Event and the Text: The Whidden Lectures 1988', transcribed and edited by Doreen DelVecchio, *Ta Panta* [published by the McMaster University Faculty Association] 6, no. 1 (1988), pp. 15–20.

Question-and-Answer Session with Tom Stoppard, Peter Wood and Roger Rees following a preview performance of *Hapgood*, The James A. Doolittle Theatre, Los Angeles, 9 April 1989. Arranged through the auspices of ACTER [A Center for Theatre, Education, and Research], the University of California at Santa Barbara.

PRINT INTERVIEWS

1966

John Knight. 'Saturday night Sunday morning'. *Sunday Mirror*, 18 December 1966, p. 13.

1967

Anonymous. 'Londoner's Diary: Worried Author'. *Evening Standard*, 8 April 1967, p. 6.

Sean Day-Lewis. 'Plays and Players: Shakespeare Plus'. *Daily Telegraph*, 8 April 1967, p. 13.

Anonymous. 'Footnote to the Bard'. *Observer*, 9 April 1967, p. 23.

Keith Harper. 'The Devious Route to Waterloo Road'. *Guardian*, 12 April 1967, p. 7.

John Dodd. 'Success is the Only Unusual Thing about Mr. Stoppard'. *Sun*, 13 April 1967, p. 3.

Hunter Davies. 'Stoppard Goes'. *Sunday Times*, 23 April 1967, p. 13.

Peter Lewis. 'How Tom Went to Work on an Absent Mind and Picked up £20,000'. *Daily Mail*, 24 May 1967, p. 6.

Shaun MacLoughlin. 'Another Moon Called Earth'. *Radio Times*, 175 (22 June 1967), p. 33.

Anonymous. '"What's All This About?"'. *Newsweek*, 70 (7 August 1967), p. 72.

Bernard Adams. 'Tom Stoppard on "Teeth"'. *Radio Times*, 24 August 1967, p. 19.

Dan Sullivan. 'Young British Playwright Here For Rehearsal of "Rosencrantz"'. *New York Times*, 29 August 1967, p. 27.

Kathleen Halton. 'Tom Stoppard: The Startling Young Author of the Play *Rosencrantz and Guildenstern are Dead*'. [American] *Vogue*, 150 (15 October 1967), p. 112.

William Glover. 'Theater Week: Enter Playwright, Successfully'. AP Wireservice, 19 November 1967. New York: Public Library, Lincoln Center Drama Collection.

Jerry Tallmer. 'Closeup: Rosencrantz' Friend'. *New York Post*, 8 December 1967, p. 55.

John Gale. 'Writing's my 43rd Priority, Says Tom Stoppard'. *Observer*, 17 December 1967, p. 4.

William Hedgepeth. 'Playwright Tom Stoppard: "Go Home, British Boy Genius!"'. *Look*, 31 (26 December 1967), pp. 92–6.

1968

Tom Prideaux. 'Uncertainty Makes the Bigtime'. *Life*, 64 (9 February 1968), pp. 75–6.

Ronald Hastings. 'Rosencrantz was not the First'. *Daily Telegraph*, 17 February 1968, p. 13.

Patricia Louis. 'See the Father. See the Baby. See the Father Playing with the Baby. Doesn't the Father Look Happy? Yes, He Does.' *New York Times*, 24 March 1968, p. D3.

Anonymous. 'The Talk of the Town: Playwright-Novelist'. *New Yorker*, 44 (4 May 1968), pp. 40–1.

Giles Gordon. 'Tom Stoppard'. *Transatlantic Review*, no. 29 (Summer 1968), pp. 17–25; repr. in Joseph F. McCrindle (ed.), *Behind the Scenes: Theater and Film Interviews from the Transatlantic Review*. New York: Holt, Rinehart Winston, 1971.

Lewis Funke. 'Tom Stoppard'. In *Playwrights Talk about Writing: 12 Interviews*. Chicago: Dramatic Publishing, 1975, pp. 217–31. [Interview conducted in 1968].

1969

William Leonard. '"R&G Are Dead" Brings Life to "Hamlet" Legend'. *Chicago Tribune*, 27 April 1969, sec. 5, pp. 7–8.

1970

Anonymous. 'The Times Diary: Non Stop'. *The Times*, 11 April 1970, p. 8.

1972

Anonymous. 'Interview with Tom Stoppard'. In the National Theatre *Jumpers* production programme, 2 February 1972, London, n. pag.

Mel Gussow. 'Stoppard Refutes Himself, Endlessly'. *New York Times*, 26 April 1972, p. 54.

Richard Natale. 'I'm Always Chasing Peacocks'. *Women's Wear Daily*, 27 April 1972, p. 12.

Jerry Tallmer. 'Tom Stoppard Pops In On the Cast'. *New York Post*, 26 August 1972, p. 15.

Robert Wahls. 'Footlights: The Stage As a Chessboard'. *New York Sunday News*, 24 September 1972, p. 8.

Peter J. Rosenwald. 'The Theater'. *Wall Street Journal,* 25 September 1972, p. 12.

Peter J. Rosenwald. 'Stoppard's Sweet and Sour'. *Time Out,* no. 142 (3 November 1972), p. 31.

Barry Norman. 'Tom Stoppard and the Contentment of Insecurity'. *The Times,* 11 November 1972, p. 11.

1973

Frances Hill. 'Quarter-Laughing Assurance: A Profile of Tom Stoppard'. *Times Educational Supplement,* 9 February 1973, p. 23.

Joseph McCulloch. 'Dialogue with Tom Stoppard'. [20 March 1973] In *Under Bow Bells: Dialogues with Joseph McCulloch.* London: Sheldon Press, 1974, pp. 162–70.

Janet Watts. 'Tom Stoppard'. *Guardian,* 21 March 1973, p. 12.

Michael Leech. 'The Translators: Tom Stoppard: *The House of Bernarda Alba*'. *Plays and Players,* 20 (April 1973), pp. 37–8.

1974

Tom Donnelly. 'Donnelly's Revue: Jumping for Joy'. *Washington Post,* 17 February 1974, sec. P, pp. 1, 5.

Michael T. Leech. 'Wave of Success for *Jumpers* Author Tom Stoppard'. *Christian Science Monitor,* 6 March 1974, p. F6.

Tom Topor. 'Lunch With a Playwright'. *New York Post,* 10 April 1974, p. 64.

Mel Gussow. '*Jumpers* Author Is Verbal Gymnast'. *New York Times,* 23 April 1974, p. 36.

Tom Stoppard. 'Ambushes for the Audience: Towards a High Comedy of Ideas' [Interview with Roger Hudson, Catherine Itzen and Simon Trussler]. *Theatre Quarterly,* 4, no. 14 (May 1974), pp. 3–17.

T.E. Kalem. 'Ping Pong Philosopher'. *Time,* 103 (6 May 1974), p. 85.

Michael Owen. 'Stoppard's New Electric Notion'. *Evening Standard,* 24 May 1974, p. 26.

Derek Mahon. 'Tom Stoppard: A Noticeable Absence of Tortoises'. [British] *Vogue,* 164 (June 1974), p. 21.

Hugh Hebert. 'Domes of Zurich'. *Guardian,* 7 June 1974, p. 10.

Mark Amory. 'The Joke's the Thing'. *Sunday Times Magazine,* 9 June 1974, pp. 65, 67–8, 71–2, 74.

A.C.H. Smith. 'Tom Stoppard'. *Flourish* [The RSC Club news-sheet] issue one (10 June 1974), n. pag.

Ronald Hayman. 'First Interview with Tom Stoppard: 12 June 1974'. In *Tom Stoppard.* 4th ed. Contemporary Playwrights Series. London: Heinemann; Totowa, N.J.: Rowman and Littlefield, 1982, pp. 1–13.

Ronald Hayman. 'Profile 9: Tom Stoppard'. *New Review,* 1 (December 1974), pp. 15–22.

Stanley Eichelbaum. '"Call Me the Thinking Man's Farceur"'. *San Francisco Examiner,* 11 December 1974, p. 69.

Robert Taylor. 'It's Really About . . .'. *Oakland Tribune,* 11 December 1974, p. 31.

Sylvie Drake. 'Stage Notes: Tom Stoppard – The Entertainer'. *Los Angeles Times*, 12 December 1974, sec. 4, p. 26.
William Hogan. 'Stoppard's Non-Absurdity'. *San Francisco Chronicle*, 13 December 1974, p. 66.
Gary Tischler. 'It Was No Day for an Interview'. *Fremont* (Calif.) *Argus*, 20 December 1974, p. 23.

1975

Charles Marowitz. 'Tom Stoppard–The Theater's Intellectual P.T. Barnum'. *New York Times*, 19 October 1975, sec. 2, pp. 1, 5.
Mel Gussow. 'Playwright, Star Provide a Little Curtain Raiser'. *New York Times*, 31 October 1975, p. 21.
Leo Seligsohn. 'Tom Stoppard: Intellect's the Thing for Playwright'. (Long Island, NY) *Newsday*, 4 November 1975, pp. 4A–5A, 17A.
Ross Wetzsteon. 'Theatre Journal: Tom Stoppard Eats Steak Tartare with Chocolate Sauce'. *Village Voice*, 10 November 1975, p. 121.
Marilyn Stasio. 'Cue Theatre: Tom Stoppard's Mad Mushrooms'. *Cue*, 44 (29 November 1975), p. 15.

1976

William Glover. 'Stoppard Leaving "Circus" for Man and Dog'. *Cincinnati Enquirer*, 11 January 1976, sec. G, p. 5.
Steve Grant. 'Serious Frivolity'. *Time Out*, no. 327 (18 June 1976), p. 7.
Anonymous. 'Stoppard's Last Words'. Brief interview regarding *Every Good Boy Deserves Favour*. *Guardian*, 19 June 1976.
Robert B. Semple, Jr. 'How Life Imitates a Stoppard Farce'. *New York Times*, 21 June 1976, p. 45.
Ronald Hayman. 'Second Interview with Tom Stoppard: 20 August 1976'. In *Tom Stoppard*. 4th ed. Contemporary Playwrights Series. London: Heinemann; Totowa, N.J.: Rowman and Littlefield, 1982, pp. 138–46.
Peter Wood. 'A conversation'. In the National Theatre *Jumpers* production programme, 21 September 1976, London, n. pag.

1977

Oleg Kerensky. *The New British Drama: Fourteen Playwrights since Osborne and Pinter*. London: Hamish Hamilton, 1977, pp. 168–71.
Bruce Cook. 'Tom Stoppard: The Man Behind the Plays'. *Saturday Review*, 4 (8 January 1977), pp. 52–3.
Lawrence Christon. 'Travesties – A Footnote Follies From Stoppard'. *Los Angeles Times*, 9 January 1977, 'Calendar' section, p. 48.
John Leonard. 'Tom Stoppard Tries On A "Knickers Farce"'. *New York Times*, 9 January 1977, sec. 2, pp. 1, 5.
Jon Bradshaw. 'Tom Stoppard, Nonstop: Word Games With a Hit Playwright'. *New York*, 10 (10 January 1977), pp. 47–51.
Tony Schwartz. 'Tony Schwartz'. *New York Post*, 12 January 1977, p. 31.
Jonathan Silver. 'Stoppard Takes the "Modest Course": Portrays a

Personal View of Theater'. *Daily Nexus* [University of California at Santa Barbara student newspaper], 17 January 1977, pp. 1, 8.

Beverley Jackson. 'Patient Tom Stoppard'. *Santa Barbara News-Press*, 18 January 1977, sec. B, pp. 6–7.

Sylvie Drake. 'The Importance of Being Stoppard'. *Los Angeles Times*, 20 January 1977, sec. 4, p. 12.

C.E. Maves. 'A Playwright on the Side of Rationality'. *Palo Alto* (Calif.) *Times*, 25 March 1977, p. 16.

Stanley Eichelbaum. 'So Often Produced, He Ranks with Shaw'. *San Francisco Examiner*, 28 March 1977, p. 24.

Barbara Bladen. 'Playwright Sees Plays as "Rational"'. *San Mateo* (Calif.) *Times*, 29 March 1977, p. 29.

Bernard Weiner. 'A Puzzling, "Traditional" Stoppard'. *San Francisco Chronicle*, 29 March 1977.

Robert Taylor. 'Tom Stoppard's Plays Are More Than Just "Clever Nonsense"'. *Oakland Tribune*, 17 April 1977, p. 2E.

Clifford D. May with Edward Behr. 'Master of the Stage'. *Newsweek*, 90 (15 August 1977), pp. 35–40.

Kenneth Tynan. 'Withdrawing with Style from the Chaos'. *New Yorker*, 53 (19 December 1977), pp. 44–111; repr. in Kenneth Tynan, *Show People: Profiles in Entertainment*. New York: Simon and Schuster, 1979, pp. 44–123.

1978

Penelope Mortimer. 'Tom Stoppard – Funny, Fast Talking and Our First Playwright'. [British] *Cosmopolitan*, January 1978, pp. 30–1, 39.

Milton Shulman. 'The Politicizing Of Tom Stoppard'. *New York Times*, 23 April 1978, sec 2, pp. 3, 27.

Anonymous. 'Tom Stoppard Puts Case for Soviet Jews'. *The Times*, 12 July 1978, p. 7.

Martin Huckerby. 'Arts Diary: KGB to Blame in the End'. *The Times*, 17 August 1978, p. 12.

Bart Mills. 'Tom Stoppard Moves into Political Writing'. (Long Island, NY) *Newsday*, 7 September 1978, p. 62.

Albert R. Glaap. 'From the Horse's Mouth: Questions from German Students to Living British Dramatists'. *Anglistick & Englischunterricht*, 5 (1978), pp. 103–14.

1979

Philip Gaskell. Interview with Tom Stoppard, 9 January 1979. Partial transcript contained in Philip Gaskell, *'Night and Day*: The Development of a Play Text'. In Jerome J. McGann (ed.), *Textual Criticism and Literary Interpretation*. Chicago and London: University of Chicago Press, 1985, pp. 162–79.

Joost Kuurman. 'An Interview with Tom Stoppard'. *Dutch Quarterly Review of Anglo-American Letters*, 10 (1980) 41–57 [Interview conducted in March 1979].

Nancy Shields Hardin. 'An Interview with Tom Stoppard'. *Contemporary Literature*, 22 (Spring 1981) 153–66 [Interview conducted in April 1979].
Carol Lawson. 'Stoppard–Previn Drama To Play at the Met Opera'. *New York Times*, 6 June 1979, sec. 3, p. 22.
Hugh Hebert. 'A Playwright in Undiscovered Country'. *Guardian*, 7 July 1979, p. 10.
Rosemary Say. 'Show Talk'. *Sunday Telegraph*, 8 July 1979, p. 14.
Mel Gussow. 'Stoppard's Intellectual Cartwheels Now With Music'. *New York Times*, 29 July 1979, sec. 2, pp. 1, 22.
Robert Berkvist. 'This Time, Stoppard Plays It (Almost) Straight'. *New York Times*, 25 November 1979, sec. 2, pp. 1, 5.

1980

Pauline Young. 'Interview with Tom Stoppard: Pauline Young Talks to Our Leading Dramatist: London, 16 January 1980'. *Madog Arts Magazine* [Published by The Polytechnic of Wales Department of Arts and Languages], Spring 1981, pp. 12–27. Available at the British Library.
Ray Connolly. 'Atticus: Stoppard in Greeneland'. *Sunday Times*, 20 January 1980, p. 32.
Daniel Henninger. 'Theater: Tom Stoppard and the Politics of Morality'. *Wall Street Journal*, 1 February 1980, p. 17.
Ronald Hayman. 'Double Acts: Tom Stoppard and Peter Wood'. *Sunday Times Magazine*, 2 March 1980, pp. 29, 31.

1981

David Gollob and David Roper. 'Trad Tom Pops In'. *Gambit*, 10, no. 37 (Summer 1981), pp. 5–17.
Pendennis. 'Dialogue with a Driven Man'. *Observer*, 30 August 1981, p. 18.
Karla Peterson. 'Public Recognition Baffles Stoppard, English Playwright'. *Daily Aztec* [San Diego State University student newspaper], 30 October 1981, pp. 5, 7.
Phyllis Ruskin and John H. Lutterbie. 'Balancing the Equation'. *Modern Drama*, 26 (December 1983) 543–54 [Interview conducted October 1981].
Welton Jones. 'Stoppard Coup Assures SDSU a Fortnight of Rare Drama'. *San Diego Union*, 1 November 1981, sec. E, pp. 1–2.
Bill Hagen. 'Today's Truth, by Tom Stoppard'. *San Diego Tribune*, 6 November 1981, p. C-1.

1982

Hilary DeVries. 'Playwright Tom Stoppard: Wit Ricochets Off Every Surface'. *Christian Science Monitor*, 8 July 1982, Western Edition, pp. B1–B4.

1983

Leslie Bennetts. 'Friendship Characterizes Stoppard Play Rehearsals'. *New York Times*, 22 November 1983, sec. C, p. 13.
Ellen Levene. 'Stoppard Looks at Love and Freedom'. (Long Island,

NY) *Newsday*, 25 December 1983. In *Performing Arts* microfiche, vol. 10 (January 1984) card 62: F1-2.

1984

Mel Gussow. 'The Real Tom Stoppard'. *New York Times Magazine*, 1 January 1984, pp. 18–23, 28.

Richard Corliss. 'Theater: Stoppard in the Name of Love'. *Time*, 123 (16 January 1984), pp. 68–9.

Jack Kroll. 'A Dazzling Gift of Play'. *Newsweek*, 103 (16 January 1984), pp. 82–3.

Samuel G. Freedman. 'Stoppard Debates the Role of the Writer: Political Duty Is Questioned'. *New York Times*, 20 February 1984, sec. C, p. 13.

Joan Juliet Buck. 'Tom Stoppard: Kind Heart and Prickly Mind'. [American] *Vogue*, 174 (March 1984), pp. 454, 513–14.

Ros Asquith. 'City Limits Interview: Tom Stoppard'. *City Limits*, 19 October 1984, pp. 79–80.

Garry O'Connor. 'Two Men on an Ocean Wave'. *Sunday Times*, 21 October 1984, p. 39.

1985

Vicki Sanders. 'He Makes You Want to Listen'. *Miami* (Fla.) *Herald*, 29 January 1985. In *Performing Arts* microfiche, vol. 11 (February 1985), card 78: D10-11.

J. Wynn Rousuck. 'In *The Real Thing*, Stoppard's Trying for Realism – For Once'. (Baltimore, Md.) *Sun*, 28 April 1985. In *Performing Arts* microfiche, vol. 11 (May 1985), card 110: D7–8.

Duncan Fallowell. 'Theatrical Incest and Acquisitive Lust'. *The Times*, 23 August 1985, p. 8.

1986

Nicholas Shakespeare. 'A New Wineskin from old Vienna'. *The Times*, 17 May 1986, p. 18.

Dan Sullivan. 'Stoppard: Getting the Right Bounce'. *Los Angeles Times*, 2 June 1986, sec. 6, pp. 1, 6.

Clare Colvin. 'The Real Tom Stoppard'. *Drama*, 43, no. 161 (1986), pp. 9-10.

Sean Mitchell. 'Just Who, Really, is Tom Stoppard?' *Los Angeles Herald Examiner*, 18 December 1986. In *Performing Arts* microfiche, vol. 13 (November 1986–February 1987), card 110: A5–6.

1987

Tom Killen. 'Stoppard Giving Answers'. *New Haven* (Conn.) *Register*, 15 March 1987. In *Performing Arts* microfiche, vol. 13 (May 1987), card 146: F2.

Janet Watts. 'Stoppard's Half-Century'. *Observer*, 28 June 1987, pp. 17–18.

Charles Champlin. 'New Day Dawns for "Sun" Writer Tom Stoppard'. *Los Angeles Times*, 10 December 1987, sec. 6, pp. 1, 9.

Bob Thomas. 'Spielberg Creates an "Empire"'. *Santa Barbara* [Calif.] *News-Press*, 18 December 1987, 'Scene' section, pp. 19–20.

Luaine Lee. 'Stargazing: The U.S. According to Stoppard'. Pasadena [Calif.] *Star-News*, 18 December 1987, p. Extra-2.

Luaine Lee. 'Writer Says He's Suited to His Craft'. Pasadena [Calif.] *Star-News*, 27 December 1987, pp. B1-4.

1988

Peter Lewis. 'Quantum Stoppard'. *Observer Magazine*, 6 March 1988, pp. [58–9].

Michael Billington. 'Stoppard's Secret Agent'. *Guardian*, 18 March 1988, p. 28.

Leslie Bennetts. 'The Arts Festival: Five Top Playwrights in a Dialogue, With Arthur Miller Adding Drama'. *New York Times*, 18 June 1988, p. 9. [Account of symposium on 'The Challenge of Writing for the Theater Today', sponsored by the First New York International Festival of the Arts.]

1989

Thomas O'Connor. 'Welcome to the World of Tom Stoppard'. *Orange County* [Calif.] *Register*, 2 April 1989, 'Show' section, pp. K3–K5.

Richard Stayton. 'The Mysterious Tom Stoppard'. *Los Angeles Herald Examiner*, 14 April 1989, sec. E, 'Weekend', p. 6.

Stephen Schiff. 'Full Stoppard'. *Vanity Fair*, 52, no. 5 (May 1989), pp. 152–7, 214–15.

RADIO AND TELEVISION INTERVIEWS

1967

'The Lively Arts'. BBC Radio Three (12 April 1967). John Bowen interview with Tom Stoppard regarding *Rosencrantz and Guildenstern are Dead*. Transcript: BBC Script Library. Recording: National Sound Archive.

'Woman's Hour: Showpiece'. BBC Radio Light Programme (13 April 1967). Gordon Gow interview with Tom Stoppard regarding *Rosencrantz and Guildenstern are Dead*. Transcript: BBC Written Archives Centre.

'Late Night Line-up'. BBC 2 (28 June 1967). Interview with Tom Stoppard regarding *Another Moon Called Earth*. Transcript not available from the BBC.

'Late Night Line-up'. BBC 2 (29 September 1967). Interview with Tom Stoppard. Transcript not available from the BBC.

1970

'Our Changing Theatre, No. 3: Changes in Writing'. BBC Radio Four
(23 November 1970; recorded 12 October 1970). John Russell Taylor
interview with Tom Stoppard and Howard Brenton. Transcript: BBC
Script Library. Recording: National Sound Archive.

1972

'Woman's Hour'. BBC Radio Two (5 April 1972; recorded 15 March
1972). Marjorie Anderson interview with Tom Stoppard regarding
Rosencrantz and Guildenstern are Dead and *Jumpers*. Transcript: BBC
Script Library. Recording: National Sound Archive.
'In Parenthesis'. BBC Radio Three (1 April 1972; recorded 23 March
1972). Discussion, entitled 'Is "Is" Is?', by Tony Palmer and Tom
Stoppard of 'Language as a Medium of Communication'. Transcript:
BBC Script Library. Recording: National Sound Archive.
'One Pair of Eyes: Tom Stoppard Doesn't Know'. BBC 2 (7 July
1972). Programme and interview with David DeKeyser and Marjorie
Anderson regarding the ideas of Tom Stoppard. Transcript: BBC Script
Library.
Peter Orr. Recorded interview with Tom Stoppard for the British
Council (21 September 1972). British Council tape.
'Scan'. BBC Radio Four (9 November 1972). Bryan Magee interview with
Tom Stoppard regarding *After Magritte*, *The Real Inspector Hound*, and
Jumpers. Transcript: BBC Script Library.
'Arts Commentary'. BBC Radio Three (10 November 1972). Richard Mayne
interview with Tom Stoppard regarding *Artist Descending a Staircase*.
Transcript: BBC Script Library. Recording: National Sound Archive.

1973

'Full House'. BBC 2 (6 January 1973). Interview with Tom Stoppard
regarding *After Magritte*. Transcript not available from the BBC.
'P.M. Reports'. BBC Radio Four (8 June 1973; recorded 7 June
1973). Giles Smith interview with Tom Stoppard regarding 'The
Ten-Minute Hamlet'. Transcript: BBC Written Archives Centre.
Recording: National Sound Archive.

1974

'Kaleidoscope'. BBC Radio Four (17 April 1974). Peter France interview
with Tom Stoppard regarding *Travesties* and *Jumpers*. Transcript: BBC
Script Library.

1975

'Critics' Forum'. BBC Radio Three (4 January 1975). Panel discussion
led by J.W. Lambert with Margaret Drabble, Tom Stoppard, and Basil
Taylor. Transcript: BBC Script Library.

'Critics' Forum, No. 3'. BBC Radio Three (16 January 1975). Panel discussion led by J.W. Lambert with Margaret Drabble, Tom Stoppard, and Basil Taylor. Transcript: BBC Script Library.

'Critics' Forum, No. 4'. BBC Radio Three (18 January 1975). Panel discussion led by Oleg Kerensky with Margaret Drabble, Tom Stoppard, and Basil Taylor. Transcript: BBC Script Library.

'The Book Programme'. BBC 2 (13 May 1975). Tom Stoppard with book choice. Transcript not available.

'Omnibus'. BBC 1 (21 September 1975). Tom Stoppard et al. at the Eleventh Hour. Transcript not available.

1976

'Profile'. Alastair Lack interview with Tom Stoppard for Topical Tapes (7 April 1974). Recording: National Sound Archive.

'Kaleidoscope'. BBC Radio Four (16 April 1976). Edwin Mullins interview with Tom Stoppard regarding *Dirty Linen*. Transcript: BBC Script Library.

'Start the Week'. BBC Radio Four (17 May 1976). Richard Baker interview with Tom Stoppard regarding *Dirty Linen*. Transcript: BBC Script Library.

'Kaleidoscope'. BBC Radio Four (22 September 1976). Paul Vaughan interview with Tom Stoppard and Martin Esslin regarding *Dirty Linen* and the process of writing. Transcript: BBC Script Library.

'The Playwright: Tom Stoppard'. 'The South Bank Show'. Thames Television (28 September 1976). Benedict Nightingale, interviewer. Transcript housed at Thames Television, London.

1977

'Tom Stoppard in Conversation with Anthony Smith'. Recorded interview. London: British Council, c. 1977. Literature study aids series. Recorded 17 December 1976 at Tom Stoppard's home in Iver, Buckinghamshire. Cassette recording and pamphlet available from the British Council.

'The World This Weekend'. BBC Radio (27 February 1977). Gordon Clough interview regarding dissidents Stoppard met on his trip to Moscow and their treatment. Recording: National Sound Archive.

'The Secret Workshop'. Ian Rodger interviews various writers about radio and the part it has played in their lives (9 March 1977). Recording: National Sound Archive.

'André Previn Meets'. BBC 1 (29 May 1977). Interview with Tom Stoppard. Transcript not available.

'Tonight'. BBC 1 (29 June 1977). John Timpson interview with Tom Stoppard. Transcript not available.

'Kaleidoscope'. BBC Radio Four (1 July 1977). Sheridan Morley interview with Tom Stoppard, André Previn, and Ronald Hayman regarding *Every Good Boy Deserves Favour*. Transcript: BBC Script Library.

1978

Stephen Banker. 'Tom Stoppard'. Interview regarding *Jumpers*. Washington, D.C.: Tapes for Readers, 1978.

'Kaleidoscope'. BBC Radio Four (10 November 1978). Michael Billington interview with Tom Stoppard regarding *Night and Day*. Transcript: BBC Script Library. Recording: National Sound Archive.

'The South Bank Show'. London Weekend Television (26 November 1978). Melvyn Bragg interview. Cited in Tim Brassell, *Tom Stoppard: An Assessment*, London: Macmillan; New York: St. Martin's Press, 1985, pp. 282, 284.

1979

'Kaleidoscope'. BBC Radio Four (17 May 1979). Michael Oliver interview regarding *Dogg's Hamlet, Cahoot's Macbeth*. Recording: National Sound Archive.

'Tonight'. BBC 1 (29 June 1979). Michael Billington interview with Tom Stoppard at the National Theatre about all plays he has on at present, especially *Undiscovered Country*. Transcript not available.

'Panorama: Under Surveillance'. BBC 1 (9 July 1979). Fred Emery and Michael Cockerell interview Tom Stoppard and Vaclav Havel regarding Czechoslovakia. Transcript: BBC Script Library.

'Kaleidoscope'. BBC Radio Four (17 July 1979). Paul Vaughan interview with Tom Stoppard regarding *Dogg's Hamlet, Cahoot's Macbeth*. Transcript: BBC Script Library.

'Kaleidoscope'. BBC Radio Four (2 August 1979). Russell Davies interview with Tom Stoppard, Otto Preminger, Nicol Williamson, Robert Morley, Sir Richard Attenborough regarding *The Human Factor*. Transcript: BBC Script Library. Recording: National Sound Archive.

'The Arts Worldwide'. BBC Radio (October 1979). Stoppard interviewed by Nigel Lewis on imprisonment of five social reformers in Czechoslovakia. Recording: National Sound Archive.

'Friday Night . . . Saturday Morning'. BBC 2 (2 November 1979). Tim Rice interview with Tom Stoppard. Transcript not available.

1981

'Drama Up to Now'. BBC Radio Four (8 May 1981). John Russell Brown, interviewer. Includes partial transcripts of Stoppard interviews 'Our Changing Theatre' BBC Radio Four (23 November 1970) and 'Arts Commentary' BBC Radio Three (10 November 1972). Transcript: BBC Script Library.

'Week's Good Cause'. BBC Radio Four (11 October 1981). Appeal on behalf of Writers and Scholars Educational Trust and its magazine *Index on Censorship*. Recording: National Sound Archive.

'Various Stages: No. 1 *On the Razzle*'. BBC Radio Three (24 October 1981). Ronald Hayman interview with Tom Stoppard, Peter Wood, Felicity Kendal, Dinsdale Landen, Mary Chilton, Harold Innocent,

Ray Brooks, and Carl Toms regarding *On the Razzle*. Transcript: BBC Script Library. Recording: National Sound Archive.

1982

'Tom Stoppard'. KPBS-TV, San Diego (26 January 1982). Re-broadcast KCET-TV, Los Angeles (1 February 1982). Interview (conducted in November 1981) by Helen Hawkins of Tom Stoppard regarding *Rosencrantz and Guildenstern are Dead* and *Mackoon's Hamlet, Cahoot's Macbeth* (Stoppard's adaptation of *Dogg's Hamlet, Cahoot's Macbeth* for San Diego State University). Videotape: Media Library, SDSU.

'Reputations'. BBC 2 (25 July 1982). Anthony Howard, moderator, of a programme on Kenneth Tynan; Tom Stoppard, participant. Transcript: BBC Written Archives Centre.

'Kaleidoscope'. BBC Radio Four (17 November 1982). Michael Oliver interview regarding *The Real Thing*. Transcript: BBC Written Archives Centre.

'Channel Four News'. Channel 4, London (15 November 1982). Stephen Phillips interview with Tom Stoppard. Cited in Tim Brassell, *Tom Stoppard: An Assessment*, London: Macmillan; New York: St. Martin's Press, 1985, p. 286.

1983

'The World Tonight'. BBC Radio Four (25 January 1983). Geoffrey Wareham interview regarding Stoppard opening an exhibition illustrating the plight of Soviet Jews. Transcript not available.

'Writers on Writing'. ITV (22 April 1983). Cited in Neil Sammells, *Tom Stoppard: The Artist as Critic*, London: Macmillan, 1988, p. 158.

'Kaleidoscope'. BBC Radio Four (8 June 1983). Brief interview by Natalie Wheen regarding writing for radio. Transcript: BBC Written Archives Centre.

'Frank Delaney'. BBC-TV (17 October 1983). Frank Delaney interview with Tom Stoppard and Christopher Hampton regarding translations and adaptations for film, television, stage and radio; also deals with *The Real Thing*. Videotape: BBC Viewing Service, Centre House.

1984

'Kaleidoscope'. BBC Radio Four (2 March 1984). Sheridan Morley interview regarding *Jumpers* and a new Manchester production of the play. Transcript: BBC Written Archives Centre.

'Gloria Hunniford'. BBC Radio Two (25 May 1984). Interview about Stoppard's career and about cast changes in *The Real Thing*. Transcript not available.

1985

'Desert Island Discs'. BBC Radio (8 January 1985). Stoppard talks to Roy Plomley about his life and work and chooses eight gramophone records to take to a desert island. Recording: National Sound Archive.

1986

'Sunday'. BBC Radio Four (16 February 1986). Trevor Barnes interview regarding Stoppard's demonstration on behalf of Soviet Jews.

'Breakfast Time'. BBC-TV (17 February 1986). Live interview by Glyn Worsnip from the National Theatre where Stoppard organised a day-long vigil reading the names of 10,000 Soviet Jews refused exit visas. Videotape: BBC Viewing Service, Centre House.

'First Night Impressions'. BBC Radio Four (14 May 1986). Robert Cushman interview regarding *Jumpers*, *Professional Foul*, and *Travesties*. Recording: National Sound Archive.

'Breakfast Time'. BBC-TV (20 May 1986). As Guest of the Day, Stoppard talks about *Dalliance*, Schnitzler, *Professional Foul*, and cricket. Videotape: BBC Viewing Service, Centre House.

'Round Midnight'. BBC Radio Two (26 May 1986). Transcript not available.

'Saturday Review'. BBC-TV (18 October 1986). Russell Davies interview regarding Vaclav Havel and *Largo Desolato* being staged at the Bristol New Vic. Videotape: BBC Viewing Service, Centre House.

1988

'Talking Theatre'. BBC Radio Four (6 January 1988). Robert Cushman interview with Tom Stoppard. Transcript not available.

'John Dunn Show'. BBC Radio Two (29 February 1988). John Dunn interview with Tom Stoppard. Transcript not available.

'Review'. BBC-TV (13 March 1988). Kate Kellaway interview regarding *Hapgood*; includes comments by Dr. Patricia Lewis, a nuclear physicist. Videotape: BBC Viewing Service, Centre House.

1989

'Morning Edition'. [American] National Public Radio (12 April 1989). Interview by Sarah Spitz of KCRW, Santa Monica [Calif.], with Tom Stoppard, actor Simon Jones, and director Peter Wood regarding U.S. première of *Hapgood*. Cassette recording: National Public Radio Cassette Service.

'Today'. NBC-TV (26 April 1989). Heidi Schulman interview with Tom Stoppard and Peter Wood regarding U.S. première of *Hapgood*.

SELECT BIBLIOGRAPHY OF CRITICISM

BOOKS

Bigsby, C.W.E. *Tom Stoppard*. Writers and Their Work Series. London: Longman, 1976, rev. 1979.

Billington, Michael. *Stoppard the Playwright*. Modern Theatre Profiles series. London and New York: Methuen, 1987.

Bloom, Harold, ed. *Tom Stoppard*. Modern Critical Views series. New York: Chelsea House, 1986.

Brassell, Tim. *Tom Stoppard: An Assessment*. London: Macmillan; New York: St. Martin's Press, 1985.

Bratt, David. *Tom Stoppard: A Reference Guide*. Boston: G.K. Hall, 1982.

Corballis, Richard. *Stoppard: The Mystery and the Clockwork*. Oxford: Amber Lane Press; New York: Methuen, 1984.

Dean, Joan FitzPatrick. *Tom Stoppard: Comedy as a Moral Matrix*. Columbia and London: University of Missouri Press, 1981.

Dutton, Richard. *Modern Tragicomedy and the British Tradition*. Norman and London: University of Oklahoma Press, 1986.

Hayman, Ronald. *Tom Stoppard*. 4th ed. Contemporary Playwrights Series. London: Heinemann; Totowa, N.J.: Rowman and Littlefield, 1982.

Hu, Stephen. *Tom Stoppard's Stagecraft*. American University Studies: Series 4, English Language and Literature. Vol. 78. New York, Bern, Frankfurt/M., Paris: Peter Lang, 1988.

Hunter, Jim. *Tom Stoppard's Plays*. London: Faber and Faber; New York: Grove Press, 1982.

Jenkins, Anthony. *The Theatre of Tom Stoppard*. Cambridge and New York: Cambridge University Press, 1987.

Londré, Felicia Hardison. *Tom Stoppard*. New York: Ungar, 1981.

Page, Malcolm, ed. *File on Stoppard*. London and New York: Methuen, 1986.

Rusinko, Susan. *Tom Stoppard*. Twayne's English Authors Series. Boston: Twayne, 1986.

Sammells, Neil. *Tom Stoppard: The Artist as Critic*. London: Macmillan, 1988.

Whitaker, Thomas. *Tom Stoppard*. London: Macmillan; New York: Grove Press, 1983.

ARTICLES AND PORTIONS OF BOOKS

Bailey, John A. 'Jumpers by Tom Stoppard: The Ironist as Theistic Apologist'. *Michigan Academician*, 11 (1979) 237–50; repr. in Harold Bloom (ed.) *Tom Stoppard*. New York: Chelsea House, 1986, pp. 31–43.

Bennett, Jonathan. 'Philosophy and Mr Stoppard'. *Philosophy*, 50 (January 1975) 5-18.

Brassell, Tim. 'Jumpers: A Happy Marriage?'. *Gambit*, 10, no. 37 (Summer 1981), pp. 43–59.

Buhr, Richard J. 'Epistemology and Ethics in Tom Stoppard's *Professional Foul*'. *Comparative Drama*, 13 (1979) 320–9.

—. 'The Philosophy Game in Tom Stoppard's *Professional Foul*'. *Midwest Quarterly*, 22 (1981) 407–15.

Camroux, David. 'Tom Stoppard: The Last of the Metaphysical Egocentrics'. *Caliban* (Toulouse), 15 (1978) 79–94.

Cave, Richard Allen. 'New Forms of Comedy: Ayckbourn and Stoppard'. In *New British Drama In Performance On The London Stage: 1970-1985*. Gerrards Cross [Bucks.], Colin Smythe, 1987, pp. 70–100.

Cobley, Evelyn. 'Catastrophe Theory in Tom Stoppard's *Professional Foul*'. *Contemporary Literature*, 25 (1984) 53–65.

Cohn, Ruby. 'Tom Stoppard: Light Drama and Dirges in Marriage'.

In C.W.E. Bigsby (ed.), *Contemporary English Drama*. Stratford-upon-Avon Series 19. London: Edward Arnold, 1981; New York: Holmes and Meier, 1981, pp. 109–20.

Crump, G.B. 'The Universe as Murder Mystery: Tom Stoppard's *Jumpers*'. *Contemporary Literature*, 20 (1979) 354–68.

Delaney, Paul. 'The Flesh and the Word in *Jumpers*'. *Modern Language Quarterly*, 42 (1981) 369–88.

—. 'Cricket Bats and Commitment: The Real Thing in Art and Life'. *Critical Quarterly*, 27 (Spring 1985), pp. 45–60.

Duncan, Joseph E. 'Godot Comes: *Rosencrantz and Guildenstern Are Dead*'. *Ariel: A Review of International English Literature*, 12, no. 4 (October 1981), pp. 57–70.

Egan, Robert. 'A Thin Beam of Light: The Purpose of Playing in *Rosencrantz and Guildenstern are Dead*'. *Theatre Journal*, 31 (March 1979) 59–69.

Ellmann, Richard. 'The Zealots of Zurich'. *Times Literary Supplement*, 12 July 1974, p. 744. [On *Travesties*.]

Gaskell, Philip. 'Stoppard, *Travesties*, 1974'. In *From Writer to Reader: Studies in Editorial Method*. Oxford: Clarendon Press, 1978, pp. 245–62.

—. '*Night and Day*: The Development of a Play Text'. In Jerome J. McGann (ed.), *Textual Criticism and Literary Interpretation*. Chicago and London: University of Chicago Press, 1985, pp. 162–79.

Gruber, William E. '"Wheels Within Wheels, etcetera": Artistic Design in *Rosencrantz and Guildenstern Are Dead*'. *Comparative Drama*, 15 (Winter 1981–2) 291–310.

James, Clive. 'Count Zero Splits the Infinite'. *Encounter*, 45 (November 1975), pp. 68–76.

Jensen, Henning. 'Jonathan Bennett and Mr Stoppard'. *Philosophy*, 52 (April 1977) 214–17.

Kramer, Mimi. 'The American Stoppard'. *New Criterion*, 2 (March 1984), pp. 50–5. [On *The Real Thing*.]

Kreps, Barbara. 'How Do We Know That We Know What We Know in Tom Stoppard's *Jumpers*?'. *Twentieth Century Literature*, 32 (Summer 1986) 187–208.

McMillan, Dougald. 'Dropping the Other Boot, or Getting Stoppard out of Limbo'. *Gambit*, 10, no. 37 (Summer 1981), pp. 61–76.

Pearce, Howard D. 'Stage as Mirror: Tom Stoppard's *Travesties*'. *MLN*, 94 (1979) 1138–58.

Rabinowitz, Peter J. '"What's Hecuba to Us?": The Audience's Experience of Literary Borrowing'. In Susan R. Suleiman and Inge Crosman (eds), *The Reader in the Text: Essays on Audience and Interpretation*. Princeton: Princeton University Press, 1980, pp. 241–73.

Rayner, Alice. 'Stoppard's Paradox: Delight in Utopia'. In *Comic Persuasion: Moral Structure in British Comedy from Shakespeare to Stoppard*. Berkeley: University of California Press, 1987, pp. 129–51.

Roberts, Philip. 'Tom Stoppard: Serious Artist or Siren?', *Critical Quarterly*, 20 (Autumn 1978), pp. 84–92.

Salmon, Eric. 'Faith in Tom Stoppard'. *Queen's Quarterly*, 86 (Summer 1979) 215–32. [On *Jumpers* and *Travesties*.]

Scruton, Roger. 'The Real Stoppard'. *Encounter*, 60 (February 1983), pp. 44–7.

Taylor, John Russell. 'Tom Stoppard'. In *The Second Wave: British Drama of the Sixties*. London: Methuen, 1971; repr. London: Eyre Methuen, 1978, pp. 94–107.

Thomson, Leslie. 'The Subtext of *The Real Thing*: It's "all right"', *Modern Drama*, 30 (December 1987) 535–48.

Tynan, Kenneth. 'Withdrawing with Style from the Chaos'. *New Yorker*, 53 (19 December 1977), pp. 44–111; repr. in Kenneth Tynan, *Show People: Profiles in Entertainment*. New York: Simon and Schuster, 1979, pp. 44–123.

Weightman, John. 'A Metaphysical Comedy'. *Encounter*, 38 (April 1972), pp. 44–6. [On *Jumpers*.]

Wilcher, Robert. 'The Museum of Tragedy: *Endgame* and *Rosencrantz and Guildenstern are Dead*'. *Journal of Beckett Studies*, No. 4 (Spring 1979) 43–54.

—. 'Tom Stoppard and the Art of Communication'. *Journal of Beckett Studies*, No. 8 (Autumn 1982) 105–23.

Zeifman, Hersh. 'Comedy of Ambush: Tom Stoppard's *The Real Thing*'. *Modern Drama*, 26 (1983) 139–49.

—. 'Tomfoolery: Stoppard's Theatrical Puns'. *Yearbook of English Studies*, 9 (1979) 204–20.

Index